FROM VICTIMS
TO SURVIVORS

FROM VICTIMS
TO SURVIVORS

Reclaimed Voices of Women
Sexually Abused in Childhood by Females

Juliann Mitchell, Ph.D.
Jill Morse

ACCELERATED DEVELOPMENT
A member of the Taylor & Francis Group

USA	Publishing Office:	ACCELERATED DEVELOPMENT
		A member of the Taylor & Francis Group
		1101 Vermont Avenue, N.W., Suite 200
		Washington, DC 20005-3521
		Tel: (202) 289-2174
		Fax: (202) 289-3665
	Distribution Center:	ACCELERATED DEVELOPMENT
		A member of the Taylor & Francis Group
		1900 Frost Road, Suite 101
		Bristol, PA 19007-1598
		Tel: (215) 785-5800
		Fax: (215) 785-5515
UK		Taylor & Francis Ltd.
		1 Gunpowder Square
		London EC4A 3DE
		Tel: 0171 583 0490
		Fax: 0171 583 0581

FROM VICTIMS TO SURVIVORS: Reclaimed Voices of Women Sexually Abused in Childhood by Females

1 2 3 4 5 6 7 8 9 0   E B E B   0 9 8 7

This book was set in Times Roman. Editing by Sharon L. Emmons. Technical development by Cynthia Long and Candise M. B. Heinlein. Cover design by Alan Hill. Author photos and photos in content by Terry Snee.

A CIP catalog record for this book is available from the British Library.
∞ The paper in this publication meets the requirements of the ANSI Standard Z39.48-1984 (Permanence of Paper)

Library of Congress Cataloging-in-Publication Data

Whetsell-Mitchell, Juliann.
    From victims to survivors: reclaimed voices of women sexually abused in childhood by females / by Juliann Mitchell, Jill Morse.
        p.   cm.
    Includes bibliographical references and index.

    1. Adult child sexual abuse victims—United States—Case studies. 2. Sexually abused children—United States—Case studies.   3. Abused women—United States—Case studies.   4. Women child molesters—United States.   I. Morse, Jill.   II. Title.
    HV6570.2.W43   1997
    362.76'4'0973—dc21   97-33606
                                                                   CIP

ISBN 1-56032-569-0 (cloth)
ISBN 1-56032-570-4 (paper)

We would like to dedicate this book to the 80 women
who shared their stories with us,
and to the children and others
who do not yet have the voices to tell.

CONTENTS

ACKNOWLEDGMENTS

First, I would like to thank our editor, Dr. Joe Hollis of Accelerated Development. I also would like to say a special thank you to Juliann Mitchell for inviting me to be part of this project. Little did I know when I began compiling data from the questionnaires four years ago that I would become so involved in its development.

I would like to thank my parents, David and Penny Morse, for loving and supporting me, for believing in my ability to write, and especially for listening when I needed to talk. (Ma, thanks for always correcting my grammar. Although I hated it at the time, I guess you realized I would appreciate it someday.) Also, thanks to Wendy and Bill Frase for their visits, times to forget about deadlines and play games. I also must thank my gram, Jean Morse, for her love, support, and prayers. I am sure they have made a difference.

I must acknowledge some of my friends—Heather Mihalic, Lynann Neel, Darcey Palm, Jennifer Rullo, Karin Tomcik, and Jill Petersson—for their words and letters of encouragement while I was writing this book and for listening when I needed to talk about it.

A huge thank you to my best friend, Paul O'Rourke. Since I cannot sum up in just a few words everything you have done for me and all that you mean to me, I can only say, thank you.

Lastly, I would like to thank God for my healthy mind and body.

—Jill Morse

This book would not have been possible without the help and participation of the survivors who contributed their life stories. Thank you seems inadequate for all that each of you were willing to share so that this book could be written.

A special thanks to my family and friends for their love and support through the writing and rewriting of this book; and to two people at Accelerated Development, Dr. Joe Hollis, my editor, and also to Cindy Long, the editorial assistant. Your belief and support of this project has meant so much to me.

—Juliann Mitchell

BACKGROUND INFORMATION AND DATA SOURCES

This book evolved from a number of years of collecting data from female survivors of child sexual abuse. The abusers in these survivors' lives were female, and many of the perpetrators were the survivors' mothers or grand-mothers.

Within the last 10 years, a proliferation of books, articles, and television shows have focused on the topic of sexual abuse. Predominantly, the abusers portrayed have been males preying on female children. While it is true that female children are more often sexually abused and violated on every level by males, it also is true that females can and do molest children.

The female survivors of these personal horror stories never really have been given a voice to speak out and be heard. *From Victims to Survivors* tells the stories of 80 women who have survived and were gracious enough to share their stories with us. No identifying data were used, so their anonymity could be maintained.

These women were abused by mothers, grandmothers, aunts, cousins, Vacation Bible School teachers, baby-sitters, neighbors, female friends of the family, youth directors, clergy, and scout leaders. Most often, the abuse began before the age of five. Some of the abusive incidents were daily, weekly, or monthly, and often the abuse continued until the survivor left home as a young adult.

Forms of sexual abuse included oral sex, digital penetration, enemas, fondling of the genitals, being forced to touch others' genitals, objects inserted into the vagina and into the anus, mutilation, Lysol douches, and being forced to participate in sexual acts with animals (bestiality). Physical and emotional abuses were always part of the sexual abuse.

The majority of these women did not tell anyone about the abuse as children; the few who did try to tell someone were not believed. None of the female abusers ever was charged with a crime. When asked what prevented them from telling, many of the women said they were threatened, believed that it was all their fault, were afraid, or were told they had imagined it.

The respondents were from 36 of the 50 United States, the District of Columbia, Puerto Rico, and other countries, including Canada, Germany, Guam, and Israel. Their ages at the time of response ranged from 19 to 69 years. Occupations included writers, musicians, nurses, teachers, administrative assistants, chemists, social workers, journalists, computer consultants, homemakers, postal service employees, artists, waitresses, occupational therapists, probation officers, mechanics, park rangers, school counselors, and sales representatives.

The purposes of this book are (a) to enrich and augment the mental health professional's knowledge of the existence of female molesters and adult female survivors of sexual abuse; (b) to understand and address the myths and the realities of this phenomenon; and (c) to present case studies of survivors, in which they share their lives, discuss how they survived, and help the reader understand what has helped in the healing process and what has not.

The women were invited to share their personal stories of abuse in the form of narrative. **Narrative** is a word that signifies a sequencing or ordering of past events or experiences in which the individual tells the experiences in his or her own words (Fanshel & Labov, 1977). Narrating is used throughout an individual's lifetime to create order out of happenings. The individual then translates those occurrences into verbal or written words that can be shared with others. Narrative helps provide meaning and understanding for events (Riesman, 1990). Many of the questions in this study were asked in an open-ended manner to provide the women with the opportunity to begin to make some meaning out of what had happened in their lives. These narratives are *reports of events*, abusive acts in this case. Therefore, the information shared is *the survivors'* reporting of what happened. The events in the text were not observed by the authors. This does not mean we do not believe the stories. However, we want the reader to be aware that we do not have corroborative evidence to back up what was written by the respondents.

Contents of the participants' responses were reviewed, and patterns were identified. One interesting piece of information garnered from this study is that many of these survivors had mothers whom they defined as compulsive overeaters. This is not to say that most women who are sexual offenders are compulsive overeaters; such a generalization cannot be made. In this group of participants, however, 33% reported that their mothers were compulsive overeaters.

The questionnaire we used was structured in three main parts. The first was designed to obtain basic demographic data about life for the survivor while growing up (e.g., number of siblings; father's and mother's occupations; type of environment—rural, suburban, or urban—and socioeconomic status). The second part contained questions that focused on when and how the abuse began, how the survivor functioned as a child, if the abuse was revealed to anyone, what type of abuse took place, who the abusers were, and what the survivor's relationship was like with anyone else during childhood. The third part of the questionnaire focused on how the woman functions as an adult: What are her relationships like? How does she feel about herself? Who has she told about the abuse? What was each person's response? What does she want others to know about sexual abuse by female molesters?

A letter of introduction was included with each packet, as were a release of information form and a telephone number and office address (see Appendix A). All packets included self-addressed, stamped envelopes to return the information to the researchers' office. Potential participants were encouraged to call or write if they had any questions or concerns. Complete anonymity was assured, in that no names were used when the data were compiled. Respondents were encouraged to share the questionnaire with anyone of their choosing (therapist, supportive friends, etc.). Any requests for returned data were honored by the authors. It was completely acceptable if a participant decided she did not want to participate in the study because she had changed her mind. No form of research grant funded this study. All moneys used for copying journal articles, purchasing books, postage, and such came from personal funds. More than 250 packets were mailed to interested persons.

The data presented in the following chapters do not constitute a representative sample of women survivors of female perpetrators. They do not represent a cross-section of the population. We did not use a control group, and this was not a randomized study. The information was collected from women who identified themselves as having been abused as children by adult women. The women who supplied the data became aware of the project through ads placed in national survivor newsletters such as *S.O.F.I.E.* (Society Of Female Incestors Emerge). We present information that was found to be true *for this group of survivors.* How much of this information can be generalized to other adult female survivors is unknown at this time.

From Victims to Survivors interweaves these survivors' stories with theory and current research data on issues such as dissociative identity disorder, Munchausen's by Proxy Syndrome, memory, self-injury, and verbal and nonverbal treatment modalities. This book also includes some of the survivors' artwork and poetry, all of which will enable the reader to better understand what the participants experienced. This is a book about the resiliency of the human spirit and the ability to heal.

REFERENCES

Fanshel, D., & Labov, W. (1977). *Therapeutic discourse.* New York: Academic Press.

Riesman, C. K. (1990). *Divorce talk: Women and men make sense of personal relationships.* New Brunswick, NJ: Rutgers University Press.

Chapter 1

ABUSERS AND SURVIVORS

DEFINITIONS OF SEXUAL ABUSE

Determining a clear-cut definition of female sexual abuse is challenging at best. There are cultural variations in what is considered abusive and nonabusive treatment of children. Finkelhor and Korbin (1988) have developed this international definition of abuse, which is applicable to all cultures: "Child abuse is the portion of harm to children that results from human action that is proscribed, proximate and preventable" (p. 3). Lawson (1993) has suggested that maternal sexual abuse should include the following categorizations: subtle, seductive, pervasive, overt, and sadistic (p. 265). She defined each of these categories as follows,

> Subtle abuse is defined as behaviors that may not intentionally be sexual in nature but serve to meet the parent's emotional and/or sexual needs at the expense of the child's emotional and/or developmental needs. . . . Seductive abuse implies conscious awareness and intention of arousing or stimulating the child sexually . . . e.g., exhibitionistic display of nudity or sexual behavior; exposure to pornographic materials, etc. . . . Abuse of the child's sexuality or perversive abuse may include behavior such as forcing the boy to wear female clothing, criticizing the child's rate of sexual development, threatening the child with fears of homosexuality. . . . Overt sexual abuse . . . behaviors included are: attempted intercourse, cunnilingus, anilingus, fellatio, genital fondling, digital penetration. . . . Sadistic sexual abuse includes maternal sexual behavior that is

1

intended to hurt the child and may be part of a general pattern of severe physical and emotional abuse. (pp. 265-266)

The National Committee for Prevention of Child Abuse (NCPCA, 1988) has defined child sexual abuse as occurring when "a child is used for the sexual gratification of an adult" (p. 5).

For an illustration of the silencing of victims by their perpetrators, see Figure 1.1.

EFFECTS OF ABUSE

Traditionally the mother or mother-figure has been thought of as comforter, nurturer, soother, protector, and champion of her children's rights. Rarely have the words sadistic, sexually abusive, cruel, and assaultive been used to describe "normal" females involved in caretaking and caregiving roles. Most often if a female was found to be sexually abusive, she was labeled psychotic. Yet nonpsychotic mothers and other females can and do sexually, emotionally, and physically abuse both male and female children. A mother wounds and violates a sacred bond of trust when she sexually abuses her child. One of the most tragic aspects of sexual violation by a mother is the flagrant disregard of the child's attachment and trust of her. It is a fact that mothers and other females can and do commit heinous acts of violence against children's bodies, souls, and spirits.

Lori's Story

Lori's earliest memory of abuse by her mother occurred when she was 2. This abuse was physical and violent and ended with her mother, whom Lori described as "mentally ill," cutting her internally with a kitchen knife. Lori's abuse continued until she was 14 years old. Although she was sexually abused by approximately eight people, Lori's mother was the only female abuser.

Here's what Lori had to say about the manner in which she was abused,

My mother forced me to do oral sex on her; she did the same to me several times. She inserted objects (an egg beater, toys of metal, a knife, etc.) inside of me and hurt me when she was raging. She forced me to "nurse" when I was six or seven—to stimulate her. When I was nine, she cut me internally with a razor blade when I rebelled against having my legs shaved. She screamed out that I'd injured her at birth and she wanted me to hurt and die. My mother also used the douche bag regularly to "clean me out" and called me a "whore" from age five up.

Lori's abuse occurred more than three times a week for 12 years.

Lori tried to tell her aunt in a letter about the abuse. She wrote about how much she hated her mother, but her aunt's reply was, "all adolescents go through that." Lori told no one else. Her mother threatened her life to keep Lori quiet. And, although Lori's grandmother walked in on the abuse once, no one intervened. Here's what Lori said about the event:

> *My grandmother witnessed my mother using the douche on me and screamed at her in Italian. I don't know what she said. . . . She never followed through to help; the abuse went on.*

Like many people who undergo traumatic events, Lori dissociated to help her deal with her mother's violent sexual abuse. She said, *"I read 20 to 25 books a week and could think about the stories while being hurt. I counted tiles on the bathroom wall, patterns on the ceiling tiles; I escaped to rainbow places full of colors."* Lori wrote this poem about these rainbows.

RAINBOW OF HOPE

At times when life felt ugly,
The pain too much to bear,
My thoughts would travel skyward
Toward the beauty waiting there.

The joyful burst of color,
The clouds of fluffy white,
Somehow the memory of the rainbow
Got me through the night.

You must have sent the rainbow,
To give me hope, it seems;
To show me there is beauty,
To keep alive my dreams.

Oh, God! I offer thanks,
For the sunshine and the rain,
For all the brilliant colors,
That help to ease the pain.

The thought of rainbow colors
Somehow shined right through;
And the splendor of your rainbow,
Kept me close to you.

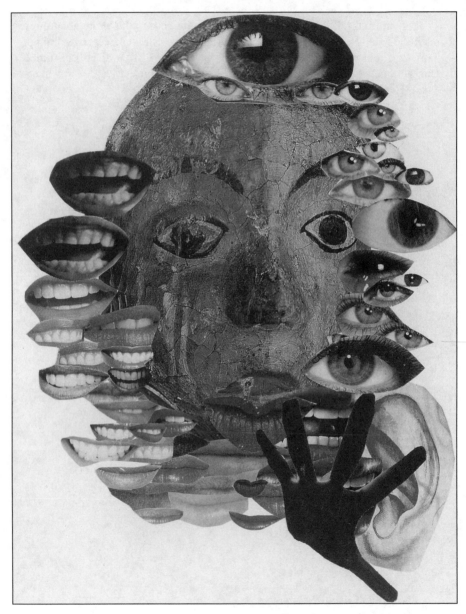

Figure 1.1.   From Victim to Survivor, by Juliann.

Figure 1.1.   This first collage is surrounded on the right by many eyes. Jacobson (1986) and Cohen and Cox (1995) have demonstrated that eyes are seen often in the artwork of sexually abused women. An ear has been placed in the lower right-hand corner with two mouths screaming into it, but a hand covers the mouths and part of the ear. This is an attempt to convey the idea that the child was silenced by the perpetrators or others who chose to ignore the abuse. The silence continued is represented by the closed mouths across the bottom of the page. Moving up the left-hand side of the collage, the mouths gradually begin to open until finally the last two mouths depicted are completely open and laughing, signifying that the survivor is no longer silenced. She has reclaimed her voice, in part by telling about the abuse.

Lori's abuse ended when she was 14 years old. She felt isolated; she had no close friends. *"I was non-trusting and lonely—always felt like I was on the outside,"* she said. Emotionally she was *"withdrawn, depressed, anxious, wanted to be anonymous, yet craved love. . . . I was in search of a real mother constantly, but didn't let myself get close enough to have a real connection."*

A major problem of early maternal abuse is the failure of the mother to be connected and responsive to what her child needs or feels. Kohut (1984) contended that all children have a basic need to be *mirrored*. Mirroring involves the mother or other caretaker acknowledging and responding to the child's need for love and approval. The mother/caretaker mirrors adequately if she validates, admires, and understands the child as the child exists in the world. If the needs of a child are met, the child will feel good about herself. If the basic needs of the child are not met, the child often feels invalidated and unloved. When a mother/caretaker responds to a child's needs of hunger, pain, and fear, the small child learns that the world (which the mother/caretaker symbolizes) is predominantly good—that it is a "safe" place in which to exist. When a mother/caretaker pays no attention to her child's needs or repeatedly responds in ways that violate the child or are hurtful, the child learns that no place is safe or secure and that the world, more often than not, disappoints and punishes. When a mother/caretaker does not soothe or nurture the child, it may be quite difficult for the adult survivor to know how to "take care" of herself.

It is not uncommon for a person who was sexually abused and whose sense of self was violated by a mother/caretaker to find it difficult in childhood and in adulthood to trust others—whether the person be a significant other, a therapist, a support group member, or even a friend. Erikson (1950) has stated that an individual needs to form a basic trusting relationship with at least one individual who assumes a caretaking role in order to progress through the other developmental stages. When a mother is not able to accept the child as she is, the child may reach adulthood feeling as if she has no inner self and is of little value. Because the mother/caretaker continually invalidated what she was experiencing as a child, the adult survivor may lack the ability to trust her thoughts and feelings and may seek out external others to tell her how she feels, what to do, and how to respond.

One participant in this study discussed the "unreality" of her experiences: *"I usually think I'm lying. When I believe it, I recoil in horror of what happened. I feel devastated."*

Another survivor commented, *"I am still blaming myself and am having a great deal of trouble accepting my returning memories. But I feel relief to know there is a reason for why I have felt so worthless."*

Finally, one woman responded by stating, *"I feel that it's surprising I am alive. I have survived my own personal Holocaust. I survived satanic ritual abuse. Few people will experience in a lifetime the suffering I endured in just one year of my childhood."*

ATTACHMENT THEORY

British psychiatrist John Bowlby has written extensively on attachment theory. He contends that attachment is a biological bond between caregiver and child. This attachment relates to survival needs:

> Thus attachment behaviour is conceived as a class of behaviour distinct from feeding behaviour and sexual behaviour and of at least an equal significance in human life. There is nothing intrinsically childish or pathological about it . . . the individual who shows attachment behaviour is usually referred to as child and the attachment figure as mother. . . . When mother is present or her whereabouts well-known and she is willing to take part in friendly interchange, a child usually ceases to show attachment behavior and, instead, explores his environment. In such a situation mother can be regarded as providing her child with a secure base from which to explore and to which he can return, especially should he become tired or frightened. (Bowlby 1979, pp. 131-132)

Other attachment behaviors in the infant include crying, smiling, walking, crawling, and saying the name of the caregiver or calling for her. These attachment behaviors are attempts on the part of the child to engage the caregiver or to stay close enough to her so that she can be seen by the child (Bowlby, 1977). Biringen (1994) said,

> Although parental attachment may exist from earlier on, the child's attachment to the primary caregiver (usually the mother) develops slowly, taking typically six months to establish a preferential relationship to that caregiver. (p. 405)

He continued,

> Once a normative attachment to the mother is established, the infant uses the mother as a secure base from which to explore the environment (Ainsworth, 1982). Because the infant feels safe and secure in the context of the mother's presence, he or she is able to go some distance from the mother and explore freely. (p. 405)

Part of Bowlby's theory was termed "the internal working model" by Main and Goldwyn (1984). According to this model, the development of the personality is based on a child's first experiences with the primary caregiver. The baby forms ideas about herself based on how she connects to others: If her needs are met, she learns she is of value and merits the care of others; if her needs are ignored, she learns she has little value.

Throughout the early developmental phases, the child learns how to take care of herself and how to care for others based on how she is treated by the attachment figure. This "internal working model" is composed of both thinking and feeling parts. Alexander (1992) wrote, "Therefore, the internal working model is both affected by and comes to affect the types of interpersonal experiences that are encoded into the concept of the self" (p. 186).

After the baby becomes attached to the primary caregiver, she uses this caregiver as a safe foundation from which to investigate her surroundings (Ainsworth, 1982). If the baby feels protected while the caregiver is in close proximity, she is capable of moving away from the caregiver and independently investigating the environment. As the child moves farther away from the caregiver, she becomes more anxious and fearful and once more moves toward the caregiver to be close to him or her. These attachment-seeking behaviors are also seen when the infant comes in contact with strangers, the dark, and animals.

Ainsworth, Blehar, Waters, and Wall (1978) supplied experiential data to support Bowlby's attachment theories in their "strange situation" research. In a laboratory setting during a 20-minute period, more than 50 12-month-old infants were separated from and then reunited with their mothers twice. The child's reaction to the mother during the reconciliations determined whether the child was categorized as secure or insecure. A securely attached infant either moved toward or welcomed the mother following a separation. Ainsworth et al. determined that these infants' mothers had responded appropriately to their babies' demands and needs during the first months of life.

An insecurely attached infant was identified as "avoidant." For the most part, the "avoidant" infant ignored or paid little attention to the mother on her reappearance in the experimental situation and did not choose her more than a stranger. These infants' mothers were identified as emotionally and physically detached from their children.

A second type of insecurely attached infant was identified as the "resistant" type. This child both sought the mother and displayed angry outbursts toward her upon her return. The "resistant" child stayed close to the mother before the separation, was quite upset during the separation, and both avoided and sought tthe mother after her return. The resistant child's mother was identified as being contradictory in her response patterns, sometimes responding to the child's needs and other times avoiding the child.

A third type of child was identified as the "disorganized/disoriented" (Main & Solomon, 1990). A child with this coping style acts in a variety of ways after the mother reappears: For example, at first the child seeks to be close to the mother, then vigorously avoids her, shows fear and anxiety when she returns, and looks at her in a bewildered manner. Loss and sexual abuse are attributes of the parent whose child uses "disorganized/disoriented" coping styles (Main & Cassidy, 1988).

Alexander (1992) reported that several researchers have categorized adults based on their attachments to others who play an important role in their lives (e.g., father, mother, husband, wife). These adults have been identified as secure, dismissing, preoccupied, or fearful. She identified secure adults as those able to think about their childhoods, at ease with an extensive array of feelings, able to trust others and themselves, and able to gain satisfaction from being close to others. Adults who have avoidant attachments (who would have been avoidant children) generally have few if any memories from childhood, do not feel comfortable being close to someone else, have low self-worth, and are isolated and angry. A preoccupied adult (who would have been a resistant child) is characterized as anxious, possessive, perplexed, envious, and suspicious. Finally, Alexander contended that the fearful adults (who would have been disorganized children) are hampered or impaired in their interactions with others, are passive, and may have some of both the avoiding and the preoccupied adult's characteristics.

Alexander (1992) suggested that insecure attachments of the parent to the child is antecedent to the child's being abused. She stated, "Attachment theory offers precise predictions as to how different types of insecure attachments are manifest in different types of parent/child interactions in the sexually abusive family" (p. 188).

Rejection is the first characteristic of the child who is avoidantly attached. This child feels as if she does not belong to the family and is not cared for by her parents. An avoidant or dismissing mother and father ignore the child and do not respond to her needs. Inaccessibility characterizes these parents. Alexander suggested, "the child who has developed an avoidant attachment pattern because of rejection may be even less able to defend himself or herself or to seek help from others either inside or outside the home" (p. 188).

Parentification (Gelinas, 1983) or role reversal is the second characteristic frequently seen in families in which sexual abuse occurs. This parentification of the child is often identified with a resistant form of attachment between parent and child.

> The experience growing up as a parentified child can lead to a sense of entitlement in either an abuser, resulting in expectations that one's child should meet one's own emotional and sexual needs, or in a nonabusive parent, resulting in expectations to be nurtured by rather than to nurture the child. (Alexander, 1992, p. 189)

Alexander continued,

> [A]lthough the resistant child's typical neediness (Sroufe, 1988) may elicit the support of other protective adults, it could also make her more vulnerable to the manipulations of an abusive adult or older child outside the home (Troy & Sroufe, 1987). (p. 189)

Finally, unresolved trauma relates to disorganized attachments in the family. A mother or father of a disorganized child may have been sexually abused and may have their own issues relating to abandonment. Alexander (1992) characterized this parent who molests as trying "to suppress or repress his own trauma or experience of abandonment through substance use or dissociation, reducing his impulse control. . . . Finally, the disorganized child may find herself in the untenable situation of seeing her abuser as her only ally" (p. 189).

Thus, an imbalance or insecurity in the attachment behaviors in members of a family are related to the inability to satisfy one's needs in socially acceptable and healthy ways, to not being cognizant of other family members' behaviors toward each other, and to not being able to ask for outside assistance to stop the abuse. So this type of insecure attachment may lay the foundation for sexual abuse in the family system (Alexander, 1992).

WHAT THE EXPERTS SAY

A number of individuals have contributed to bringing child abuse to our attention (Forward & Buck, 1979; Herman, 1981; Herman & Hirschman, 1977; Kempe et al., 1962; Meiselman, 1978; Miller, 1990; Rush, 1980). The vast majority of the data on child sexual abuse has focused on males as perpetrators and females as victims. The idea that females rarely are sexually abusive toward children continues. Olafson, Corwin, and Summit (1993) commented on female perpetrators, writing, "Recent surveys and studies indicate that men outnumber women among child molesters by very large percentages, especially when victims are girls" (p. 16). Freund and Kuban (1993) stated, "female pedophilia is very rare . . . and the question remains open whether in (nonschizophrenic) heterosexual females true pedophilia exists at all" (p. 315).

In contrast, Allen (1991) has suggested that about 1.5 million females in this country have been sexually abused by other females. His statistic is based on prevalence rates and 1989 U.S. Census Bureau total population statistics. He obtained his results using the following calculation: 127,300,00 (represents the total number of females in the United States) × 23% (represents the number of women experiencing abuse in childhood) × 5% (the percentage of females of male/female perpetrators who sexually abuse children; p. 20). Kendall-Tackett and Simon's (1987) retrospective study of adult survivors identified 3% of their study participants (total n = 365) as having been sexually abused by females. The American Humane Association's 1981 study determined that 6% of the female participants and 14% of the male participants had been sexually abused by females.

Myth #1: Women Don't Abuse Their Children

Our minds and physical bodies recoil at the thought of a mother sexually abusing her child. The very idea of a mother penetrating her daughter's vagina with a broomstick handle or giving her little girl Lysol douches causes us to cringe inside. The brutality some of these survivors experienced is almost unimaginable. Yet women do sexually abuse their own and others' children.

A few studies have validated that females do perpetrate acts of sexual abuse against male and female children (Allen, 1991; Faller, 1987; Fehrenbach & Monastersky, 1988; Knopp & Lackey, 1987; Mathews, Matthews, & Speltz, 1989; McCarty, 1986). But given how many studies are completed each year on sexual abuse, these few represent a very small portion indeed. This is not to suggest that female sexual abuse is rare; rather, it simply is not often addressed in the research literature.

A number of authors have taken issue with the myth of the female perpetrator. Miller (1990) had this to say:

> Mothers also abuse their children. Only the truth, even the most uncomfortable, endows a movement with the strength to change society, not the denial of the truth. . . . Hence young children, male as well as female, can become victims of adults of either sex. . . . Psychoanalysts protect the father and embroider the sexual abuse of

the child with the Oedipus, or Electra, complex, while some feminist therapists idealize the mother, thus hindering access to the child's
first traumatic experiences with the mother. Both approaches can
lead to a dead end, since the dissolving of pain and fear is not
possible until the full truth of the facts can be seen and accepted. (p.
78-79)

Welldon (1988) was in agreement with Miller when she stated, "Are we
blocked from perceiving this by our own idealization of motherhood? Surely
we are, and this is why even in the original Oedipal situation we fail to notice
Jocasta's responsibility. Hers is the most important case of incest" (p. 85).

Banning (1989) also addressed the issue of female sexual abusers:

The incidence of female sexual offenders will probably remain much
lower than that of males. However it is highly likely that we have
underestimated the true incidence due to our disbelief that this can
occur. In Freud's time father-daughter incest could not be accepted.
Child physical abuse was not recognized or acknowledged until the
1960's and child sexual abuse in the mid 1970's. Not until the 1980's
were male victims recognized and studied and their victimization
found to be more frequent than previously recognized. Mother-son
and mother-daughter incest could well be not as unusual as we had
thought or hoped. (p. 569)

Myth #2: Only Mentally Ill Women Abuse Children

The idea that only mentally ill women sexually abuse children is a fallacy.
None of the women in Mathews, Matthews, and Speltz's (1989) study of
women offenders were identified as out of touch with reality or having had
psychotic breaks. Very few of the women in this study identified their abuser
as being mentally ill. Perhaps the women offenders brought to the attention of
the legal authorities are not representative of the typical female offender, who
never is caught. None of the female molesters in this study was ever processed
through the legal system. This does not mean that seemingly normal appearing
women do not sexually abuse children. It might mean that they simply do not
get caught.

Denial that sexually abusive acts are committed by females is pervasive in
our society. Allen (1991) has suggested three reasons why female sexual abuse
of children has not been addressed:

First, professionals have overestimated the strength of the incest
taboo, particularly true for adherents of psychoanalytic traditions that

explain differences between women and men on the basis of innate, psychogenic characteristics. These characteristics, according to orthodox psychoanalytic theory, contribute to keeping women passive and docile, without sexual needs. Thus they are incapable of sexually abusing children. . . . A second reason is overextension of feminist explanations of child sexual abuse. Although similar to psychoanalytic explanations in that both perspectives are founded on the notion that only men—and not women—sexually abuse children, feminist explanations stem from a very different base. These explanations hold that men sexually abuse children, not because of inherent, individual differences between the two genders, but because of male-dominant social structures which socialize men to be aggressors and women and children to be victims. A third reason is overgeneralization of the empirical observation that the sexual abuse of children by women is rare. This occurs when professionals assume that if female child sexual abuse is not reported in the literature, it is not occurring. It also occurs when professionals assume that the low proportions of reported female-perpetrated child sexual abuse indicate low numbers in absolute figures. (p. 61)

Finkelhor (1986) suggested that certain kinds of sexually abusive experiences are not reported or are underreported because (a) experiences are not available to conscious memory and therefore are not retrieved; (b) experiences are partially blocked but can be brought to conscious awareness; (c) experiences are in conscious memory but do not fit the criteria being asked for in studies; or (d) experiences are not shared because of shame or other feelings associated with the sexual abuse (p. 48).

Sgroi (1982) had this to say about mothers and sexual abuse:

The socially accepted physical intimacy between a mother and her child may serve to mask incidents of sexual exploitation and abuse on the part of a mother. It may be that only sexually abusive mothers who are handicapped by serious mental illness or intellectual deficiency are detected since, by reason of their psychological impairment, they lack the skills to conceal successfully this behavior. (p. 230)

Myth #3: Only Low-Income Women Abuse Children

Another pervasive myth is that abuse by females occurs only in families of low socioeconomic status. Many of the survivors in our study reported growing up in a middle or upper socioeconomic bracket.

Current research indicates that one of every four females and one of every five males will have some type of sexual experience with an adult before the age of 18 (Bagley & Ramsey, 1986; Herman, Russell, & Trocki, 1986; Kilpatrick, Saunders, Veronen, Best, & Von, 1987). These data are not for just those of low socioeconomic status but hold across all socioeconomic groups.

Ann's Story

Ann is in her early 40s. She grew up in a middle-class family that was active in the church. Her father was a perfectionist. He always looked good and was concerned with public opinion and being respected. He was absent from the home often because of his career, and was withdrawn from the family when he was there. Ann's mother was viewed by the community as "a sweet women." Ann stated, *"So many people have told me, 'Your mother is so sweet.'"* For Ann, the "ultimate sin" was to embarrass her mother in public, because public appearances were extremely important to her mother as well as to her father. Ann remembers her mother being sweet in public and wicked in private:

> *This attitude of changing sides—nice one minute and cruel the next— which had nothing whatsoever to do with my behavior at the time generated incredible confusion and fear and feelings of being without any security. (Only recently have I begun to see that her criteria of which attitude to manifest was associated with what would make her look good—this realization has cleared away so much of this chronic confusion).*

Keeping up public appearances was important so that no one would become suspicious of what was going on at home. For as long as Ann can remember, she was sexually, physically, and emotionally abused by her mother. *"There was always an underlying undercurrent of threat of sexual abuse. It could erupt from my mother at any time."*

From the time Ann was an infant and up into preschool, her mother would starve her, then take off her own clothes and force Ann to suck on her breasts. Ann said, *"Sometimes she would masturbate herself while I 'nursed.' If I resisted, she would toss me to the floor and leave me with bruises."*

As Ann got older, the abuse continued. Upon coming home from school each day, Ann had to take off her clothes and beg her mother for forgiveness for leaving her for the day. Ann was supervised whenever she was dressing or using the toilet, and her mother would bathe with Ann and make her suck her breasts.

In addition to the sexual abuse, Ann suffered much verbal and emotional abuse. Her mother told her that she was "retarded" and "trash" and "a bad, bad girl." Ann said, *"She told me repeatedly that she wished I had died as a baby so that she could have had another daughter—who would have been a 'good girl.'"* Her mother also would tear apart the stuffed animals to which Ann showed an attachment and "severely punish" Ann for sucking her thumb. All of this happened before Ann was 10.

Also during this time, Ann's mother claimed that Ann had a number of medical problems and often took her for check-ups. This is what Ann had to say about it:

> *She said I had a lot of health problems and took me often (one to two times a month) to the pediatrician and had him examine my vagina while she watched. Then she would talk about this exam for days and examine me herself. She would call me a whore (I didn't know what this meant until I was much older) and said that I enjoyed having my legs apart.*

Another form of abuse during her early childhood occurred with a female cousin three years younger than Ann. *"Many times I was tied up and made to watch while she was abused, and they would switch and hurt me while she watched. Witnessing another girl's abuse was awful,"* Ann stated.

When Ann was 11 years old, her father became very ill and was hospitalized for months. Ann had this to say about the time her father was out of the home: *"This isolation from my father (or rather his physical presence in the home) and the pressure on my mother during this time triggered major abuse which ushered in a whole new wave of chronic patterns."*

The family moved into a new home, in which Ann was not allowed her own room. In fact, she was forced to share a room with her abusive mother. Even when her father came home from the hospital, Ann had to share a room with the two of them, sleeping in a twin bed with her mother. Ann had this to say: *"I would lie awake and most nights I would manage to disentangle myself (she would hold me tight like a stuffed animal), and I would go into the living room and sleep on the floor."*

Ann's mother became obsessed with Ann's sexual development during this time. She often "inspected" Ann's breasts and talked frequently about menstrual cycles, and about how Ann would become a "whore" when hers began. She would make Ann strip down to her underwear and get on her knees to ask permission to do anything, and she laughed at Ann if she cried.

Although a sixth-grade teacher noticed that Ann was depressed, there was no intervention other than a phone call home to her mother. *"My mother was enraged at me for 'being a problem' and beat me,"* Ann said.

Because the family didn't have much money due to her father's poor health, Ann's mother made her clothes.

> She always bought ugly colors—oranges, browns—and made weird clothes that I hated. I wasn't allowed to pick out anything because I was "too stupid to know what I wanted." While she was making a dress, she would have me stay in the room with her in my underwear ready to "try it on." She would try to make me point to my nipples to "place the point of the dart." I would get really upset, and she would pin me against the wall and threaten to "call the doctor" about me.

Ann's mother continued to schedule appointments for her to be examined by the doctor. *"She would tell me explicit stories of physical examinations and became sexually excited as she talked,"* Ann remembered. During this time, her mother also talked often about death.

> She told explicit (real or imagined) stories of rape where the woman died after the abuse. . . . She read the obituaries to me every morning and talked about illness and funerals. She would plan my funeral often—writing the order of the service, songs, etc

The sexual abuse continued through adolescence; however, Ann cannot yet remember much of her life from the ages of 16 to 25. She remembers her mother and her mother's sister forcing her to take showers with them. They would look at Ann's body and "make fun" of her sexually.

During this phase, Ann finally got her own room. *"However, she would 'visit' whenever she wanted, and I had no privacy,"* she stated. A separate, secluded room also made Ann more vulnerable to sexual abuse from her brother, who had abused her for most of her life. He wanted Ann to be his maid and sexual slave.

When Ann was in college, the abuse continued. Her mother refused to let Ann leave home, but she made Ann pay rent for the privilege of living there. When Ann was 22, she got a yeast infection. Ann's mother found out about it from a friend's mother and forced Ann to go to her mother's doctor. *"It got cleared up, but my mother insisted it had been sexually transmitted and repeatedly humiliated me in front of her friends about it."*

Ann finally moved out at age 25, even though moving out caused "World War III." However, after an accident and illness when she was 27, Ann ended up spending about two months at her mother's house again. *"She gave me large amounts of Valium and sexually assaulted me several times,"* Ann remembers.

Ann was at her mother's house again in her early 30s. Her father had died, and she spent a week there after the funeral. This time her mother verbally and physically abused her. That was Ann's last visit.

Ann repressed her sexual abuse. When asked how she dealt with the sexual abuse at the time it occurred, she answered, *"Dissociated—I just 'left' didn't become someone else—just numbed out and felt like I didn't exist. Distinct perception of myself as a wind-up toy, inanimate object."* However, Ann's mother hated it when Ann "numbed out" and would beat her to make her "come back."

Memories about the sexual abuse by her brother began to surface first. Ann was in group therapy for this abuse with a woman who had been sexually abused by a female. Hearing the woman's story triggered Ann's memories of her mother's abuse.

Ann has been severely affected by her mother's sexual abuse: *"My sexuality is really messed up. There are phases I go through when I'm not sure I'm a woman—I think maybe I'm an it."*

She is chronically depressed and often thinks about suicide: *"I feel hopeless most of the time—mostly I feel guilt for my existence. . . . I have a hard time being present. I'm numbed out, spaced out a lot."*

Ann is in individual and group therapy. She feels that she is fortunate to have found a group of female survivors of sexual abuse perpetrated by women. *"This experience validated me and supported me in my process more than anything else"* she said.

Myth #4: Most Sexual Offenders Are Strangers

Another prevalent myth is that almost all sexual offenders are strangers to the children they molest. A review of the general research literature indicates that 80% to 90% of the time, the child knows his or her abuser (Seattle Institute for Child Advocacy, 1984). In out study, all of the participants knew their abuser.

Myth #5: Child Abuse Is a Recent Development

Many individuals have purported that child sexual abuse is a modern day occurrence. This is a myth. Adults have been documented using and abusing children for hundreds of years. In Europe it was common practice for adults to be sexual with children during the 16th, 17th, and 18th centuries (deMause, 1974).

Freud gives a classic example of how professionals have perpetuated the myth that sexual abuse is a rare phenomenon. Freud's Oedipus theory was developed because his documentation of sexual abuse by his patients was considered scandalous by his colleagues in Austria. When Freud discussed his findings linking hysteria and sexual abuse, he was met with derision and hostility from his professional peers. Following this, Freud reworked his ideas, and the Oedipus theory was born. It was much more acceptable to blame the child for desiring the opposite-sex parent than to believe that adults, often parents or other caretakers, could and did sexually abuse children.

"I'm late! I'm late! For a very important date," said the White Rabbit in Walt Disney's version of the children's story, *Alice in Wonderland,* authored by Lewis Carroll. Carroll was the pen name for Charles Dodson, a clergyman at Oxford University's Christ Church College in Great Britain. One of his favorite hobbies was to photograph nude children. In fact, Carroll kept diaries in which he meticulously documented his photographic exploitation of children (Tyler & Stone, 1985).

Myth #6: Child Sexual Abuse Is a One-Time Event

Another myth is that sexual abuse of a child usually is a one-time occurrence. Only one of the participants in our study documented her sexual abuse by a female as a one-time occurrence. Other studies of the sexually abusive behaviors of female perpetrators document that the large majority of abusive incidents happened repeatedly.

Often when a male is the abuser, the child is "groomed." Some of this behavior was reported in the Mathews, Matthews, and Speltz (1989) study of female offenders, as well. In one case, for example, the female offender and her husband began to play spin-the-bottle with their children and would French-kiss the children. This progressed to strip poker and eventually to sexual intercourse. During the grooming process, the child is desensitized to behaviors that become more openly and progressively sexual as time passes. Sometimes a child is exposed to sexually explicit videos or pornographic magazines or the abuser exposes his or her genitals to the child. This may progress to fondling, kissing, and so forth, until sexual intercourse occurs. Most of the survivors in our study did not report being groomed, especially if the perpetrator was the mother.

Sgroi (1982) reported five phases in abuse that occurs inside the family unit.

> First is *the engagement phase*. Sgroi wrote, "How does he or she get the child to participate in some type of sexual behavior? Usually in a low-key nonforcible fashion, possibly by presenting the activity as a game or something that is 'special' and fun" (p. 13).
>
> Next is *the sexual interaction phase*, during which the sexual activity progresses from the perpetrator exposing his or her genitals to vaginal and maybe even anal penetration of the child.
>
> During the next stage, *the secrecy phase*, the offender wants to keep his or her activity a secret. Sgroi wrote, "the perpetrator is unlikely to wish to be caught and held responsible for the sexual abuse. Secrecy also enables repetition of the behavior" (p. 15).
>
> Following the secrecy phase is *the disclosure phase*. According to Sgroi, there are two types of disclosure, accidental and purposeful. With accidental disclosure "the secret was revealed accidentally because of external circumstances. The key factor here is that none of the participants decided to tell the secret" (p. 17). In purposeful disclosure, "A young child may tell the secret to share it. . . . An older child usually tells the secret for very different reasons. Often he or she is trying to escape or modify some family pressure situations" (p. 19).
>
> The last phase Sgroi identified is *the suppression phase:*

> [T]he child's immediate and extended family are likely to react by trying to suppress publicity, information, and intervention. . . . When sexual abuse has occurred within the family circle, suppression is likely to be intense. . . . Feeling isolated and perhaps even ostracized, the child may give in and withdraw the complaint or simply stop cooperation with those who are trying to assist him or her. (p. 25)

Sgroi's suppression phase ties in with the myth that children often lie about being sexually abused. Most persons who are abused as children do not share their secret with anyone. The survivors in our study often did not tell anyone; when they did, they were not believed. No child protective agencies became involved. Reasons for not telling varied from being emotionally terrorized by the abuser to being threatened with physical beatings if anyone found out about the abuse. Sexual abuse is an underreported phenomenon.

ADULT SYMPTOMATOLOGY

Frequently, adult survivors of sexual abuse describe feelings of rage, shame, fear, stigmatization, helplessness, guilt, grief, and isolation long after the abuse had stopped (Courtois, 1988; Herman, 1981). Survivors in our study expressed feeling "different" in their survivor support groups when the other group members were abused by males. One survivor said this:

> *Oh tell me, tell me, please tell me that there are other women out there who have been abused by their mothers. I feel so alone, so different from the others in my survivor support groups. All those women were abused by men. I feel different, like I don't belong.*

This book explores the details of 80 women's lives, how they have coped and survived, what has been helpful and healing to them. It gives them a chance to have a voice and to share their stories.

Some readers will believe, others will choose to negate or deny that sexual abusers can be female. Certain individuals will minimize the abuse by insisting that sexual abuse by females happens only in rare situations. We differ with this claim, and suggest that sexual abuse by females is one of the most under-reported acts of violence committed against female children.

Last night I told my story;
Twelve pages of unspeakable acts against your child!
And when I finished weeping, mother,
I burned you up!

My sister survivors held me up,
As we watched the brilliant flames
Charbroil the edges of my now-spoken rage
And I watched you melt away!

The heat fueled my pain, tho';
I feared I, too, would die,
As I stepped up close and witnessed your fury
Reduced to harmless ash!

Oh mother, why do I so fear
That letting go of you
Will be the death of me . . .
Reducing me to lifeless ashes too!

What invisible cord, toxic mother,
Keeps me bound to you,
And chokes me now,
In violent rage?

REFERENCES

Ainsworth, M. D. S. (1982). Attachment: Retrospect and prospect. In C. M. Parkes & J. Stevenson-Hinde (Eds.), *The place of attachment in human behavior* (pp. 3-30). New York: Basic Books.

Ainsworth, M. D. S., Blehar, M. C., Waters, E., & Wall, S. (1978). *Patterns of attachment: A psychological study of the strange situation.* Hillsdale, NJ: Erlbaum.

Alexander, P. C. (1992). Application of attachment theory to the study of sexual abuse. *Journal of Clinical and Consulting Psychology, 60*(2), 185-195.

Allen, C. M. (1991). *Women and men who sexually abuse children: A comparative analysis.* Orwell, VT: Safer Society Press.

American Humane Association. (1981). *National study on child neglect and abuse report.* Denver: Author.

Bagley, C., & Ramsey, R. (1986). Sexual abuse in childhood: Psychosocial outcomes and implications for social work practice. *Journal of Social Work and Human Sexuality, 4,* 33-47.

Banning, A. (1989). Mother-son incest: Confronting a prejudice. *Child Abuse & Neglect, 13,* 563-570.

Biringen, Z. (1994). Attachment theory and research: Application to clinical practice. *American Journal of Orthopsychiatry, 64*(3), 404-420.

Bowlby, J. (1977). The making and breaking of affectional bonds: I. Aetiology and psychopathology in the light of attachment theory. *British Journal of Psychiatry, 130,* 421-431.

Bowlby, J. (1979). *The making and breaking of affectional bonds.* New York: Tavistock.

Cohen, B. M., & Cox, C. T. (1995). *Telling without talking: Art as a window into the world of multiple personality.* New York: Norton.

Courtois, C. A. (1988). *Healing the incest wound.* New York: Norton.

deMause, L. (1974). *The history of childhood.* New York: Psychohistory Press.

Erikson, E. (1950). *Childhood and society.* New York: Norton.

Faller, K. (1987). Women who sexually abuse children. *Violence & Victims, 2,* 263-276.

Fehrenbach, P., & Monastersky, C. (1988). Characteristics of female adolescent sexual offenders. *American Journal of Orthopsychiatry, 58,* 148-151.

Finkelhor, D. (1986). *A sourcebook on child sexual abuse.* Newbury Park, CA: Sage.

Finkelhor, D., & Korbin, J. (1988). Child abuse as an international issue. *Child Abuse & Neglect, 12,* 3-24.

Forward, S., & Buck, C. (1979). *Betrayal of innocence: Incest and its devastation.* New York: Penguin.

Freund, K., & Kuban, M. (1993). Toward a testable developmental model of pedophilia: The development of erotic age preference. *Child Abuse & Neglect, 17,* 315-324.

Gelinas, D. J. (1983). The persisting negative effects of incest. *Psychiatry, 46,* 313-332.

Herman, J. (1981). *Father-daughter incest.* Cambridge, MA: Harvard University Press.

Herman, J., & Hirschman, L. (1977). Father-daughter incest. *Signs: Journal of Women in Culture and Society, 2,* 735-756.

Herman, J., Russell, D., & Trocki, K. (1986). Long-term effects of incestuous abuse in childhood. *American Journal of Psychiatry, 143,* 1293-1296.

Jacobson, M. (1986, September). *Managing anger in the multiple personality patient: Therapeutic approaches through art therapy.* Paper presented at the Third International Conference on Multiple Personality/Dissociative States. Chicago.

Kempe, H., Silverman, F. N., Steele, B. F., Droegmueller, W., & Silver, H. K. (1962). The battered child syndrome. *Journal of the American Medical Association, 181,* 17-24.

Kendall-Tackett, K. A., & Simon, A. F. (1987). Perpetrators and their acts: Data from 365 adults molested as children. *Child Abuse & Neglect, 11,* 237-245.

Kilpatrick, D. B., Suanders, B. E., Veronen, L. J., Best, C. L., & Von, J. M. (1987). Criminal victimization: Lifetime prevalence, reporting to police, and psychological impact. *Crime and Delinquency, 13,* 479-489.

Knopp, F. H., & Lackey, L. B. (1987). *Female sexual abusers: A summary of data from 44 treatment providers.* Orwell, VT: Safer Society Press.

Kohut, H. (1984). *How does analysis cure?* Chicago: University of Chicago Press.

Lawson, C. (1993). Mother-son sexual abuse. *Child Abuse & Neglect, 1,* 261-269.

Main, M., & Cassidy, J. (1988). Categories of response to reunion with the parent at age 6: Predictable from infant attachment classification and stable over a one-month period. *Developmental Psychology, 24,* 415-426.

Main, M., & Goldwyn, R. (1984). Predicting rejection of her infant from mother's representation of her own experience: Implications for the abused-abusing intergenerational cycle. *Child Abuse & Neglect, 8,* 203-217.

Main, M., & Solomon, J. (1990). Procedures for identifying infants as disorganized/disoriented during the Ainsworth strange situation. In M. Greenberg, D. Cichetti, & M. Cummings (Eds.), *Attachment in the preschool years* (pp. 121-160). Chicago: University of Chicago Press.

Mathews, R., Matthews, J., & Speltz, K. (1989). *Female sexual offenders: An exploratory study.* Orwell, VT: Safer Society Press.

McCarty, L. (1986). Mother-child incest: Characteristics of the offender. *Child Welfare, 65,* 457-558.

Meiselman, K. (1978). *Incest: A psychological study of cause and effects with treatment recommendations.* San Francisco: Jossey-Bass.

Miller, A. (1990). *Banished knowledge: Facing childhood injuries.* New York: Doubleday.

National Committee for Prevention of Child Abuse (1988). *Basic facts about child sexual abuse.* Chicago: Author.

Olafson, E., Corwin, D. L., & Summit, R. C. (1993). Modern history of child sexual abuse awareness: Cycles of discovery and suppression. *Child Abuse & Neglect, 17,* 7-24.

Rush, F. (1980). *The best kept secret: The sexual victimization of children.* New York: McGraw-Hill.

Seattle Institute for Child Advocacy. (1984). *Understanding child abuse.* Seattle: Author.

Sgroi, S. M. (1982). *Handbook of clinical intervention in child sexual abuse.* Lexington, MA: Lexington Books.

Sroufe, L. A. (1988). The role of infant-caregivers attachment in development. In J. Belsky & T. Nezworski (Eds.), *Clinical applications of attachment* (pp. 18-38). Hillsdale, NJ: Erlbaum.

Troy, M., & Sroufe, L. (1987). Victimization among preschoolers: Role of attachment relationship history. *Journal of the American Academy of Child Psychiatry, 26,* 166-172.

Tyler, R. P., & Stone, L. E. (1985). Child pornography: Perpetuating the sexual victimization of children. *Child Abuse & Neglect, 9,* 313-318.

Welldon, E. V. (1988). *Mother, madonna, whore: The idealization and denigration of motherhood* New York: Guilford Press.

Chapter 2

DISSOCIATIVE IDENTITY DISORDER

A BRIEF HISTORY

The first detailed report of Dissociative Identity Disorder (DID) is from 1791 (Crabtree, 1993). At that time, theories about the disorder were based on the Marquis de Puysegur's theory of **magnetic sleep**. In 1784, Puysegur had attended several seminars on healing taught by Franz Anton Mesmer, a Viennese physician. Using Mesmer's ideas of healing by laying hands on a patient (*animal magnetism*), Puysegur developed a method he termed magnetic sleep, which he likened to sleep-walking. Magnetic sleep "revealed a world of mental activity separated from normal awareness. It pointed to a second or alternate consciousness that possesses distinct personal qualities and a separate memory chain" (Crabtree, 1993, p. 67).

The first reported case of DID was us a 21-year-old woman in Stuttgart, Germany, who took on the personality of a typical Frenchwoman of that day. She believed herself to be from Paris and spoke perfect French (and had a French accent when she spoke German). Neither personality had any knowledge of the other. Her doctor, Eberhard Gmelin, was able to control these personalities by applying what he knew about magnetic sleep. When he induced the magnetic sleep, the woman's French personality would come forward (Crabtree, 1993).

While the concept of an alternate consciousness that could be reached in magnetic sleep was a crucial step forward, it was lacking in two ways. First, although it very nicely explained dual personality, it could not easily account for multiple personalities. Second, it did not specify a precipitating cause of the disorder." (Crabtree, 1993, p. 68)

Nearly 20 years later, in 1811, Dr. Benjamin Rush presented lectures to medical school students on dissociative disorders. Rush, an American physician, was the first to write about dissociation and DID (Carlson, 1984). In 1816, S. L. Mitchill published a case on dissociative disorder. The name of the woman in the case study was Mary Reynold. Both Pierre Janet and Alfred Binet discussed the case of Mary Reynold, but they used the pseudonym "la dame de Macnish" (Carlson, 1984).

From 1880 to 1952, there was a growing awareness of dissociation, and of "the fact that the psyche is capable of partitioning off segments of experience" (Crabtree, 1993, p. 68). There also was an awareness that "dissociation often occurs in response to trauma, and that in the process any number of psychic centers may be formed. These insights provided the basis for understanding how it is possible to have multiple personalities and for pinpointing what causes the formation of the personalities" (Crabtree, 1993, p. 68).

In the early 1880s, there was a noted cases of DID: Louis Vivé, a young man from Rochefort, France, displayed six distinct personalities, each of whom held memories from different periods of his life. His doctors, Bourru and Burot, hypnotized Vivé to induce him to switch personalities by incorporating memories from different phases of his life to each personality. "They considered this discovery to be of great importance, because it allowed retrieval and restoration of the blocked memories that caused the formation of each personality" (Crabtree, 1993, p. 68). Drs. Bourru and Burot considered Vivé's personalities to be different trance states (i.e., "successive hypnoid states of one individual, successive variations of one personality" [Crabtree, 1993, pp. 68-69]).

In 1887, Pierre Janet went a step further. Using his work with hysterics, he developed a concept of dissociation (Crabtree, 1993; Putnam, 1989; van der Hart & van der Horst, 1989). He learned that some people formed psychic centers that coexisted, "each thinking and reacting simultaneously with the others" (Crabtree, 1993, p. 69), unlike Drs. Bourru and Burot, who believed that trance states occurred one after the other. Also, Janet discovered that these subconscious personalities were products of traumatic events. These events sparked the ideas of the new personalities. "As it turned out, Janet's system was equally effective for understanding and treating multiple personality disorder, in which the various personalities spontaneously emerge to interact with the world" (Crabtree, 1993, p. 69).

In the 20th Century, the general public was introduced to such famous cases as Mortin Prince's "Miss Beauchamp," Drs. Thigpen and Cleckley's "Eve," and Cornelia Wilbur's "Sybil."

DISSOCIATION DEFINED

What researchers used to call **Multiple Personality Disorder (MPD)** is now termed **Dissociative Identity Disorder (DID)**, according to the fourth edition of the *Diagnostic and Statistics Manual* (APA, 1994). Dissociation has been described as such:

> The exclusion of an experience from conscious awareness. For sexually abused children dissociation often serves as a primary defense and coping strategy (Courtois, 1988). By dissociating, the child can be protected against the overwhelming traumatic feelings and experiences he or she is helpless to stop. Then, to preserve the original sense of self, the traumatic experience is split off and forgotten, and the child continues to develop, although often with a sense of self-fragmentation. (Sheiman, 1993, p. 14)

Calof (1995) described this phenomenon this way:

> Dissociation lets us step aside, split off from our own knowledge (ideas), our behavior, emotions, and body sensations, our self-control, identity, and memory. Dissociation, the splitting of the mind and the pigeon-holing of experience, is a natural adaptation to the complex demands of daily life. . . . At the farthest end of the dissociative continuum lies dissociative identity disorder (DID, formerly MPD), with its characteristic amnesia, derealization, depersonalization, and personality-splitting. (pp. 6-7)

Survivors in our study shared the following strategies when asked how they dealt with the abuse at the time it happened:

"I divided my brain. I indulged in dissociation enough to be able to function in both the real world and its underside—my family—without remembering the other."

"I completely forgot it."

"I never forgot completely—but began remembering details at age 22."

"I always remembered the enemas and the sex at 28."

"I usually ended up being admitted to the hospital and the abuse stopped. I therefore became a sick child. . . . I also participated in the sexual act and felt this was an expression of love when it felt good. Whenever it hurt, I left my body and just numbed."

"I dissociated and told myself that I would never be that being again. In other words, I took the blame."

"I knew what happened, but I did not know it was abuse until I went to therapy at age 39."

"I dissociated. She [the mother] convinced me I was a demon. The world would kill me if they knew who I really was."

"I went into myself."

"I learned how to dissociate."

"I have one memory when I am out of my body on the ceiling watching. I forgot afterwards. I hid in the closet a lot. I accepted responsibility. I tried to be invisible."

"I could escape my body. . . . I would become an empty human with only a shell."

"Blocked it out, repressed it, split it from feelings and awareness."

"Dissociated as much as possible. After each specific incident, I 'forgot it' as if it never happened."

"I watched from a distance. I thought is was someone else."

"Totally giving in to her. We merged in a sick kind of way and I was trained to fulfill her needs—emotional, physical, whatever. I was like a slave."

"I dissociated and got MPD."

"Dissociated."

"Dissociated. We are many. I have MPD. We began dissociating when we were very little. There are many little ones in our system. We became trees, leaves, clouds, moons, anything that wasn't our body to deal with the abuse."

"I dissociated always."

"Dissociation and not remembering the details."

"Created blackness inside my mind, into which I would go every time I was hurt."

"Blanked out, had endless nightmares. I wet the bed until I was a teenager, I cried a lot."

Van der Kolk and Fisler (1995) suggested that the term dissociation is a descriptor for four different experiences. The first involves "the sensory and emotional fragmentation of an experience" (p. 510). Second are those phenomena that happen when the trauma occurs. These experiences are called "depersonalization and derealization" (p. 510). A third type of dissociative experience identified by these authors is "ongoing depersonalization and 'spacing out' in everyday life" (p. 510). Fourth are those dissociative events "containing the traumatic memories within distinct ego-states" (p. 510).

Briere (1989) discussed the seven most typical manners in which people may use dissociation:

- **Disengagement** is the first type. The individual withdraws from experiencing any thoughts or feelings. Briere described these as "brief time-outs," and they may occur often throughout the day.
- Second is **detachment**. Briere described this aspect of dissociation as "turn-ing down the volume control." This also has been called "numbing." Detachment or numbing may create situations in which the survivor is unaware of her feelings or does not feel anything because the feelings are too painful for her.
- **Observation** is the third type of dissociation. Briere described this as being on the "outside of oneself looking in." Thoughts and feelings are not connected, the survivor sees herself talking or engaging in activities but does not participate in the affective component of the experience.
- **Postsession amnesia** is the fourth form of dissociation. It is not uncommon for therapists to discover that clients have no memory of significant information from prior sessions. This amnesia protects the client from becoming overwhelmed during treatment. Postsession amnesia is a way for the client to regulate the therapeutic process. It also can be used by the survivor of abuse to modify her level of intimacy with the mental health professional.

- **As if** is the fifth form of dissociation. Clients using this mechanism *pretend* to feel emotions and experience insights—but it is simply a pretense. A client may be too overwhelmed and panicked at the thought of being close to someone else.

- **Shutdown** is the sixth form of dissociation described by Briere. It is, "a very basic, primal state during which he or she is unaware of his or her surroundings." These shutdown behaviors range from a client's decreased awareness of herself, her surroundings, or others in the same room to swaying, wailing, groaning, or crying. In this form of dissociation, the client is attempting to escape from the situation. Grounding techniques should be used by the therapist.

- **Total repression** is the seventh form of dissociation. An individual in a completely repressed state presents long blank spaces in her early life history but denies being abused (Briere, 1989).

One of the survivors who participated in our study sent us an article from the survivor newsletter *MPD—Reaching Out*. This excerpt is from a reader who suggested another name for dissociative disorder and her reasons for the proposed category.

> Rather than using the term Multiple Personality Disorder, I personally prefer to use my own term of Fragmented Identity Syndrome for the following reasons: Personalities reflect the division of oneself into many, not the multiplication of oneself into many; 2) MPD is a dissociative disorder and should not have a name that confuses it with the personality disorders such as "borderline." The word "identity" is nearly synonymous with "personality"; 3) "syndrome" is a less offensive term to survivors of abuse than "disorder" as well as not implying that one's inner workings are a mess. MPD is in fact an orderly, systematic means of dealing with what would otherwise be unbearable; 4) For those new to the diagnosis, Fragmented Identity Syndrome does not sound nearly as frightening as Multiple Personality Disorder, to ourselves and others; Finally, 5) FIS is a more inclusive term for the other forms of multiplicity. (*MPD— Reaching Out*, June 1992, p.18)

ETIOLOGY OF DID

Having just described the seven types of dissociation, it is critical to determine, or at least attempt to understand, the etiology of Dissociative Identity Disorder. Both Ross and Braun have proposed explanations for this phenomenon.

Figure 2.1. Many Faces, by Jill. This is our impression of how a person with dissociative identity disorder feels. We tried to represent the alters as being male, female, babies, children, and dark figure or the perpetrator in this drawing.

Ross (1994) wrote,

> Two basic psychological maneuvers form the foundation of multiple personality disorder. First, the little girl who is being repeatedly sexually abused has an out of the body experience of what is going on. . . . Second, an amnesia barrier is erected between the original child and the newly created identity. Now not only is the abuse not happening to the original little girl, she doesn't even remember it. (p. viii)

Ross (1993) suggested that 5% of the general adult psychiatric inpatient population has DID that has not been diagnosed.

Braun (1988a, 1988b) developed the BASK model of dissociation to explain the memory disruption of persons who have experienced long-term abuse intermittently dispersed with love from the caregiver. Courtois (1992) wrote this about the BASK model:

> [It] posits that an individual's domains (Behavior, Affect, Sensation, Knowledge) occur within a time continuum which are split off or separated from each other by the process of dissociation in the interest of making the trauma bearable. Thus, the overwhelming experience is defensively fragmented and disorganized and emerges in disjointed form. In treatment, the dissociated individual is assisted to access all four domains for the information they contain about the trauma. The information is then reintegrated into consciousness in its totality. (p.21)

MISDIAGNOSIS OF DID

An increased awareness of DID has led to a corresponding increase in its misdiagnosis. This type of misdiagnosis falls into three categories, according to Chu (1991): "patients with other dissociative or trauma-related disorders, patients with no dissociative disorders but other major psychiatric disorders, and patients with factitious disorders or who are malingering" (p. 200).

Dissociative and trauma-related disorders can be easy to confuse. "Many . . . patients have severe dissociative experiences, including a fragmented sense of self, but do not have true multiple personalities" (Chu, 1991, p. 200). Under situations of stress, dissociative symptoms may seem more severe than they actually are, and a patient may fit the critieria for DID. However, when the stressor has been removed, the severity of the symptoms decreases, and the criteria for DID will not be met. Also, patients with dissociative disorders may "consciously or unconsciously exaggerate their dissociative symptoms" (p. 201). This occurs most often in people who are hospitalized with DID patients. Another factor that can lead to a misdiagnosis of DID is "overenthusiastic" clinicians or family members who influence the patient and encourage fragmentation.

When nondissociative disorders are diagnosed as DID, patients often have psychotic disorders or severe mood disorders instead, and the "belief that they have MPD proves to be completely delusional" (Chu, 1991, p. 201). Other times, a patient might have a dissociative disorder and some other psychiatric disorder. "In general, clinical experience has suggested that a mood or psychotic disorder which coexists with a dissociative disorder may increase dissociative symptomatology" (p. 202).

According to Chu, it is not difficult for a patient to simulate DID over a brief time period by using information she has learned about the disorder from the media, in the scientific literature, and through patient networks and self-help groups. A clinician needs to make certain that the criteria have been met over a period of time. Often, malingerers have stereotypical alter-personalities such as good/bad and exaggerate their symptoms.

> It is always a clinical problem when patients, family members, or clinicians are encouraging more fragmentation rather than less. In fact, this essentially reinforces the basic psychopathology, where stress is managed by psychological distancing through dissociation. Good and effective clinicians must be able to acknowledge the extent of existing dissociation and personality fragmentation. . . . Rather, clinicians must acknowledge the extent of dissociative phenomena, and help patients to gradually move to states of less fragmentation and more integration. (Chu, 1991, p. 203)

Jan's Story

Jan has dissociative identity disorder as a result of the severe sexual, physical, and emotional abuse that she suffered as a child at the hands of many female as well as male perpetrators. She is currently in her early 40s and is disabled due to posttraumatic stress disorder.

Jan believes that her abuse began as early as six months. While babysitting Jan, her aunt would tie Jan to the toilet with a belt and leave her there until she urinated because she didn't want to change dirty diapers. This aunt also was involved in an all-women's cult that perpetrated extreme sexual abuse against Jan.

Jan's mother was overly involved with Jan's bowel movements and gave Jan frequent enemas. She also insisted on taking Jan's temperature rectally to make sure she got the "correct temperature" until Jan was 10 years old.

Jan's other abusers included a female cousin, a male cousin, her father, her maternal grandfather, a maternal uncle and the members of a cult (different from the aunt's cult) the uncle was involved with, and her maternal grandmother. About her grandmother's abuse, Jan said, *"Grandmother would place me in a moist dirty potato box, close the lid, and lower me somewhat into the ground."*

Jan told her mother about her abusers, but her mother did not believe her and never tried to stop or report the abuse. Jan felt like an *"invisible child"* most of the time. No one interacted with her except during the abuse, and no one who knew about the abuse would help her.

Jan's abuse was the most severe until she was 5 years old. At that point her extended family moved away, and the abuse by her aunt and the women's cult occurred only when Jan was visiting her.

Jan dealt with the abuse by "becoming multiple." She developed a different, distinct identity for each different form of abuse. This was the only way she could survive in a family in which she had not one protector.

Understandably, Jan has had difficulty trusting anyone since she was a child. She broke contact with her family when she remembered the abuse. Jan has developed a trusting relationship with a "surrogate mother"—but even with her, Jan sometimes feels she cannot trust: *"I think I had a mistrust of females in general. I did have a surrogate mother who I still trust. She's never been anything but honest with me and open and trustful. I still see her and trust her as much as I'm capable of trusting."*

As a result of the abuse, Jan has many phobias, an inability to concentrate, and major depression. She also has injured herself physically. She stated, *"(I) don't like caring for the Body. I don't know whose body this is, but it ain't ours!"* Jan feels like a *"freak, flawed, and defective"* sexually, and she has many questions about her sexuality.

When asked how she feels about herself, Jan responded,

My memories began surfacing in late 1990. It's been a difficult road for me, incest to ritual abuse. . . . However, I feel much better about myself today than before the memories began. My self-esteem is higher today. I'm more likely to talk about my issues. However, I still feel flawed and defective and very less than. [I also have] periods of helplessness and hopelessness.

Jan feels that it is more traumatic for a female to be abused by a female, and a male to be abused by a male: *"The worst abuse is that done by a person's own sex. They know beyond a reasonable doubt what hurts and will really get to someone. The opposite sex can only guess. The KNOWING isn't there."*

TRAUMATIC MEMORIES

Traumatic memory plays a key role in dissociated states. As early as 1907, Janet described a phenomenon similar to dissociation. He called it a "disorder or nonrealization." In dissociated states, traumatic memories continue to plague the individual and certain events are fractionally or totally reexperienced. Blank (1985) has identified this phenomenon as "intrusive recall"; others have called it "spontaneous abreactions" (van der Hart & Brown, 1992). Van der Hart, Steele, Boon, and Brown (1993) described traumatic memory this way:

> [It] is characterized by a sense of timelessness and immutability, has no social function, and is reactivated by trigger stimuli. It also follows the principle of restitution ad interim, the tendency of all elements of the trauma to be reactivated, once one element is called into play (Janet, 1907, 1928). (p. 163)

Trigger stimuli can be certain tastes, smells, touches, sights, or sounds. Triggers also can be certain times of the day, the month, or the year. Therapy, physical states, traumatic events happening in the present, or feeling threatened also can trigger previous traumatic memories. Almost anything can be a trigger.

Goldman (1995) wrote,

> Traumatic memory differs from ordinary memory in its "prenarrative" quality (Herman, 1992). It has a frozen, wordless and static aspect. Although some high percentage (60%) of those recently studied prospectively can remember trauma or recover memories spontaneously, amnesia for abuse is associated with more severe symptoms, molestation at an earlier age, extended abuse, violent abuse,

physical injury, and more perpetrators. (L. M. Williams, 1993, in
Goldman, 1995, p. 53)

Van der Kolk and Fisler (1995) compared traumatic memory and narrative
memory. They described traumatic memory as consisting "of images, sensations, affective and behavioral states that are invariable and do not change over
time. . . . These memories are highly state-dependent and cannot be evoked at
will. They are not condensed in order to fit social expectations" (p. 520). On
the other hand, narrative memory is "semantic and symbolic, social and adaptive, evoked at will by narrator, (and) can be condensed or expanded depending
on social demands" (p. 520).

DIAGNOSTIC INSTRUMENTS

The Dissociative Experiences Scale

The **Dissociative Experiences Scale (DES)** was designed as a screening
tool for clinicians to use with persons suspected of having a dissociative disorder. It is a self-report scale that measures traits of dissociation. Although it has
been used in nonclinical groups, it was designed for use on an adult clinical
population. It is not a diagnostic instrument. High scores (30 >) do not provide
conclusive evidence that the individual has a dissociative disorder.

Items of the DES include problems relating to identity, awareness, and thought
processes. Dissociation of moods or impulses are not included on this scale.
Scores on each of the 28 items can range from 0 to 100. Selecting 0% means
the symptom never occurs; choosing 100% means that it always happens. A
mean score is obtained by adding the scores for all of the items and dividing by
28.

Research studies have determined that individuals with **post-traumatic stress
disorder (PTSD), dissociative disorder not otherwise specified (DDNOS),** and
DID score high on the scale (Carlson & Putnam, 1993). Carlson et al. (1993)
suggested a total score of 30 or more will accurately determine over 70% of
those persons who have some form of dissociative disorder. Again, the DES
should not be used to make a diagnosis of DID or other dissociative disorders.
Rather, it is a screening instrument to recognize individuals who have elevated
levels of dissociation.

Paulsen (1995) wrote, "Recommended cutoff scores on the DES for sus-
pecting dissociative disorders range from 25 (Saxe et al., 1993) to 40 (Frischholtz,

Braun, Sachs, & Hopkins, 1990). A score of 15 is the mean for psychiatric inpatients, and is well above the 'normal' population" (p. 35).

However, there are some drawbacks to self-report measures. Draijer and Boon (1993) reminded clinicians, "Some patients with a dissociative disorder are unable to give an accurate self-report, because they are unaware of their symptoms or deny them" (p. 35). Thus, if an individual is in strong denial or cannot remember if she has the symptoms, her score on a self-report measure such as the DES would be low.

Structured Clinical Interview for Dissociative Disorders

Another measure used to make a diagnosis of a dissociate disorder is the **Structured Clinical Interview for Dissociative Disorders** (Steinberg et al., 1990, 1991).

The **Structured Clinical Interview for DSM-IV Dissociative Disorders** **(SCID-D)** is defined this way:

> [A] semistructured diagnostic interview that systematically assesses the severity of five dissociative symptoms (amnesia, depersonalization, derealization, identity confusion, and identity alteration) in all psychiatric patients; and diagnoses the dissociative disorders according to DSM-IV criteria. (Steinberg, Rounsaville, & Cicchetti, 1993, p. 4)

There are many advantages to this form of testing. First, because the questions are open-ended, the interviewee can go into as much detail as she wants, instead of just replying "yes" or "no." Through the course of the interview, the client often reveals details of her trauma. Therefore, the clinician can learn a history of the client's abuse without directly asking. Another advantage is that the SCID-D can be used to diagnose dissociative symptoms in clinical and non-clinical populations. Information garnered from these interviews can be used to learn more about dissociative disorders not otherwise specified (DDNOS). Finally, although it takes between two and three hours to administer the SCID-D, it is "highly cost-effective in terms of its demonstrated ability to detect previously undiagnosed cases of dissociative disorders" (Steinberg et al., 1993, p. 4). On average, a dissociative client is in therapy for seven to ten years before a proper diagnosis is made (Chu, 1991; Steinberg et al., 1993). The SCID-D "allows for rapid implementation of appropriate treatment strategies" (Steinberg et al., 1993, p. 4).

The first of the five core symptoms of dissociation and dissociative disorders that the SCID-D diagnoses is **amnesia**. This occurs when an individual cannot remember what she did during large spans of unaccounted-for time or necessary personal information such as a name or address. Amnesia can last for only a second or for years. It is not the result of substance abuse or an organic brain dysfunction (Steinberg, 1995; Steinberg et al., 1993). "Amnesia may be regarded as the foundational system of the five dissociative symptoms in that it is the 'building block' on which the others rest" (Steinberg, 1995, p. 9).

A childhood trauma often causes severe amnesia in adults. However, according to information garnered from the SCID-D, individuals with histories of repeated child abuse should have a range of amnesia from "normal, occasional forgetfulness to recurrent or persistent episodes" (Steinberg, 1995, p. 10).

It is common for individuals to wake from amnesia states with self-inflicted injuries and no memory of inflicting the wounds (Steinberg, 1995)

Depersonalization is the second core symptom of the dissociative disorders. This occurs when the individual experiences episodes of feeling detached from her body and emotions. She may feel lifeless, like a doll. Depersonalization may be difficult for the survivor to describe; she may be so used to these feelings that they seem "normal" (Steinberg, 1995; Steinberg et al., 1993). Because of this difficulty in describing episodes of depersonalization, the SCID-D has been structured to elicit patterns of depersonalization by both direct and indirect questions (Steinberg, 1995). Brief periods of depersonalization are common with substance use, in times of severe emotional distress, and in dream states; as a side effect of certain types of medications; and with sleep deprivation (Steinberg et al., 1993).

"Depersonalization episodes may echo memories of verbal abuse" (Steinberg, 1995, p. 11), in that individuals may see images of themselves insulting themselves, as their perpetrators had. For those with an abuse-created dissociative disorder, the dialogue they hear during depersonalization episodes is between an observing and a participating self (Steinberg, 1995).

Self-injury also may occur during depersonalization episodes. Individuals may injure themselves in order to feel **alive again.**

Derealization, the third symptom, occurs if an individual experiences her friends, family, home, or workplace as unfamiliar or unreal (Steinberg, 1995; Steinberg et al., 1993). This is particularly true for those who have undergone severe childhood abuse (Steinberg, 1995; Steinberg et al., 1993). However, even though her surroundings may be unfamiliar, she usually knows her actual identity.

"Derealization often occurs in the context of flashbacks, in which a person regresses in age and re-enters a past experience, as if it were current reality" (Steinberg et al., 1993, p. 5). While a flashback is occurring, the present feels unreal to the individual. Derealization also may cause a change in the client's visual perception of her environment. For example, colors may become more or less intense or objects may change in size or shape (Steinberg, 1995).

Blank (1985) delineated between conscious and unconscious flashbacks. When a conscious flashbacks occurs the traumatic memory is reactivated and the visual image usually is quite clear. Flashbacks happening at a conscious level are remembered after they occur. An unconscious flashback happens when the trauma survivor is unaware of the trauma being reactivated during or after it happens. These flashbacks have been described as "a sudden discrete experience leading to actions, where the manifest psychic content is only indirectly related to trauma" (van der Hart, Steele, Boon, & Brown, 1993, p. 164).

Derealization can occur as a result of stress, lack of sleep, or substance abuse (Steinberg et al., 1993). However, it is a "posttraumatic symptom and, in dissociative disorders, it is a predictable by-product of persistent and recurrent child abuse (p. 150).

The SCID-D is designed so that episodes of derealization can be described in an open-ended manner, which makes the reporting less threatening. Also, the SCID-D research shows that derealiztion often coexists with amnesia, and that it is more common for derealization to occur with depersonalization than alone (Steinberg, 1995).

Identity confusion is the fourth symptom. It occurs when an individual has episodes of not knowing who she really is (Steinberg, 1995; Steinberg et al., 1993). There may be severe internal conflicts in the individual concerning important events and issues. In DID, the **alters** who grapple for control of the individual are a result of identity confusion (Steinberg et al., 1993).

An alter is sometimes identified as a personality. This personality has been described by Cohen and Cox (1995) as "an entity with a firm, persistent, and well-founded sense of self, and a characteristic and consistent pattern of behavior and feelings in response to given stimuli. It must have a range of functions, a range of emotional responses, and a significant life history (of its own existence)" (p. 295).

This type of confusion can be mild, moderate, or severe. Mild levels are common in our society following transitions such as graduation, marriage, or retirement. Mild levels also will occur before or after making important decisions such as whether to relocate, marry, divorce, or go public about one's sexual orientation (Steinberg, 1995).

Moderate levels of identity confusion cause problems in functioning socially or at work and are accompanied by feelings of dysphoria. Moderate levels do not necessarily occur because of a transition or important decision (Steinberg, 1995).

Severe levels of identity confusion have the characteristics of moderate levels, but they are more intense and last longer. Severe levels are common in individuals who have a dissociative disorder, histories of unstable employment, marital problems, and been hospitalized (Steinberg, 1995).

Information garnered from the SCID-D shows that individuals who were sexually abused may have severe identity confusion about their sexual identities (Steinberg, 1995).

Identity alteration, the last symptom, occurs when an individual assumes a new identity. This could manifest itself in a new language learned or new items acquired without knowledge of how this occurred. DID clients alter their identities when they refer to themselves individually as "we" or "us" (Steinberg et al., 1993).

The difference between identity confusion and identity alteration is this: With identity confusion, the changes are subjective (i.e., the individual "feels" different); with identity alteration, the changes are behavioral (i.e., the individual "acts" different; Steinberg, 1995).

As with identity confusion, there are three levels of identity alteration. The mildest level occurs in "normal" individuals and is manifested in the switching from "home personality" to "work personality," and so on. In this mild form, the individual is aware of the switching and feels in control of it. Mild levels are not typically associated with amnesia or lack of functioning (Steinberg, 1995).

More moderate levels of identity alteration occur in individuals who have a nondissociative psychiatric disorder or dissociative disorder not otherwise specified (DDNOS). At the moderate level, an individual may act like at least two different people, but it is not clear how much control the alters possess. At this level, there will be minor intra-interview cues, such as slight changes in vocal pitch or speech patterns (Steinberg, 1995).

With severe cases of identity alteration, an individual loses control of her actions to one of the alters. These alters often have their own names, ages, and sexual orientations. The intra-interview cues at this level would be distinct changes in speech patterns, vocal pitch, dress, posture, and so forth. Many individuals with this level of identity alteration have lost work or relationships because their drastic behavioral changes are often confusing and upsetting (Steinberg, 1995).

After the interview is complete, the clinician rates the severity of each of these five core symptoms to determine what (if any) dissociative disorder the patient has. "The scores are labeled as: absent, mild, moderate, or severe. The individual symptom severity scores are added together to yield a total SCID-D symptom score which ranges from 5 (no symptomatology) to 20 (severe manifestations of all five dissociative symptoms)" (Steinberg et al., 1993, p. 10).

The dissociative disorders the SCID-D can diagnose are dissociative amnesia, dissociative fugue, Dissociative Identity Disorder, depersonalization disorder, and dissociative disorder not otherwise specified. The **DSM-IV** (APA, 1994) characterizes dissociative disorders as "a disruption in the usually integrated functions of consciousness, memory, identity, or perception of the environment. The disturbance may be sudden or gradual, transient or chronic" (p.477).

Dissociative Amnesia. The main feature of someone with dissociative amnesia is the lack of ability to remember important personal information, too extreme to be considered normal forgetfulness (APA, 1994). The memory loss for dissociative amnesia does not occur because of another disorder (i.e., DID, dissociative fugue, posttraumatic stress disorder, acute stress disorder, or somatization disorder). It also is not a result of substance abuse or a medical condition caused by head trauma. Also, these symptoms must cause a significant amount of "distress or impairment in social, occupational, or other important areas of functioning (APA, 1994, p. 478).

Four types of memory loss may occur in dissociative amnesia. Most commonly, there is **localized amnesia**, during which an individual is not able to remember anything for a "brief" period (usually hours to days) resulting from a specific event. The second type of memory loss is **generalized amnesia**. With this, an individual cannot remember anything that occurred during her lifetime. Either localized or generalized amnesia may be **selective** (the third type). This means that the memory loss may not be for all events. The last type is **continuous amnesia**, which affects only memories following a specific event—so that the individual is no longer capable of forming new memories.

Dissociative Fugue. In a state of dissociative fugue, on the other hand, an individual suddenly leaves her home or work and has a loss of memory for all or part of her past. This is in conjunction with confusion concerning her identity and possibly involves the establishment of another identity. These cases of dissociative fugue are not the result of DID, substance abuse, or a medical condition (APA, 1994).

Fugue comes from the Latin verb *fugere*, meaning "to flee." The only identified predisposing factor of dissociative fugue is heavy alcohol abuse. A fugue episode may be caused by severe psychosocial stress. Typically, an episode will last only for a short time, a few hours to a few days.

Dissociative Identity Disorder. APA (1994) defines DID this way:

> The essential feature of Dissociative Identity Disorder is the presence of two or more distinct identities or personality states that recurrently take control of behavior. There is an inability to recall important personal information, the extent of which is too great to be explained by ordinary forgetfulness. The disturbance is not due to the direct physiological effects of a substance or a general medical condition. (p. 484)

Alters often are opposite in personality from the host. For example, if the host is shy and reserved, one alter may be extroverted and wild. Also, each alter may have his or her own mental or physical disorder. Usually, one of the alters is dominant over the others during the course of DID.

A **dominant personality** serves a specific purpose in an individual with DID: a child's personality whose primary role is to provide caretaking. Certain personalities are so dominant they "stay out" and are in control for months and sometimes years. Also, when one personality or alter assumes control, the others may not be aware of what is occurring or where they are.

Nondominant personalities are numerous and diverse. These personalities are formed during the course of abusive acts.

A **cluster** is composed of more than two personalities. Most often these personalities are children of the same age but different genders. Each personality in a cluster was created for dealing with a certain part of the abuse (i.e., one for terror, one for rage, one for pain).

Individuals who have a dissociative disorder usually have both male and female personalities. Bryant, Kessler, and Shirar (1992) tell us why:

> (1) During an abusive event, the child may have identified with the abuser. . . . When the child is a girl and the abuser is male, she may create a male part to complete the identification. . . . (2) Extreme discomfort in a sexual situation with a same sex abuser may lead to creation of an opposite sex personality. . . . (3) A male may be seen as stronger and better able to protect. . . . (4) The abusers may require a child victim to be both male and female. . . . (5) Feelings that are not acceptable or which cause too much anxiety for the child to own as part of being a boy or a girl can be dissociated into a personality of the opposite sex. (pp. 81-82)

Groups are different than clusters. They are composed of personalities of varying ages who serve developmental purposes. Most of the groups are formed during the individual's adolescence. Some common bond binds them together.

Transition from one personality to another usually is a result of stress and may be sudden and dramatic (APA, 1994). These transitions are called "switching behaviors." Most often what causes switching is a trigger of some type. Bryant, Kessler, and Shirar (1992) reported that at around 30 years of age, more and more switching begins to occur, and this may be when the individual with a dissociative disorder seeks treatment.

A **negative introject** is an adult personality *that does not belong to the individual.* It is not a true part of her personalities. While some of the personalities within the client will be negative, toxic, or persecutory, the clinician needs to work with these, reframe their functions, and facilitate their integration into the whole personality (Putnam, 1989; Ross, 1989). A negative introject's primary function, on the other hand, is to destroy and control the person. In a skewed sense, the negative introject becomes the perpetrator incarnate living within the inner system (Bryant, Kessler, & Shriar, 1992) The other negative personalities' primary functions are to protect the system, even if in a misguided way.

In the beginning phases of treatment there is no sure way to determine if a negative introject lives within. A clinician's job is to reframe the negative personalities into positive personalities. Abusive personalities often are angry or rage-filled children or adolescents, and these parts may even talk about punishing other personality parts. However, if reframing is impossible after many months of trying, the clinician may be dealing with a negative introject.

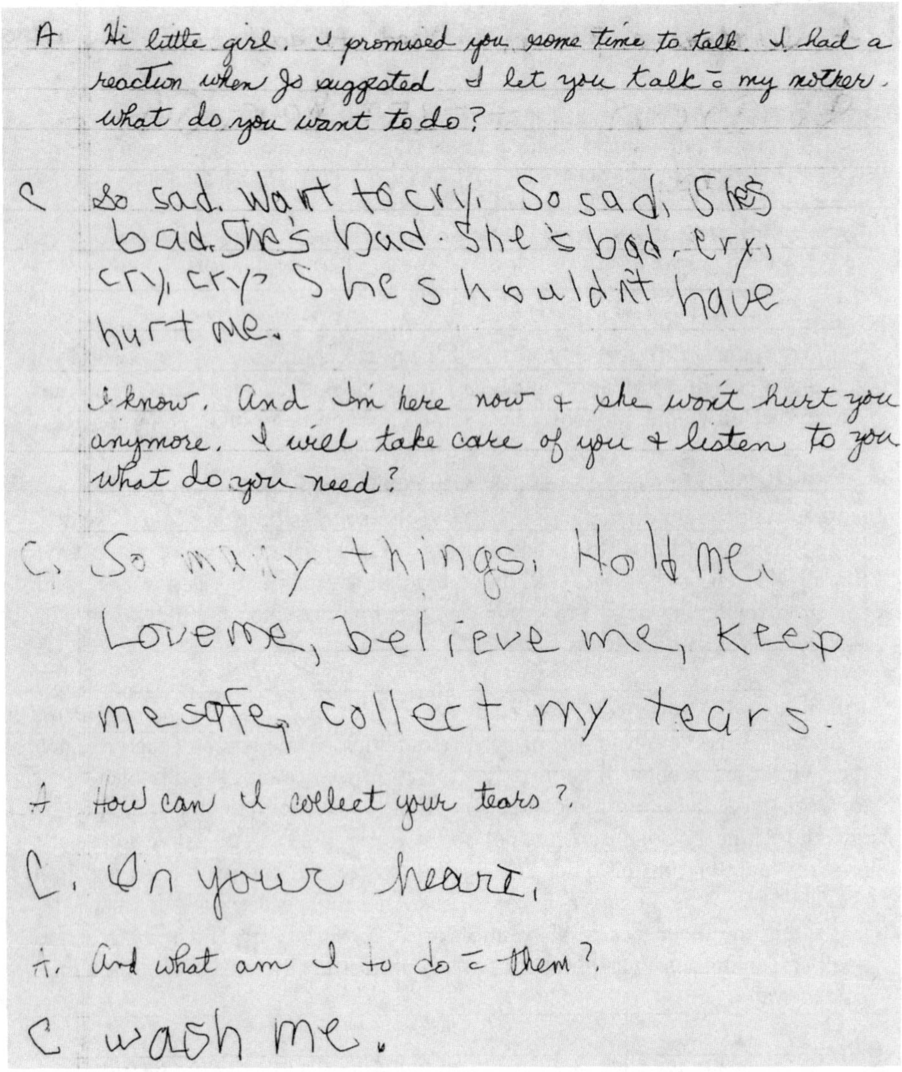

A   Hi little girl. I promised you some time to talk. I had a
reaction when Jo suggested I let you talk to my mother.
What do you want to do?

C   So sad. Want to cry. So sad. She's
bad. She's bad. She's bad. Cry,
cry, cry? She shouldn't have
hurt me.

I know. And I'm here now & she won't hurt you
anymore. I will take care of you & listen to you
What do you need?

C.   So many things. Hold me.
Love me, believe me, keep
me safe, collect my tears.

A   How can I collect your tears?

C.   On your heart.

A.   And what am I to do = them?

C   wash me.

Figure 2.2.   Conversation with inner child, by survivor.

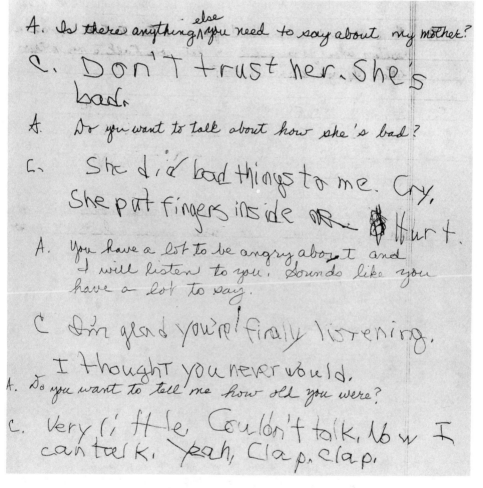

A. Is there anything else you need to say about my mother?

C. Don't trust her. She's bad.

A. Do you want to talk about how she's bad?

C. She did bad things to me. Cry. She put fingers inside or ~~Hurt.~~

A. You have a lot to be angry about and I will listen to you. Sounds like you have a lot to say.

C. I'm glad you're finally listening. I thought you never would.

A. Do you want to tell me how old you were?

C. Very little. Couldn't talk. Now I can talk. Yeah, clap. clap.

Figure 2.2, continued.

There are no good parts to the negative introject. It is all bad, and its only agenda is to hurt and control. There is no right or wrong. This negative introject would rather annihilate the other personality parts than lose control over the system.

There are many dangers in doing in-depth clinical work with a negative introject. Our intent here is simply to introduce the concepts, make the reader aware of the complexities of treating dissociative disorders, and provide suggestions for other reading material.

Finally, the **core personality**, which is the original child, will not appear until it is safe for her to do so. She is surrounded by multiple layers of personalities. The core differs from the host. The host is a dominant personality who has most control over the body (Putnam, 1989). A personality called the **Essence** usually is the same chronological age as the client who presents in therapy. *She is a reflection of the core* but often is unaware that a core personality or other personalities exist. She usually is quite confused because she has no memories and lives only in the present.

Grellert (1992) had this to say about the constellations of alters,

> The customary assortment of internal alternate personalities in Multiple Personality Disorder is not a random collection. MPD has a distinct organizational structure at its core. Typical psychogenic MPD systems organize into alters of the following general types:
>
> - Fixated children
> - A somewhat depleted and confused "original"
> - Antisocial and/or
> - Persecutory/protective and/or
> - Sexualized
>
> . . . . Thus, the original/core personality recapitulates victimization and presents in treatment as passive, depleted, confused, and/or helpless. Protector/persecutor personalities reject identification(s) with the aggressor(s) and present as angry, hostile, uncooperative and in direct conflict with the original personality. Children alters preserve the self of the original personality at times of excessive stress and present as innocent, trusting, loving and idealizing. (p. 5)

Depersonalization Disorder. Depersonalization is characterized by repeated episodes of feeling separate from one's self. The individual may feel like she is an observer or in a dreamlike state or in a movie (APA, 1994). "Various types of sensory anesthesia, lack of affective response, and a sensation of lacking control of one's actions, including speech, are often present" (APA, 1994, p. 488). However, the individual realizes that these feelings are not reality. Many other mental disorders have depersonalization as a characteristic. Depersonalization is not the diagnosis if the symptoms are in conjunction with schizophrenia, panic disorder, acute stress disorder, or another dissociative disorder. Depersonalization also is not the diagnosis if it occurs as a result of another medical condition (APA, 1994).

Depersonalization episodes come on suddenly and last for brief periods of time; however, it may take much longer for the symptoms to disappear.

Depersonalization symptoms are not always caused by dissociative disorders.

> Some other causes of depersonalization are: neurological disorders (epilepsy, migraine, brain tumors, cerebral trauma, dementia [Alzheimer's], and Huntington's disease); toxic and metabolic disorders (hypoglycemia, hypoparathyroidism, carbon monoxide poisoning, botulism, hyperventilation, mescaline intoxication, hypothyroidism); other (exhaustion, boredom, emotional trauma). (Cummings, 1985, p.123)

Dissociative Disorder Not Otherwise Specified. DDNOS is the diagnosis if the disorder meets the criteria for dissociation but does not meet the criteria for one of the specific disorders (APA, 1994).

Cheryl's Story

Cheryl's abuse began at about age 2. She was sexually, physically, and emotionally abused by her mother and has DID as a result. An early memory of her abuse is as follows:

> *I remember waking up in the morning in the bed I shared with my grandfather. The sheets were wet and sticky, and my mother said that I did it, but I didn't. He did when he rubbed me, but it got all over me. She took me to bed and yelled at me for being a nasty girl and then either took me to the bathroom and hit me with a belt through the crotch or tied me to the bed with my face in the wet and hit me with the belt and poked in my rectum and vagina with something hard.*

If Cheryl resisted her mother's sexual abuse, her mother would *"attack me with her fists and anything else available until I passed out,"* Cheryl stated.

Cheryl believes that her mother also had DID. She is convinced that her mother may honestly not remember perpetrating the abuse. However, as a child, Cheryl created a different alter for each type of abuse she suffered from her mother, who could be loving one minute and torturous the next.

Cheryl never fit in socially at school because of the alters emerging. No one understood her. Also, she never expressed emotions, and most of her alters had extremely low self-esteem.

As an adult, Cheryl still is greatly affected by the abuse. Until seeing a psychiatrist who prescribed a medication, she had *"extreme sleep disturbances with some parts being up all night while others thought we were resting. I would discover appliances broken, significant extra mileage on the car, and other scary stuff."* She also is working with a therapist and can now express some of the emotions she buried as a child. She has major respiratory problems, which she attributes partly to her childhood:

> *This I relate at least in part to feeling smothered by adult bodies on top of me and to holding back screams and to feeling smothered by having cloth stuffed in my mouth to keep me quiet. Frequently when I get to heavy issues, I lose my voice all together for that hour or for weeks at a time, which is a nuisance.*

As an adult, Cheryl also is confused about her sexuality and her sexual preference.

Cheryl finds support in a group she attends for persons with DID; however, when she revealed that she had been sexually abused by her mother, she sensed the other members' shock, so she quickly changed the subject.

Intra-Interview Cues

In addition to the client's replies to standardized questions during the interview, intra-interview cues can be useful to the clinician for detection of DID. Putnam (1989) defined the following as intra-interview cues: psychological changes that include cognitive flow, emotional expressions, and behaviors. Physical changes is the second category of intra-interview cues Putnam identified. These physical changes include alterations in vocal patterns and verbal articulations, facial expressions, bearing or stance, body movements, conduct, and mannerisms. A notable change occurs in these areas when a person switches from one alter to a different alter or back to the host personality.

Kluft (1987) determined a number of factors that can be indicative of Dissociative Identity Disorder, including previous unsuccessful, treatments; three or more different diagnoses; congruent psychological and physical symptoms (i.e., raging headaches nonresponsive to painkillers); lost blocks of time that cannot be accounted for; acting in a manner which the client has no recollection of; changes in speech, actions, or voice inflections; hearing voices in the head; finding material effects the client has no memory of purchasing; using "we" instead of "I" when responding to questions; and accessibility of other personalities through drugs or hypnosis.

SONG FOR JEFF

My therapist, his name is Jeff,
Making sense of scattered thoughts,
Showing me what I can't see,
That my mind is whole.

Don't ask me for his name or phone
I keep him for myself.
For I am only six years old,
And he's my only friend.

TREATMENT ISSUES

Slower Is Faster

Kluft (1993) discussed his treatment model for work with DID clients, stressing that treatment providers need to proceed gently and cautiously. Kluft shared what happened when he attempted to quickly integrate the alter personalities of his DID clients.

> I found myself struggling with crises, regressions, inappropriate behaviors, suicidality, and the vicissitudes of managing MPD within a hospital setting. My patients' minds, bodies, and lives all too often had become veritable battlefields, devastated by the reliving of painful events and the destabilizing impact of the treatment process. I rapidly came to see that my original concentrations, however comprehensible, were misdirected. My unwitting focus on the MPD phenomena and their resolution had, in effect, given precedence to the disorder rather than to the patient who suffered it. (p. 145)

Treatment of DID cannot begin with lengthy focusing on traumatic events. If the clinician chooses this path, he or she will find a client who begins to rapidly decompensate. First and foremost, the client needs to be stabilized and safety needs to be established. Herman (1992) identified a three-phase treatment model that adapts well to work with DID clients. Phase 1 involves establishing safety. Phase 2 includes remembering the trauma and the process of mourning. Phase 3 centers on reconnection.

These are the tasks of the therapist in successful treatment of DID:

1. Maintain and set clear boundaries.
2. Assume an active role in the treatment process and encourage the client to do the same.
3. Deal with traumatic memories after safety is established.
4. Establish and maintain strong therapeutic partnership and affiliation.
5. Diminish distinctiveness of alters and communicate the message that this is a partnership of all for one and one for all.
6. Validate the client's distress at what has happened but not necessarily accept at face value everything she says.
7. Communicate in a clear and simple manner.
8. Never, ever show favoritism between the alters. Be consistent. Follow through.
9. Pace the sessions so as not to deal with heavy duty issues during the last third of the treatment hour.
10. Help the client to restore and rebuild assumptions about herself and the world. Give assignments that are workable and can be completed.
11. Be responsible and expect responsibility.
12. Be warm, caring, and real.
13. Address cognitive distortions again and again. (Adapted from Kluft 1993, pp. 87-101).

Kluft (1993) reminded us of the vulnerability and fragility of the DID client:

> No one would trivialize a rape, and recovery for rape may require considerable treatment over protracted periods of time. If we make the estimate that the average MPD patient is misused twice a week, perhaps 50 weeks of the year, and use the statistic from Schultz, Braun, and Kluft's 1989 study of 355 MPD patients, that the average MPD patient reports having been abused an average of ten years, then an average or model MPD patient may have endured 2 × 50 × 10 = 1,000 exploitations. (p. 97)

Safety Is the First Treatment Goal

Safety must be established if the treatment is to have any hope of succeeding. This can be achieved in a number of different ways. Questions and concerns should be invited, so that any issue can be addressed. Questions should be answered as truthfully as possible, but the clinician may need to set limits regarding questions about his or her private life. Answering these kinds of questions will not enhance the treatment process. It is important to remember that the client already believes she is functioning in a less powerful position and that the power may be used against her, as it has been in the past.

The clinician should set the ground rules. The client may ask the therapist to promise never to commit her or to use medications or to refuse to continue to treat her; it is counterproductive to the treatment process to promise any of these things.

Agreeing to work with a DID client does not mean that the clinician will automatically accept and believe everything the client reveals. Indeed, Kluft wrote, "it has been my experience that many MPD patients knowingly misrepresent significant issues and facts for a variety of reasons, and the exploration of these misrepresentations is crucial for their recovery" (p. 149).

The clinician should set and maintain firm limits. Kluft advocated making it clear up front that anyone making any type of threat toward the therapist's family will be dropped as a client and that legal charges will be pursued. Clients should be expected to provide reassurance that this will not occur. Alters should be asked to "hear" what is being said about violence directed toward the helper and his or her family.

Other issues that should be discussed up front include how telephone calls will be handled from significant others, insurance carrier requests for or managed care organizations' review of records, and confidentiality issues. The clinician should be clear that intent to harm self or others are grounds for breaking confidentiality.

Availability between sessions also should be discussed:

> I try to communicate that while I am on call for genuine emergencies. I am not available for general companionship, ongoing reassurance, or as a moment-by-moment consultant, confidant, or guide. I emphasize that an emergency is an unforeseen situation that calls for immediate action, not a period of discomfort during which the patient feels badly. I work with the patient to establish a hierarchy of things to do at such times, the last of which is to call me. . . . The essential communication is that the therapist is on call, but not on tap. (Kluft, 1993, p. 151)

Therapy should be a joint effort between clinician and client. During the early stage of treatment, how the client feels about her diagnosis of DID should be explored. If denial is persistent and treatment is impeded because of this denial, the client may not be ready to pursue treatment with the current clinician. The clinician may need to refer the client to another professional—one who did not make the diagnosis of DID—because so many strong feelings are identified with the clinician who provided the diagnosis.

The client and therapist should generate a list of "safety valves" that the client can use to inhibit self-injury and suicidal tendencies (M. B. Williams, 1993). This list can be written on paper or on an index card and defines what the client can do when she wants to engage in any form of self-destructive behaviors.

Safe places also need to be determined. The client's place of residence should be evaluated for safety (i.e., are knives and guns kept in the house?). If dangers exist, the discussion should focus on how they can be removed to make home a safer place. The therapist should ask about partner abuse, how anger is managed, and if suicidal or homicidal impulses are present. Williams encouraged her clients to engage in body-strengthening activities such as body-building or karate.

Kluft (1993) suggested nine phases of therapeutic work to follow with dissociative clients. He formulated his approach based on the work of Braun (1986), Kluft (1991b), and Putnam (1989). The phases are as follows:

> 1) establishing the therapy; 2) preliminary interventions; 3) history gathering and mapping; 4) metabolism of trauma; 5) moving toward integration/resolution; 6) integration/resolution; 7) learning new coping skills; 8) solidification of gains and working through; 9) follow-up. Of these, stages 1-3 are designed to maximize safety and communication, stage 4 involves intense work with traumatic material, and stages 5-9 involve reconnection, both within the alter system and interpersonally. (Kluft, 1993, p. 89)

It is important for the survivor to know that she is not the only one with a dissociative disorder. In our study, one survivor commented on what has helped in her healing: *"Knowing other survivors, especially those with MPD."* Another survivor said,

> *The same determination that made me a survivor against all odds continues to compel me to go forth with therapy . . . group, reading everything to know and understand and to know what help is*

available/my alters, inner strength and decision-maker . . . making
dolls, which for me is creating my system in reality.

Finally, a survivor said

The last few months the most helpful thing I did was to seek out a
psychologist to help me quiet the internal voices-I honestly felt that
I was going insane. Turns out—I'm quite sane—I just have MPD.
In fact, if it wasn't for the MPD, I probably would be insane.

The Second Phase of Treatment

Assuming that trust has been established, in the next phase the client and
therapist together deal with the surfacing memories and begin connecting feelings to those memories. The abuse stories begin to be more complete. Some
concerns for the client during this phase are increased internal chaos and feeling like she is losing control. Physical symptoms connected to the original traumas return in full force. She may experience intense pain in the genital areas.
Nightmares may increase, and she may believe she is regressing. Memories and
feelings need to be processed again and again. This repeated reprocessing
diminishes their power. However, the survivor may feel almost constantly de-
pleted. It is not helpful to tell the client to nurture herself during this phase,
because she is struggling simply to survive and probably will not have those
self-soothing skills at this point in time. Plans need to be made and revised as
necessary for what she will do when she returns to the outside world after the
therapy sessions.

Each client with a dissociative disorder has developed a unique way of
coping. Most coping responses have a cyclical quality. Something or someone
acts a trigger for the client. This trigger creates confusion and disorganization in
the internal system. The external behavior mirrors the internal state. Switching
behaviors escalate and confusion reigns. More and more memories and feelings
may begin to surface. She may feel as if her psyche has become a war zone.

Headaches are common during memory work. Pain medication may do little
to relieve the discomfort. The survivor may try to deny or repress what she is
experiencing—and, in her attempt to block or deny the memories, she may become manic. During this phase she may self-mutilate or push herself physically
to the point of exhaustion in an attempt to avoid the memories.

As the memories continue to surface, the survivor may be deluged with
both angry personalities and scared personalities berating her on a continual

Figure 2.3.   Drawing of child holding bunny, by survivor.

basis. These fragile personalities believe their world is spiraling into chaotic madness, and the fragile equilibrium they all worked so hard to maintain is in jeopardy. At this point, the survivor begins to relive the trauma as it originally happened.

During this time the survivor may become paranoid and agoraphobic. Following this she begins to connect her thoughts and feelings. The pain during this part of the cycle is overwhelming and suicide may look like the most attractive option. Next, there may be intense transference toward the therapist. The survivor attempts to please, then withdraws and denies what is happening. She feels intense loneliness and her anxiety is high. She may attempt to shut down emotionally in order to regain some sense of balance in the internal system.

In the last phase of this cycle, she either reverts to denial or she reconnects with the clinician and the memory becomes assimilated and integrated into the system. Both survivor and clinician need to identify the cycle and plan accordingly.

The Third Phase of Treatment

Integration is the third phase of therapy. A number of years usually have passed before this point is reached. Both Putnam (1989) and Ross (1989) provided in-depth information on this treatment process. Integration of personalities cannot be coerced, and the clinician needs to listen to the client and allow her to move at her own pace. Integration may begin to take place in a safe place inside the client. The sequencing of the integration of personalities is a unique process and individualized for each survivor. Bryant, Kessler, and Shrier (1992) have suggested that when the essence and the core child are united, integration can begin.

ISSUES INVOLVING FAMILY MEMBERS

Persons with DID have a number of different problem areas in their marital relationships and with their children. One problem is amnesia. Amnesia affects the family because it is not possible for the person with a dissociative disorder to be existent and available in a relationship. Depersonalization is another problem, because the individual often believes her responses and reactions are unmanageable, that it is beyond her ability to regulate affect. This may cause improper and embarrassing behaviors on her part. Derealization is a problem because the individual may not be able to identify her own family members when an episode occurs. This can be greatly distressing for them.

Figure 2.4.   DID Collage, by Juliann.

Figure 2.4. Of all the collages created, this one is the most complex. The mask over part of the face is representative of how the dissociative disorder may go undiscovered for years. The fence inside the head represents the survivor's struggle to keep the alters contained inside. The baby sleeping represents the core personality—innocent and well-guarded by the other alters. Many personalities live inside this woman, both males and females. The eyes once again are representative of the repeated sexual abuse she experienced as a child. Notice at the left-hand side of the collage a female figure is sitting. She signifies the negative introject of the mother-figure.

Identity disturbances are a common feature with DID, and these can be quite problematic for the family as well. Most individuals with DID do not have firmly established awareness and recognition of their own selves. Alter personalities and switching behaviors can create havoc in intimate and familial relationships. Transference is another problem area. At its best, transference is a difficult phenomenon to sort out, and this issue becomes even more complicated as a result of the many different personality states.

Unresolved traumas from childhood and adolescence often have helped to create or generate a dissociative disorder. Cognitive distortions abound for persons who have been sexually abuse: *"It was all my fault,"* or *"I know I must have liked it the way my body responded,"* or *"I guess I really wanted it to happen because I didn't even try to tell anyone."* These unresolved traumas also greatly affect the relationship with a spouse and children. Attachment disorders are common. Persons with DID often experienced disorganized/disoriented attachments as children, and these carry over into adulthood (Liotti, 1992). At times, the individual may seem to have no affect; at other times, she may be on emotional and sensory overload from flashbacks and intrusive memories (Braun, 1988a, 1988b). This causes great distress for the family.

Shame is another prominent factor for an individual with DID. She feels inherently flawed. This sense of being blemished and always "less than" can cause her to become uncommunicative or assaultive toward others, to retreat from interactions with family and friends, and to internally denigrate herself. (See Chapter 7 for more on shame and its treatment.)

Finally, significant relationships are not possible without trust. Persons with dissociative disorders live in a world where others are not to be trusted. For most of them, trust has been violated since early childhood by acts of malevolence by family members and other caretakers. For an abused child, the world is not a safe place. Love usually means violations and heinous, hurtful actions against the child's soul and spirit.

Herman (1992) wrote,

> Many abused children cling to the hope that growing up will bring escape and freedom. But the personality formed in an environment of coercive control is not well adapted to adult life. The survivor is left with fundamental problems in basic trust, autonomy, and initiative. She approaches the tasks of early adulthood—establishing independence and intimacy—burdened by major impairments in self-care, in cognition and memory, in identity, and in the capacity to form stable relationships. She is still a prisoner of her childhood;

attempting to create a new life, she reencounters the trauma. . . . Thus the survivor develops a pattern of intense, unstable relationships, repeatedly enacting dramas of rescue, injustice, and betrayal. (p. 110)

Since families suffer the ill effects of abuse the survivor has experienced, they need to be part of the treatment process. A client with DID cannot be treated in a therapeutic vacuum. Part of the therapeutic process is educating the family members about DID. Together partner, survivor, and clinician determine how much in-depth information the partner can handle.

Partners often are shocked at the diagnosis of DID. They may have suspected or even known their spouses were struggling, but a diagnosis of DID still may be startling. Williams (1991) wrote,

Acknowledging the existence of multiplicity changes the lives of the family. Suddenly partners and children must become aware of "who is out" and to whom they are talking. Helping partners to identify those alters and to recognize certain signs and evidences of switching, as well as what triggers the switching, is another part of the educative process. (p. 94)

A number of other issues need to be addressed in work with families. Family members need to learn appropriate responses to a variety of situations. Physical violence by alters is not to be accepted by the partner or children. Concrete ways of dealing with violent alters should be determined: for example, removing all firearms, securing knives in a safe place, and hiding the matches or lighters. Williams (1991) suggested having families learn to use an expression, a specific movement, or a reaction to reactivate the "host" personality.

Williams also suggested helping the partner to identify all the alters and each of their behaviors and idiosyncrasies. Significant others may need to develop specific ways of interacting with each of the alters until they are integrated (e.g., child alters need to engage in forms of play).

Intimacy needs should be explored and discussed. Switching behaviors are common during sexual intimacy. Specific caresses, smells, sounds, or tastes may trigger dissociative episodes. Triggers may cause a child alter to come out, especially one who was brutalized by the abuser. How to respond to and deal with these occurrences during sexually intimate times must be discussed during the treatment process (Williams, 1991).

Other issues, such as financial responsibilities, family rules, and household chores, also need to be defined and delineated.

Partners themselves may have histories of abuse. They may also abuse substances or be addicts. All of these issues can be addressed in treatment. Significant others have many different feelings to sort out and cope with. It is common for them to feel rage toward the perpetrators of their spouses' abuse or intense emotional pain for what the survivors have lived through. Recognizing the atrocities and violations the survivor has experienced can cause the significant other to feel helpless. Angry feelings often are present. Family members have described their lives as being turned upside after they found out about the abuse. Never knowing what to expect takes its toll on family life. If the partner is a "fixer," he or she may experience disappointment or disillusionment.

Fright is another normal feeling for family members. Coming home from work or school and finding the survivor huddled behind a chair, screaming every time she is approached is frightening. A significant other and the survivor need to determine how the survivor can be comforted when these flashbacks occur.

Children need to be educated as well. However, the clinician walks a fine line between parentifying the child and teaching him or her reassuring and calming ways to respond to an upset child alter.

All types of social skills training can be facilitated in the middle to later stages of treatment.

Families need to know there is hope, and that healing is possible. Healing doesn't mean forgetting. It means that couples have hope for the future. Williams (1991) wrote,

> Coping with the trauma of multiplicity is easier if the family learns to manage tension, develops an external support system, takes time out to play, cooperates, reduces demands on members who have the highest levels of pain, uses humor, expresses emotions openly in a non-blaming manner, and reframes the situation into a positive growth-oriented, more manageable Gestalt. (p. 97)

Benjamin and Benjamin (1994a) identified seven types of significant others who are often involved with DID clients: "new abusers, caretakers, 'damaged goods,' obsessives, paranoids, schizotypal roommates, and closet dissociatives" (p. 193).

- A **new abuser** is a significant other who reminds the client of an abuser from her childhood. The original abusive dynamics are reenacted in the current relationship. Substance abuse often is another dynamic present in the significant other.

- A **caretaker** role played by the significant other often is a result of his or her own abuse from childhood or impaired behaviors that cause him or her to act out in the relationship (i.e., alcoholism). the caretaker sees him- or herself as the "rescuer." Caretakers often are nurses or mental health professionals. They may feel threatened when the DID client begins to heal and becomes more functional.
- **Damaged goods** is the third type of partner identified by Benjamin and Benjamin (1994a). This significant other is a caring person but, for a number of different reasons, believes he or she is "less than" the rest of society. He or she may find the diagnosis of DID difficult to understand or accept. This significant other may fear that when the DID client begins to heal, she will be abandon her "damaged goods" partner.
- **Obsessives** are the fourth type of partner often chosen by an individual with DID. The obsessive partner is affectively limited but marries a person who is overly emotional, sometimes to the point of hysteria. An obsessive partner is fearful of being abandoned and is convinced that he or she must rescue the DID partner from all types of situations. Overtly the significant other complains about the DID client, but internally he or she fears the spouse will improve and life, as it is known and experienced, will be changed for the worse.
- A fifth type of partner Benjamin and Benjamin (1994a) identified is the paranoid. This significant other sees the world as an unsafe and hostile place. Those whom the paranoid considers unsafe may be the DID client's mental health providers. The paranoid type is not invested in the partner recovery, because a recovered partner would not be as supportive in the paranoid's crusade against the world.
- **Schizotypal roommate** is the sixth type of significant other often involved with the DID client. This person is uninvolved and isolated from society. He or she may be unaware that the partner has a disorder. Little intimacy of any kind exists in this relationship. The schizotypal roommate may believe this to be a normal relationship. The roommate may be depressed, addicted, or psychotic. The mental health treatment provider may discern that the schizotypal roommate is extremely nonfunctional. This type of partner is not invested in his or her own recovery or in that of the DID client.
- Finally, Benjamin and Benjamin (1994a) identify the **closet dissociative**. As the client with a dissociative disorder progresses in her treatment, she may be the first to identify that her partner has many of the same types of symptoms that she had in the initial stages of treatment.

These authors wrote,

> The purpose of this typology is not to "label" partners in a negative manner, but to point out that partners often play a vital role in helping the client to maintain certain behaviors. This awareness is crucial in helping clinicians appreciate that the MPD client and partner operate as a complimentary system to maintain not only marital patterns but patterns of relating to others. (Benjamin & Benjamin, 1994a, p. 195)

Benjamin and Benjamin (1994b) and Goldberg (1982) also identified six issues that arise again and again in couples therapy: power or control, nurturance, intimacy, trust, fidelity, lifestyle, and sense of order. Benjamin and Benjamin (1994b) wrote, "While couples that contain a dissociative partner have the extraordinary task of dealing with the dissociative symptoms and past traumas, they also have the ordinary dilemas that face all couples. . . . In work with couples, it behooves the therapist to locate any hidden resources" (pp. 234-235).

The research literature is not cohesive, however, in terms of agreed upon treatment for family members of the DID individual. Chiappa (1994) wrote,

> Some of the suggestions . . . keep the dissociative individual in the sick role, by encouraging the family's preoccupation with the person and their symptoms. For example, using the family to "map the system" of alters, teaching children to look out for and respond differentially to different alters, playing with child alters, and working flashbacks at home are all interventions that skew the system toward preoccupation with the symptomatic member.
>
> The disorder becomes the family's focus, obscuring the roles of spouse, parent, and child, which are the foundation of a well-functioning family. Children in particular should be spared having to cope with a parent's alters and flashbacks, because this dissolves the parent-child boundary and reenacts incest at a psychological level. The family and individual therapists both must make clear to the MPD/DD member that he or she is responsible for controlling symptomatic behavior at home, particularly around the children. (p. 187)

REFERENCES

American Psychiatric Association. (1994). *Diagnostic and statistic manual of mental disorders* (4th ed.). Washington, DC: Author.

Benjamin, L. R., & Benjamin, R. (1994a). A group for partners and parents of MPD clients: Marital types and dynamics. *Dissociation, 7*(3), 191-196.

Benjamin, L. R., & Benjamin, R. (1994b). Issues in the treatment of dissociative couples. *Dissociation, 7*(4), 229-238.

Blank, A. S. (1985). The unconscious flashback to the war in Vietnam veterans: Clinical mystery, legal defense, and community problem. In S. M. Sonnenberg & J. A. Talbot (Eds.), *The trauma of war: Stress and recovery in Vietnam veterans* (pp. 293-308). Washington, DC: American Psychiatric Press.

Braun, B. G. (1986). *Treatment of multiple personality disorder.* Washington, DC: American Psychiatric Press.

Braun, B. G. (1988a). The BASK model of dissociation. *Dissociation, 1,* 14-23.

Braun, B. G. (1988b). The BASK model of dissociation: II. Treatment. *Dissociation, 1*(2), 16-23.

Briere, J. (1989). *Therapy for adults molested as children: Beyond survival.* Newbury Park, CA: Sage.

Bryant, D., Kessler, J., & Shirar, L. (1992). *The family inside: Working with the multiple.* New York: Norton.

Calof, D. (1995). Dissociation: Nature's tincture of numbing and forgetting. *Treating Abuse Today, 5*(3), 5-8.

Carlson, E. B. (1984). The history of multiple personality in the United States: Mary Reynolds and her subsequent reputation. *Bulletin of the History of Medicine, 58,* 72-82.

Carlson, E. B., & Putnam, F. N. (1993). An update on the *Dissociative Experiences Scale. Dissociation, 6*(1), 16-27.

Carlson, E. B., Putnam, F. W., Ross, C. A., Torem, M., Coons, P., Dill, D., Loewenstein, R. J., & Braun, B. G. (1993). Validity of the *Dissociative Experiences Scale* in screening for multiple personality disorder: A multicenter study. *American Journal of Psychiatry, 148,* 1548-1551.

Chiappa, F. (1994). Effective management of family and individual interventions in treatment of dissociation disorders. *Dissociation, 7*(3), 185-190.

Chu, J. A. (1991). On the misdiagnosis of multiple personality disorder. *Dissociation, 4*(4), 200-204.

Courtois, C. A. (1988). *Healing the incest wound.* New York: Norton.

Courtois, C. A. (1992). The memory retrieval process in incest survivor therapy. *Journal of Child Sexual Abuse, 1*(1), 15-31.

Crabtree. A. (1993). Multiple personality before "Eve." *Dissociation, 6*(1), 66-73.

Cummings, J. L. (1985). *Clinical neuropsychiatry.* New York: Grune & Stratton.

Draijer, N., & Boon, S. (1993). The validation of the Dissociative Experiences Scale against the criterion of the SCID-D using receiver operating characteristics (ROC) analysis. *Dissociation, 6*(1), 28-37.

Frischholtz, E. J., Braun, B. G., Sachs, G. R., Hopkins, L., Shaeffer, D. M., Lewis, J., Leavitt, F., Pasquotto, F. N., & Schwartz, D. R. (1990). The *Dissociative Experiences Scale*: Further replication and validation. *Dissociation, 3*(3), 151-153.

Goldberg, M. (1982). The dynamics of marital interaction and marital conflict. *Psychiatric Clinics of North America, 5,* 449-467.

Goldman, J. G. (1995). A mutual story-telling technique as an aid to integration after abreaction in the treatment of MPD. *Dissociation, 8*(1), 53-60.

Grellert, E. A. (1992). Once-multiple therapist countertransference to multiple personality disorder. *Treating Abuse Today, 2*(2), 5-9.

Herman, J. (1992). *Trauma and recovery.* New York: Basic Books.

Janet, P. (1887). L'anesthésie systématisée et la dissociation des phénomènes psychologiques. *Revue Philosophique, 23,* 449-472.

Janet, P. (1907). *The major symptoms of hysteria.* London & New York: Macmillan. Reprint of second edition, 1920. New York: Hafner.

Janet, P. (1928). *L'evolution de la mémoire et la notion du temps.* Paris: Chahine.

Kluft, R. P. (1987). Parental fitness of mothers with multiple personality disorder: A preliminary study. *Child Abuse & Neglect, 11,* 273-280.

Kluft, R. P. (1991). Multiple personality disorder. In A. Tasman & S. Gold-finger (Eds.), *American Psychiatric Press Annual Review of Psychiatry, 10,* 161-188.

Kluft, R. P. (1993). The treatment of dissociative disorder patient's: An overview of discoveries, successes, and features. *Dissociation, 7*(2/3), 87-101.

Liotti, G. (1992). Disorganized/disoriented attachment in the etiology of the dissociative disorders. *Dissociation, 5*(4), 196-204.

Mitchill, S. L. (1816). A double consciousness or a duality in the same individual. *The Medical Repository, 3,* 185-186.

MPD newsletter. (1992, June). *Reaching Out.* Ontario, Canada: Royal Ottawa Hospital.

Paulsen, S. (1995). EMDR and reprocessing: Its cautious use in the dissociative disorders. *Dissociation, 8*(1), 32-44.

Putnam, F. (1989). *Diagnoses and treatment of multiple personality disorder.* New York: Guilford.

Ross, C. (1989). *Multiple personality disorder: Diagnosis, clinical features and treatment.* New York: Wiley.

Ross, C. (1993). Scientific state of the dissociative disorders field. *Treating Abuse Today, 3*(5), 4-9.

Ross, C. (1994). *The Osiris complex: Case-studies in multiple personality disorder.* Toronto, ON: University of Toronto Press.

Saxe, G. N., Van der Kolk, B. A., Berkowitz, R., Chinman, G., Hall, K., Lieberg, G., & Schwartz, J. (1993). Dissociative disorders in psychiatric inpatients. *American Journal of Psychiatry, 150*(7), 1037-1042.

Schultz, R., Braun, B., & Kluft, R. (1989). Multiple personality disorder: Phenomenology of selected variables in comparison to major depression. *Dissociation, 2*(1), 45-51.

Sheiman, J. A. (1993). "I've always wondered if something happened to me": Assessment of child sexual abuse survivors with amnesia. *Journal of Child Sexual Abuse, 2*(2), 13-21.

Steinberg, M. (1995). *Handbook for the assessment of dissociation: A clinical guide.* Washington, DC: American Psychiatric Press.

Steinberg, M., Cicchetti, D., Buchanan, J., Hall, P., & Rounsaville, B. (1993). Dissociative symptoms and disorders: The Structured Clinical Interview for DSM-IV dissociative disorders. *Dissociation, 6*(1), 3-15.

Steinberg, M., Rounsaville, B., & Cicchetti, D. (1990). The structured clinical interview for DSM-III-R dissociative disorders: Preliminary report on a new diagnostic instrument. *American Journal of Psychiatry, 147*, 76-82.

Steinberg, M., Rounsaville, B., & Cicchetti, D. (1991). Detection of dissociative disorders in psychiatric patients by a screening instrument and a structured diagnostic interview. *American Journal of Psychiatry, 148*(8), 1050-1054.

van der Hart, O., & Brown, P. (1992). Abreaction re-evaluated. *Dissociation, 5*(4), 127-138.

van der Hart, O., Steele, K., Boon, S., & Brown, P. (1993). The treatment of traumatic memories: Synthesis, realization and integration. *Dissociation, 6*, 162-180.

van der Hart, O., & van der Horst, O. (1989). The dissociation theory of Pierre Janet. *Journal of Traumatic Stress, 2*, 399-314.

van der Kolk, B. A., & Fisler, R. (1995). Dissociation and the fragmentary nature of the traumatic memories: Overview and exploratory study. *Journal of Traumatic Stress, 8*(4), 505-525.

Williams, L. M. (1993). Adult memories of child sexual abuse: Recent developments. Paper presented at the 10th International Conference on Multiple Personality/Dissociative States, Chicago.

Williams, M. B. (1991). Clinical work with families of MPD patients: Assessment and issues for practice. *Dissociation, 4,*(2), 92-99.

Williams, M. B. (1993). Establishing safety in survivors of severe sexual abuse in posttraumatic stress therapy. *Treating Abuse Today, 3*(1), 4-11.

Chapter **3**

MEMORY

So why seek out this memory? Why not leave "well enough" alone?
So you've happened to build your house on top of a toxic waste
deposit: just don't dig around, stir things up, or plant a garden. Sell
and don't tell. Not possible. (Client's voice, quoted in Courtois, 1992,
p. 23)

In our study, over half the survivors repressed the memories of their abuse.
Sixty-six percent ($n = 53$) remembered the abuse only after they had left home
and the abuse had ended.

The level of details remembered varies with each woman. One survivor
vividly remembered:

> *My stepmother made me use vegetables on myself. She was also on
> top of me and made me suck her breast and/or oral sex and finger
> her. She did the same to me. I was tied in bed every night for three
> years because I masturbated. While I was tied, my stepmother would
> finger me.*

However, another survivor stated, *"I'm not sure. . . . My memeories are
shadows, and it was very early in my life."*

A third woman had these memories:

> *I don't remember much detail. She would lay me down on my back
> with my hands together above my head and my knees bent. She*

would rub me and put things in my vagina. I don't know what. I have an image of being able to see nothing but her two breasts hanging over me and bright red lipstick. I think she used to kiss me all over, in a smothering kind of way. It's like she invaded every cell of my being, totally overwhelming me, completely enmeshed.

Steinberg (1995) has called memory the "language of identity." Who we are and how we define ourselves is based on our memories. Our identity is related to how we recall and chronicle previous happenings, alliances, associations, and events. Rosenfeld (1988) wrote, "Memories are not fixed but are constantly evolving generalizations—recreations—of the past, which give us a sense of continuity, a sense of being, with a past, a present, and a future" (p. 76).

Janet was one of the first to study memory. He presented a concept he called "stream of consciousness," which is sustained by feeling at home with and recognizing one's environment, and which then is moderated by committing to memory what has happened in the environment. Janet (1925) wrote that when memories produce anxiety and cannot be offset, they are banished from the stream of consciousness by dissociation. These memories often return later as "flashbacks," triggered by emotional or sensory cues.

A constructivist view describes memory as a contingency composed of cognitive schemas, individuality, and temperament grounded in cultural realities. Mayman (1968) studied the reconstructive processes of early childhood memories. He was convinced that memories from early childhood are reconstructed later in life so as to reveal "psychological truths" instead of objective truths. He believed individuals develop universal beliefs regarding the self and other people that frame their views of the world. Since Mayman first postulated this theory other authors have agreed (Barclay & DeCooke, 1988; Barclay & Wellman, 1986; Barclay, Pettito, Labrum, & Carter-Jessup, 1991). Mayman theorized that themes of early childhood memories provide the clinician with information about the client's primary motivations, types of neuroses, and her unconscious conflicts in adulthood.

Mayman (1968) collected data on early memories from his study population by inquiring about 16 specific memories. He began by asking the client to identify his or her earliest memory from childhood, and then his or her next earliest memory. Other questions were connected to the subject's early memories eliciting happiness, anger, fear, and snugness. Tapping into a client's earliest memory of being "snug" provides information on how the client experiences feeling safe, is able to be reassured, and forms her elementary ego-relatedness (Winnicott, 1958). A question focusing on the memory of a special object (e.g., a blanket or a favorite stuffed toy) provides data about the clients fantasies and the presence of a transitional object (Winnicott, 1971).

Fowler (1994) developed some suggestions for dealing with a client's memories. First, he believed it is critical for the clinician to be impartial about the accuracy of memories. Second, when the clinician responds, he or she should use the client's own words and forms of language, so as not to contaminate the client's memories. Third, the clinician needs to be cognizant of topics or subjects revealed in the memories. Finally, Fowler asserted that the clinician needs to be "firmly grounded in reality." This means the clinician's role is to facilitate the client's sorting through of events, suppositions, and misconceptions surrounding her memories so that her own reality can be determined.

Spence (1984) believed the process of psychotherapy involves the client "informing" the clinician about her life, which then becomes "narrative truth" rather than "historical" or "objective truth." The clinician's role is to formulate data into a consonant pattern. This pattern is then mirrored back to the client by the clinician's elucidations, paraphrases, and summaries. Through this illuminating process, the client gains an increased awareness of her narrative truth, which facilitates more exploration and enables her to reach new levels of understanding herself.

STUDIES RELATED TO MEMORIES
OF SEXUAL ABUSE

Elliott and Briere (1995) conducted a study of 505 subjects in a random stratified sample of the general population. Of respondents who had been abused as children, 42% identified a time when they had had less recollection of the abuse than they had at the time the survey was completed, and 20% identified a time when they were completely unaware of the abuse. These individuals also reported threats of physical harm by the perpetrator. Elliott and Briere's study did not find a connection between severity of the abuse and a likelihood of amnesia. Instead, this study found that amnesia was connected to bullying, psychological intimidation, and fear of violent reprisals against the victim.

Psychological instruments used in Elliott and Briere's (1995) study were abridged versions of the *Traumatic Events Scale* (Elliott, 1992), *Trauma Symptom Inventory* (Briere, 1995), *Impact of Event Scales* (Horowitz, Wilner, & Alvarez, 1979), and the *Symptom Checklist* (Foy, Sipprelle, Rueger, & Carroll, 1984).

Elliott and Briere believe that, because this study was conducted in the general population, it confirms that there is not a "repressed memory syndrome" seen only in well-educated females from an upper socioeconomic background. Participants in this study reported delayed memories regardless of educational level, race, or income.

In a study by Herman and Schatzow (1987) of 53 women who were incest survivors, 64% were not able to remember everything about the abuse, and 28% had difficulty remembering details of the abuse. Two factors seem to be related to repression: (a) the abuse began during the preschool period and stopped prior to adolescence; (b) abuse that was more brutal was more likely to cause incomplete memories.

Briere and Conte (1989) found that about 60% of the women in their study of abuse survivors (*n* = 468) had some type of amnesia for sexual abuse that happened before the age of 18. Subjects in their study had more amnesia if the abuse occurred at an early age and if it was violent.

Loftus, Polonsky, and Fullilove (1994) studied 105 women receiving out-patient treatment for substance abuse. Of these women, 54% reported being survivors of childhood sexual abuse. Of that 54%, 81% had always remembered being abused. However, 19% did not report that they had always remembered.

Williams (1994) did a study of 129 women who had been sexually abused in childhood and for whom documentation was available from hospital records. Study participants had been between 10 months and 12 years of age when they were brought to the hospital emergency room. These women were interviewed 17 years later. Although all of the participants had been sexually abused in childhood, *only 62% reported the abuse* when questioned by the interviewer. An astonishing 38% did not report the abuse. Reasons for not reporting abuse in either the Loftus et al. (1994) study or Williams's study are unclear. Perhaps the victims had repressed the knowledge, had childhood amnesia, or simply chose not to reveal the information.

Williams (1995) suggested one reason that young children have no memory of abuse:

> [T]he memory may have been laid down or constructed in a way that was not verbally mediated but based on images, actions, or feelings . . . events which occur in childhood may be forgotten because they are incomprehensible to the child at the time. Eventually the child may realize the significance of the event. (p. 651)

Additionally, having little or no support from the mother after the abuse occurred seems to affect memory retrieval.

One survivor in this study stated, *"I always remembered but didn't have a name for the sexual abuse. . . . My earliest awareness is being in my crib, unable to move (she tied me in various ways)."*

Williams (1995) reported that 45% of the survivors who were 3 years old or younger at the time of abuse reported being able to recall the abusive incident or other abusive incidents by the same offender. Williams did not find a correlation between a prior history of psychological treatment and whether the reported abusive incident was remembered or not.

MEMORY TRIGGERS

Amnesia can be one of the effects of trauma. Amnesia that is related to trauma may persist for weeks, months, or years. Memories may return when the survivor is exposed to "sensory or affective stimuli that match sensory or affective elements associated with the trauma" (van der Kolk & Fisler, 1995, p. 509).

Courtois (1992) discussed the various ways in which memory returns: physiologically (body memories, colors, visualizations, sounds, smells, tastes); somatically (pain, illness, paralysis, numbing); and emotionally (flashbacks, dreams, nightmares). She stated,

> Organized triggers (or associational cues) for recall and reaction fall into five categories: (1) normative developmental events or developmental crises of an incremental type (such as the development of an intimate relationship or the birth of a child) or ceremonial type (such as the death of the perpetrator or other significant kin); (2) exposure to events which symbolize or resemble the original trauma (such as a specific person, body type, sound, smell, body position or movement, childhood picture, media account phrase or image, anniversary reaction, medical or dental procedure, and sexual activity or sexual event); (3) crises associated with recollection, disclosure, confrontation, reporting, and criminal justice concerning the client's personal abuse experiences or the abuse of other family members or acquaintances; (4) issues within the therapy (such as support, trust, validation, the encouragement to associate and disclose); and (5) life stages or cumulative life events (such as the "empty nest syndrome" or mid-life crisis of the middle-aged woman and "hitting bottom"

and/or achieving sobriety or another from of recovery from a substance or process addiction/compulsion). (p.22)

A therapist could suggest a client use the following to help recall memories: journaling about her life in the family as a child, making collages, drawing
a lifemap that pinpoints significant happenings to her from birth, drawing the
childhood home, genogramming, and bringing items into the therapy session
from childhood, including pictures (Courtois, 1992).

Clients need to be prepared for the emotional effects once memories are
triggered. Supports need to be established prior to engaging in any of the afore-
mentioned activities. Sessions should be paced, and memory work should never
be started in the final phase of a session. Group work can be quite helpful and
powerful in this respect. These treatment suggestions are not for those persons
diagnosed with DID or DDNOS.

In our study population, one survivor's memory was triggered when she
was taking a bath: *"She started forcing me to play with her genital area, and
she touched my genital area. She did this in the bathtub by holding my head
under water until I would do as she asked."*

TRAUMA RESPONSES

A trauma response has two parts: denial and intrusion (Horowitz, 1986;
van der Kolk, 1988). Denial occurs when memories are repressed. The individual may feel nothing emotionally. Intrusion occurs when thoughts and feelings
arise suddenly, without any warning. Intrusive symptoms can include both flashbacks and body memories, both of which are distressing for the survivor.

Information about post-traumatic stress disorder (PTSD) and triggers should
be provided to the survivor if it is determined she has this disorder. The clinician also needs to focus on the survivor's ability to manage her symptoms,
asking her not to avoid the intrusive thoughts and images but to practice tolerating them for short periods of time in the beginning.

It is the clinician's responsibility to structure the sessions so that the survivor does not leave in a hyperaroused emotional state and is not so overwhelmed
and flooded with emotions that she cannot function after leaving the session.

Remembering must be planned ahead. This allows the survivor to feel more
control over the memory. It also may be appropriate to allow 90 minutes for

sessions involving memory work rather than the average 50-minute sessions. Concrete and explicit plans should be made ahead of time for how safety will be created within the therapeutic environment and also outside the treatment room after the survivor leaves. The survivor needs to be able to verbalize and identify what helps her feel safe in the therapy room—for example, sitting on the floor with her back resting against her favorite chair and holding a safety object of her choice.

Together therapist and survivor should identify a signal the survivor can use to make the therapist aware that she is feeling overwhelmed and needs to stop. This can be practiced a couple of times so that the survivor becomes comfortable giving the signal.

Briere (1992) suggested that the clinician should begin working with memories that are already in conscious awareness. His abuse-focused psychotherapy suggests the clinician should obtain information on features of the abuse, including the survivor's past and present ways of responding. Second, the therapeutic environment should provide the survivor with the chance to verbalize the details of victimization. This will weaken and deprecate the memories associated with the abuse.

Extreme emotional responses can be characterized as "normal" because of the traumatic situations the survivor has encountered. She can be asked to focus on her body: "What do you observe about yourself at this moment?" She may be able to recognize that she experienced nausea or gagging, and then be able to connect it with a certain event in the past. Survivors have revealed that certain fragrances or other smells trigger intense emotional reactions. After identifying the roots of these intense responses, the survivor might be able to relate them back to abusive experiences in childhood.

The survivor can be asked to identify current experiences that produce feelings of rage, intense pain, and overwhelming fear. These intense feelings may cause her to feel overwhelmed and disconcerted. Often survivors describe overreacting to news segments, parts of movies, or sections in magazine articles and books. Once they are able to understand the roots of their reactions, they can better manage the emotional responses.

These triggers (e.g., the movies or books) can be explored by having the client identify what it was about the event that precipitated her strong emotional response. Each client needs to move at her own pace. Following this, the clinician might ask, "If your responses are connected to your memories, what do these memories mean to you?" or "How do you interpret this?"

As the survivor becomes more and more aware of the connection between past events and current intense reactions, prior repressed memories may surface. Recovery needs to proceed at the survivor's pace, not the clinician's.

The survivor may or may not identify abusive experiences. If she does verbalize that she believes she has experienced some abuse, the following question can be asked, "What do you need to be able to deal with these memories?" This can lead to identification of needs such as support from others or some form of exercise to deal with the feelings or sense of restlessness she might be experiencing.

One survivor stated,

> As a child I vowed to never be like my mother or act like her, so after I got to college I began reading about psychology, searching about behavior that was normal—trying to be around "normal" people —then when a doctor recommended around the time of my mother's last schizophrenic episode to see a psychiatrist—1960 I began my healing—my therapist helped to clear my thinking, I found Transactional Analysis provided the framework-infrastructure to work from that I had never had. . . . In those early days no one dealt with sexual abuse, since my mother was mentally ill it seemed logical that I was fouled up by her treatment of me—BUT sexual abuse never entered the picture. I have been in and out of individual and group therapy for over thirty years. . . . I was suspicious about 12 years ago that my father had sexually abused me when I broke out crying when I read an article about a woman suing her father. I read the article and said to myself, "What is so unusual about that" and then wept because then I realized it was abuse. My mother's abuse (sexual) only entered my thoughts after all my childhood relatives (aunt, mother, father) had died and it was "safe" for it to "bubble up" into my conscious.

The next phase of memory work focuses on the client expanding her coping repertoire. Consistent overreactions can be indicators of traumas involving persons, places, and events from the past. It may be important to differentiate between the signs and the symptoms of intrusiveness. Signs are "hypervigilance, startle reactions, verbal or behavioral repetition, emotional ability, confusion, inability to concentrate and readiness to flee" (Claridge, 1992, p. 248). Being aware of these signs can help a client identify symptoms of intrusiveness, which are "sensations, images, illusions, physiologic arousal, recurrent dreams, and compulsive repetitions" (Claridge, 1992, p. 249). If the survivor determines that these symptoms are related to prior traumas, this understanding can facilitate her becoming more engaged in the process of living. Her verbalization of the abuse may help her to see the situation differently than she did as a child (i.e., *"It was all my fault"*). She now can say, *"I survived and did what I needed to do to get through it. As a child I had no choice."*

Using this method of memory retrieval does not culminate in quick recovery of memories, nor does it always provide complete memories. Instead, it often seems that a variety of memory fragments are produced. Sensory or body memories often surface first. Visual memories usually are the last to be experienced. All memories of abuse do not need to be remembered by the survivor for her to heal (Briere, 1992).

The survivor must be prepared before engaging in memory work. The clinician should ask her, "What do you anticipate will occur when your memories begin to surface?" A distancing technique such as the "movie screen" approach may be appropriate and helpful to the client when she begins to do memory work. With this approach, the memories or events from the past are projected onto an imaginary screen. The clinician asks the survivor to provide the details of the abusive events in the third person, using the words "she" and "her." This helps decrease the impact of what she is remembering. For example, instead of describing the scene as, "He is stroking me right now," the survivor would say, "He always started by stroking her." Grounding postures should be used as much as possible during this process. Objects that represent safety may be brought to the sessions and held or placed in the survivor's lap while she is doing this type of work.

In Briere's (1992) abuse-focused psychotherapy, he encouraged exploration of and dealing with the memories already in the survivor's conscious awareness. He recommended acquiring information on features of the abusive incidents, how the survivor responded then, and how she has survived and responds currently. This process enables the survivor to confront the denial that the abuse occurred.

Other repressed memories may rise to the surface of conscious awareness. If the client perceives the therapeutic environment to be safe, these hurtful, excruciating emotions become desensitized within the confines of the "holding environment."

Gil (1988) suggested using photographs of the client from as many ages as possible, having the survivor bring one photo to each session, and asking these questions about each photo:

- "At this time in the child's life, who are the significant persons in her life?"

- "What does the child do during the day and in the evening?"
- "Where did she call home?"
- "Who did the child feel closest to?"
- "What does the child enjoy doing?"

Gil (1988) also recommended asking the client to draw the house where she lived when the abuse occurred, putting as much detail as possible into the drawing, including colors, furniture, and so on. The therapist should pay attention to the client's responses and emotional reactions. It is not unusual for clients to experience trembling, shaking, twitching, or rapid eye blinking. Gil suggested taking a detailed history of school, friends, teachers, and reports.

Normalizing the memory retrieval process is another component of treatment. Again, this involves a judgment call on the part of the therapist, who must determine if current crises are avoidance mechanisms the client uses to deal with past trauma. Flashbacks remind the client that the abuse took place in the past and is not happening now. During dissociation episodes, Williams (1993) advocated asking the client what would help her return to the session. She gave examples of items her clients used to facilitate grounding: pieces of artwork, toys, stuffed animals, and a glow worm. Part of the therapeutic agenda is to help the client integrate the memories into her life, "reframing, decatastrophizing, and defusing" (p. 15) them.

There are several reasons why clients don't willingly share memories with the therapist: feelings of shame, rage, revulsion, and loathing; fear of submergement and of being out of control; believing the therapist will respond in a hurtful manner; attempting to lessen the impact of what has occurred by not speaking the unspeakable.

AN ECOLOGICAL VIEW
OF RECOVERED MEMORIES

A first indicator of healing in psychological trauma is that the survivor begins to feel in control of new and emerging memories. "The recovered individual can choose to recall or not recall events that previously intruded unbidden into awareness, the amnesiac aftermath of trauma is largely repaired" (Harvey, 1996, p. 11).

The second step of recovery is integrating memories and emotions. Some survivors are numb emotionally while recalling memories. "In recovery, memory and affect are joined. The past is remembered with feeling" (Harvey, 1996,

p. 12). As the survivor remembers, she connects emotions and memories. She will experience all emotions at the same level of intensity as in the original encounters. Both client and clinician need to be prepared for this abreaction before it occurs.

The third step of recovery is tolerating the effects. After recovery, the feelings connected to the trauma no longer have the same intensity. Feelings can be identified and tolerated "without overwhelming arousal, without defensive numbing, and without dissociation" (Harvey, 1996, p. 12).

The fourth step of recovery is mastering the symptoms. Triggers have been identified and are avoided (e.g., violent and sexually graphic movies). The survivor has learned how to reduce symptoms of arousal. "The emphasis in this domain is not on the abatement of all symptoms, but on the survivor's ability to predict and manage symptoms" (Harvey, 1996, p. 12).

In the fifth step of recovery, the survivor evolves a more cohesive sense of self. There is a corresponding reduction of self-defeating and self-mutilating behaviors (Harvey, 1996).

In the sixth step of recovery, the survivor is able to form and maintain healthy attachments to others. Before reaching this phase in the recovery process, the survivor will have had to do a significant amount of grief work around important relationships in her life and all the losses the sexual abuse has entailed, both primary and secondary (Harvery, 1996).

Finally, the survivor ascribes new meaning to the traumatic events in her life. Harvey (1996) wrote, "Whatever the process, the recovered survivor will have named and mourned the traumatic past and imbued it somehow with meaning that is both life-affirming and self-affirming" (p.13).

SOME SURVIVORS SPEAK OUT

A number of high-profile persons have "recovered memories" of abusive experiences during childhood. Marilyn Van Derber, a former Miss America, recalled at age 24 memories of sexual abuse by her father. Dr. Ross Cheit, a professor at Brown University, sued the San Francisco Boys' Chorus after remembering being sexually abused as a child by a staff member at the organization's summer camp. In this instance, the perpetrator corroborated the account of the abuse in a taped confession.

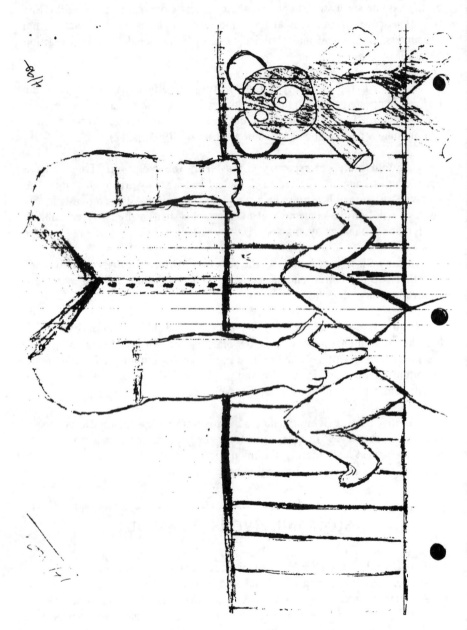

Figure 3.1.   Drawing of crib, perpetrator, child, and bear.

Frank L. Fitzpatrick, founder of the newsletter *Survivor Connections*, remembered being sexually abused by a Roman Catholic priest, who later confessed and pled guilty to molesting 28 children.

Jennifer Freyd also did not remember being sexually abused by her father until she was in her 30s. Jennifer's parents' response to her memories of being sexually abused as a child was to form The False Memory Syndrome Foundation.

The Backlash

The False Memory Syndrome Foundation was founded on March 14, 1992, by Pamela and Peter Freyd. Pamela already had published a story about being falsely accused by her daughter under the pseudonym "Jane Doe" in 1991.

False memory is not a new term. But **false memory syndrome** is. Freyd (1993) defined false memory syndrome this way:

> A person who is disturbed, a distressed individual, enters therapy for that distress. . . . Then, in some way, the notion becomes embedded that the reason for the distress isn't anything having to do with their present life but that it's the result of some kind of past trauma, except that nobody knows just what that trauma was. (p. 33-34)

Proponents of the False Memory Syndrome Foundation contend that these repressed memories of sexual molestation are simply "confabulated pseudo memories" embedded in the minds of vulnerable clients by power-seeking mental health professionals who are out to destroy families and make money in the process. Supposedly, clinicians use mind-control techniques to facilitate this process.

Pamela Freyd described to Whitfield (1995) how a case of "false memory" is documented.

> When the Foundation states that we have documented a certain number of cases, it means that the report we received fits the pattern described in our literature, that the people calling have asked to have their case investigated, and that we know how to get in contact with these people so that a further study can either substantiate or not what has been claimed. (p. 75)

Whitfield (1995) then posed the question: Since "at least 95% of child molesters initially deny their abusive behaviors, how can untrained lay people like Pamela Freyd and her staff 'document' a 'real' or 'unreal' case of 'FMS,' which usually occurs over the telephone or by letter?" (p. 76).

According to Whitfield (1995), the False Memory Syndrome Foundation says there are three reasons why people create delayed memories of abuse. The first scenario goes like this: An angry, hostile adolescent is seeking independence from her parents, but also feels guilty for her dependence on them. This adolescent begins to receive treatment from a mental health professional, who helps her to determine that her parents have sexually abused her. Now that she has been provided with an explanation and a justification for the anger and hostility she feels toward her parents, she is able to distance herself from them without feeling guilty (Whitfield, 1995; Ganaway, 1989; Wylie, 1993).

A second explanation the Foundation gives for these repressed memories is "projection" (Whitfield, 1995). In these instances, a woman says her father sexually abused her, but in reality he has not. Instead, she has projected her own sexual feelings for her father onto him (Gardner, 1992; Gardner, 1994; Wylie, 1993). The woman's therapist (in this scenario, also a woman) had been sexually abused in childhood and so wants to chastise men, so she believes her client.

The third theory espoused by the Foundation is that of the "good achiever." This theory says that the family is happy. The children always do their best, are high achievers, and want to please others. When these persons begin therapy with a therapist who is convinced that sexual abuse is the root of most problems in his or her practice, the clients fabricate stories of abuse to please the therapist (Freyd, 1993; Wylie, 1993).

Bloom (1995), a practicing psychiatrist, made this tongue-in-cheek response to the repressed memory debate:

> Now women (what about all the male victims?) are falsely accusing innocent people of past deeds that never happened, although since they are sick (weak? stupid?), it is not their fault but the fault of money-grubbing psychotherapists who are foolish enough, poorly trained enough, or greedy enough to actually believe what these sick (weak, stupid), women say. (p. 275-276)

Bloom (1995) suggested that the backlash actually is a result of "lawsuits that adult survivors started bringing against their perpetrators" (p. 282). These lawsuits infuriate the perpetrators, who then sue the therapists. Bloom points out that it would not look good for the perpetrator to bring litigation against his or her own flesh and blood, so the only way to retaliate is against the mental health provider. Bloom wrote, "Then it is no longer the adult patient who was raped, beaten, and betrayed as a child, who is the victim seeking restitution. Now the real victim is the accused perpetrator. It is a brilliant legal strategy" (p. 282).

MEMORY AS A SYSTEM

Memory is a reconstructive process. It is the end result of the interplay of complicated neural pathways in the brain. Memory systems are complex (van der Kolk & Fisler, 1995). Memory is not one unified system but consists of a number of different areas of the brain. Squire (1987) has suggested two basic types of memory: **skill memory** and **fact memory**.

Skill Memory

Nondeclarative memory (Zola-Morgan & Squire, 1990), or **implicit memory** (Schacter, 1987), consists of memories composed of proficiencies, habits, affective responses, reflexes, and responses that have been conditioned (Squire, 1994). An example of this type of memory is when an individual demonstrates a change in behavior without being consciously aware of exactly how this change took place (Zola-Morgan & Squire, 1990). Nondeclarative memory is slow, consistent, and unchanging (Squire, Knowlton, & Musen, 1993). Implicit memory involves the basal ganglia and amygdala areas of the brain (Schacter, 1987; Squire, 1992; Squire, Zola-Morgan, & Cave, 1990). Implicit memory is not directly stated and is appraised by circuitous means. A survivor's phobic reactions to people, places, and items are examples of implicit memories (Steinberg, 1995). Implicit memory does not involve a conscious awareness of how the information was learned but is recognizable by performance on certain tasks.

Certain phenomena affect the relationship between intact implicit recall and impaired explicit recall: benzodiazepines, anesthesia, and amnesia induced by hypnosis. All of these illustrate how explicit memory can be impaired while implicit recall remains intact (Kihlstrom & Barnhardt, 1993). A man may not remember anything about an operation except a needle being stuck in his vein, yet the surgeon says that the man carried on a conversation throughout the entire process.

Metacognitive processing (or **reality processing**) enables an individual to determine the difference between memories that result from perceptions and memories based in the imagination (Cohen, 1990)—the difference between dreams, hallucinations, and reality (Whitehouse, Orne, Orne, & Dinges, 1991). Foulkes (1993) ascertained that young children are not able to discriminate between dreams and waking states. After the age of 7 or 8, however, the child is able to describe the sequence of events in dreams and also his or her behaviors during dream states. Thus suggesting that the child would definitely be able to differentiate between dreams and memories.

There are reports of adults having memories of events that occurred when they were only 2 years old (Usher & Neisser, 1993). A few persons have scattered memories of their lives between 3 and 6 years of age (Nelson, 1993). But some people remember very little about their childhoods. Some researchers suggest that children whose parents have dismissing parental styles do not do narrative autobiographical memory work. In other words, the parents do not talk about events in the child's life, and there is little dialogue between parent and child about happenings in the child's life or events that take place in the family. Thus the individual might have very few memories retrievable from childhood.

Benningfield (1992) wrote this about memory retrieval:

> Current research on memory retrieval has shown that one cannot hypnotically refresh exact memories of past events. As with all memories, information recalled during hypnosis is altered by the emotional and mental state of the individual, the setting in which recall occurs, and personal motivation of the patient. (p. 22)

Fact Memory

Fact memory is declarative memory, involving information that is available by conscious recall (Squire & Zola-Morgan, 1991). Declarative memory is affected when amnesia occurs as a result of impairment in the medial temporal lobes.

Declarative memory (Cohen & Squire, 1980; Mandler, 1990) happens when the individual is cognizant of occurrences that have taken place (Squire & Zola-Morgan, 1991). It is what we "remember," and it enables us to consciously recall the names of places, persons, and happenings. It is quick, sometimes unreliable, and flexible. This type of memory also has been called **explicit memory**. Images can be brought to mind without a visual cue. Explicit memories can be appraised by direct means. Explicit memories of a traumatic event would include details that were involved with the trauma (for example, the color of bathroom carpet or the lamp in the bedroom where the molestations occurred).

Van der Kolk (1987) said that during times of intense emotional arousal, explicit memory may be unsuccessful and overwhelmed. Van der Kolk and Fisler (1995) wrote,

> However, while traumatized individuals may be unable to give a coherent narrative of the incident, there may be no interference with implicit memory: they may "know" the emotional valence of a stimulus and be aware of associated perceptions, without being able to articulate the reasons for feeling or behaving in a particular way. (p. 511)

Each category of memory is dependent on diverse neural routes. The hippocampus is responsible for performing explicit memory tasks (Squire, 1992). For information learned and stored, the individual must focus his or her attention on the data presented. It has been suggested that during traumatic events, hippocampal processing is impaired. Although this affects explicit memory, implicit encoding still occurs. Traumatic reenactment has its roots in implicit memory.

Traumatic reenactments occur as flashbacks on all levels: visual, olfactory, affective, auditory, and kinesthetic—but not all simultaneously. The trauma bursts into consciousness with great intensity.

> Initially the traumatic experiences were not condensed into a narrative. It appears that as people become aware of more and more elements of the traumatic experience, they construct a narrative that "explains" what happened to them. This transcription of the intrusive sensory elements of the trauma into a personal narrative does not necessarily have a one-to-one correspondence with what actually happened. (van der Kolk & Fisler, 1995, p. 519)

Complete memories include an affective component, a verbal component (who, what, where, when, and a story line), and a sensory component (visual images and body memories). Traumatic events create fragmentation or a disjointedness between these elements of memory.

Declarative memory can be divided into episodic and semantic memories. **Episodic memory** also has been called autobiographical memory. It involves knowledge about the self; it is, in essence, one's mental knowledge about one's life.

Autobiographical memories are recalled quite easily (Herman, 1992). Other memories are recovered more slowly. A number of factors were found to influence this retrieval process: how the incident was experienced (i.e., personally or through second-hand information); the individual's comprehension of the memory; the individual's affective condition during encoding and retrieval; and the amount of time since the memory was encoded.

Autobiographical memories also are affected by "memory talk." When adults talk to children about their memories (Nelson, 1993), some autobiographical memories actually are constructed by parent and child. Memories of these events then evolve from both a significant other and the child.

Autobiographical memories are revealed in the form of narratives. Usually, after the age of 2 years, the child can articulate some basic narrative forms of communication (Fivush & Hudson, 1990; Nelson, 1993). Narratives are expressed in different ways: autobiographical stories, fictional stories, and schematic sequences. These different forms of narrative help children make sense of their world.

Brewer (1994) suggested four different types of autobiographical memory: personal memory, generic personal memory, nonimaginal memory, and non-image forms of memory. **Personal memory** is used to recall a certain incident from one's past. It is analogous to "reliving" the initial experience and usually coexists with optical pictorialization. Brewer (1988) contended that personal memory embodies data involving places, people, and actions of others, but the individual has minimal knowledge regarding absolute time. When survivors describe abusive situations, they may remember who, what, and where—but exactly when may not be clear. For instance, the molestation may have taken place in the evening when it was dark or after the survivor was in bed. Remembering that bedtime was nine o'clock every night might help the survivor pinpoint when the abuse would begin, but it is not an absolute. Some nights, for whatever reason, bedtime might have been at ten o'clock.

Generic personal memory is the second type of autobiographical memory. This type of memory involves visual imagery and occurs because of a recurrence of the same or corresponding events. As an example, a survivor may be able to describe the bathroom in which her abuse took place, down to the color and even the number of tiles she counted while the abuse was occurring; but she may be unable to identify who was in other parts of the house each time the abuse took place.

Nonimaginal or autobiographical fact is the third type of autobiographical memory. Autobiographical fact occurs when one is able to remember facts about events, but no visual pictures are involved (Brewer, 1994).

Brewer (1994) has called the last form of autobiographical memory **non-image**. This form of memory happens from repetitions of a number of comparable happenings. Everyone formulates and arranges data relative to the self (i.e., favorite colors, vacation spots visited). Data about the nonself also are formulated into schemas (Brewer & Nakamura, 1984). Schemas include reactions, experiences, and affects the survivor believes to be true about herself, others, and the world (McCann & Pearlman, 1990; Share, 1994).

Sandy's Story

Sandy was abused from the age of 5 until she was 13 years old. She said she *"never forgot completely, but began remembering details at age 22."* Sandy's abuser was the nurse in her pediatrician's office. Sandy remembers being abused on at least five separate occasions.

Sandy described the abuse this way:

> *I was touched inappropriately during exams from age 5 until about 12 or 13 years. I was subjected to unnecessary embarrassments, such as being forced to be naked on the table with the door wide open . . . and (these are my worst memories) I was treated abusively during painful medical procedures, such as leering glances (that I still see when I shut my eyes!), inappropriate remarks, tension, fear, and anxiety-producing comments. My worst memory is of her giving me an extremely painful penicillin injection in which she was cruel through dragging out the agonizing minutes before [the shot] while she teased me about my physical and emotional reactions to my fear (I was 5 and had never had a large injection before), made a display of showing me the injection, when I cried (beforehand) she said things, such as, "I haven't even touched you yet" etc., etc. . . . Additionally I was subjected to unnecessary procedures such as her taking my temperature rectally when I was 12 years old. And I was penetrated anally.*

When asked to describe her feelings about what happened to her as a child, Sandy said,

> *I feel sometimes still confused, also some acceptance, but sometimes it feels like resignation. I still wonder "Why me?" And the memories are still frightening. They just do not come as often. I feel*

angry that this sort of thing happened. It really messed up and changed
the course of my life.

SURVIVORS

Alone, full of rage and self-pity,
    I wandered through the park with seven lakes,
Barely connecting with the beauty of the sun-dappled water,
    Or the bright blue sky.
Struggling to integrate memories of childhood trauma,
    Only now coming into consciousness, I wandered blindly on,
Grieving, then cursing the fact that I was alive,
    Nearly missing God's message waiting there.
But then a patch of purple caught my eye,
    And I was drawn back to take a closer look.
My breath caught in my throat and tears flooded by eyes,
    With the simple reminder of my inherent strength there before me.
Oh, wild purple iris, how I identify with you!
    Each of us born and rooted in stagnant, swampy places,
Yet living, vibrantly, colorfully, as survivors do,
    Our faces uplifted, seeking the light.

THE DUAL-STORAGE THEORY OF MEMORY

Prince (1995) conceptualized memory as a process, not as concrete stages
of consciousness. According to Prince, there are a variety of forms of memory,
and conscious memory is just one type. Memory is composed of three parts:
"registration, conservation, and reproduction" (Prince, 1995, p. 30). This memory process involves unconscious and conscious factors, and even may be
wholly unconscious. "Two of its factors—registration and conservation—are responsible for the building up of the unconscious as the storehouse of the mind
and, therefore, primarily for all subconscious processes." (Prince, 1995, p. 30).
Short-term memory and long-term memory are descriptive categories of the dual-
storage model of memory.

Short-term or recent memory involves the individual's ability to recall
memories from previous hours or days—for example, what you had for lunch
yesterday. Limited amounts of information are stored in short-term memories.
For instance. it might be almost impossible for you to recall what you ate for
lunch two weeks ago on Wednesday, unless it was a highly significant day for
you.

Memory is affected by personal experiences. Trauma may affect memory processing on four levels: encoding, registration, retrieval, and sharing (van der Kolk & Fisler, 1995). It is possible that traumatic memories are not encoded in the same way as are memories for commonplace events. Emotional arousal might affect hippocampal memory operations. Therefore, affect at the time of memory encoding may impact on one's ability to retrieve those memories later (Bower, 1987). The encoding process includes intake, perceptual processing, and working memory. After the memories are stored, a process called **retrieval inhibition** acts as the gatekeeper to prohibit large amounts of information stored in long-term memory from deluging the conscious level of memory (Bjork, 1989). The amygdala is involved in storing memories that are highly charged with emotion (Conway, 1995; LeDoux, 1992; McGaugh, 1992).

Information from **long-term memory** is put in working memory, processed some more, and then placed in storage in a new configuration. Therefore, retrieval acts can be described as memory reshapers. There are two kinds of retrieval: direct and indirect. Recognition, spontaneous recall, and cued recall are examples of direct retrieval. Free association and quickness in relearning a task are ways to assess indirect retrieval (Richardson-Klaveien & Bjork, 1988).

FLASHBULB MEMORIES

Another type of memory was described by Brown and Kulik (1977) as **flashbulb memories** or **FM**. Their hypothesis for flashbulb memories is based on Livingston's (1967) **"Now Print"** theory, which contends that a memory is encoded for every recent brain event that occurs above a specific level of organization. However, this level of organization is unknown.

Livingston (1967) suggested that flashbulb memories occur in the limbic and reticular systems. Conway (1995) described the theory this way:

> Structures in the reticular formation respond to novelty (surprise), and other structures in the limbic system evaluate the "biological significance" of an event. When the "biological significance" of an event passes some criterion, the limbic system discharges into the reticular system, which responds with a diffuse discharge distributed throughout the cortical hemispheres. (p. 13)

For a flashbulb memory to be forced, it must have relevance for the individual and it must be unexpected (Brown & Kulik, 1977). Rubin and Kozin (1984) found that flashbulb memories are constructed for significant life events, as opposed to events with societal or universal relevance. Emotion seems to be the most important component in structuring flashbulb memories.

People also may have flashbulb memories of significant national events (i.e., the assassination of John F. Kennedy, the explosion of the space shuttle Challenger, Richard Nixon's resignation) or of traumatic personal events. These memories are unusually clear, with much detail. But flashbulb memories actually are fragmentary accounts of past happenings, and they have a number of common features. People usually are quite confident about the accuracy of these memories. Conway (1995) wrote, "The intense emotions associated with traumatic events do not always lead immediately to highly accessible FMs" (p. 78).

INFANT MEMORIES

Share (1994) discussed the current controversy surrounding memory reconstruction in early childhood and infancy. There are those who believe it is possible for traumas (based on emotional and perceptual events) to be retained in the unconscious and conscious mind of the infant (LeDoux, 1992; Nachman & Stern, 1984; Terr, 1988).

LeDoux (1992) is convinced that the amygdala, not the hippocampus, is responsible for emotional learning in infants. According to LeDoux, the amygdala reaches maturity much earlier than the hippocampus. He contends that the process for infant memory works in the following manner: The amygdala is sent information from both the thalamus and the cortex. "The thalamo-amygdal circuits, then, may be the structural container, so to speak for affective experiences and the place where affective 'memory traces' are registered and stored prior to cognition in the infant" (Share, 1994, p. 26).

Terr (1979, 1983) studied the manner in which infants and young children recall meaningful trauma. She examined the files of 32 children who had experienced some form of trauma before the age of 5 years. Twenty of the children had external corroborating evidence of the abuse (e.g., police reports, perpetrator confessions, pictures of the injuries).

Each child in the study played, drew pictures, or talked about his or her trauma. The children ranged in age from 6 months to 4 years at the time of the trauma. The time between the trauma and the memory appraisal done by Terr ranged from 5 months to 12 years. Based on her findings, Terr (1988) reported "virtually universal behavioral memory."

Terr and LeDoux are not the only ones to validate the ability of infants to recall memories for certain events. Myers, Clifton, and Clarkson (1987) have documented its existence. And a study by Nachman and Stern (1984) confirmed that infants have memories for affective experiences. Stern (1985) said that infants store scenes. He called these scenes, "Representations of Interactions that have been Generalized" (or **RIGS**). Because of these representations of interactions, the infant formulates or establishes criteria for life. These internal prescriptions help the infant anticipate what will occur in circumstances that are similar to those already experienced. So RIGS are culminations of a variety of experiences from which the infant develops preconceived expectations about a new but similar experience.

RIGS are consolidated into what Stern called **working models**. These working models evolve from generalized memories related to specific occurrences between child and caregiver. Working models are developed for the self, the caregiver, and the type of relationship established between them. These working models help to form the infant's belief about self, others, and the world. Stern contended that the infant's "core self" is established between the ages of 2 and 7 months. At about 15 months of age, the infant begins to develop the "verbal self." By the age of 3, the child develops what Stern called the "narrative self." This narrative self can relate stories about self.

On the other side of the controversy over infant memory is Piaget (1969), who was convinced that, cognitively, a child cannot have evocative memory before 18 months of age, when "symbolic function" begins. **Evocative memory** is the child's ability to summon or elicit a memory related to an individual or object without a cue related to the individual or the object. In other words, according to Piaget (1969), the child at 18 months can recall the person or object without the cue.

Share (1994) suggested two separate forms of memory, and said that the two types are different. The memory described by LeDoux (1992) is what Terr called "behavioral memory" of the infant. This type of memory is what Freud (1923) called "perceptual image" memory.

Verbal memory is the second type described by Terr (1988). This form of memory is what Freud (1923) described as "memory image." Share (1994) wrote, "A 'verbal memory' or 'memory image' becomes modified, distorted, and overlaid with current experience and development issues over time. It does not lend itself easily to veridical reconstruction" (p. 143).

Therefore, when Piaget (1969) and Dowling (1985) referred to the unattainability of specific infant memories, they were referring to "verbal memories."

The memories Terr (1988) and LeDoux (1992) described were "behavioral" or "perceptual image" memories

A REASON NOT TO TELL

Courtois (1992) contended that many adult incest survivors do not remember abuse from childhood because they have been in the denial-numbing phase of a posttrauma response. This denial is reinforced by family proscriptions of "Don't tell." Courtois described this numbing-denial phase as composed of a variety of phenomena: "repression, dissociation, partial, selective, or total amnesia (discontinuous memory), emotional construction, self-anesthesia, self-hypnosis, emotional and social withdrawal, anhedonia, and avoidance of emotions or situations related to the trauma" (pp. 17-18).

SUGGESTIONS FOR HELPING
WITH MEMORIES OF TRAUMA

1. **Do an initial intake interview.** Include screening for substance addiction. Consider using the *SCID-D* to determine if dissociative disorders are present (Steinberg, 1993). Also consider using Briere's (1995) *Trauma Symptom Inventory*, which measures four groups of trauma related symptoms: dysphoric mood (anxious arousal, depression, and anger/irritability), posttraumatic stress (intrusive experiences, defensive avoidance, and dissociation), sexual difficulties (sexual concerns and dysfunctional sexual behavior), and disturbance in self-regulation (impaired self-reference and tension-reduction behavior). Another scale frequently used is Horowitz et al.'s (1979) *Impact of Event Scale,* which has 15 items. (Seven of the statements are related to avoidance, 8 are related to intrusive thoughts.) Determine a support system. Do a family genogram, and identify family members who were substance abusers, had problems with boundary violations, and so on.
2. **Work on establishing trust with the client.** Let her move at her own pace.
3. **Never assume there has been a trauma in the past;** likewise, do not assume there has *not* been a trauma.
4. **Do not tell the client she was abused.** Never make statements such as, "Based on the information you have provided me with today, I'd say you have definitely been abused, even though you have no memories of any trauma." Instead, ask the client if she has any thoughts

on why these symptoms persist. Or, "What are your thoughts about the possibility of having been abused as a child?"

5. **If the client is in crisis, the first step is to stabilize her.** Screen for acute suicidal tendencies.

6. **Explore all possible outcomes.** If the abuse has been intrafamilial, the family may not validate anything for the survivor. Denial is often rampant. Confronting family members should be addressed but neither encouraged nor discouraged by the therapist. Fantasies about responses should be explored, as well as expectations for outcomes by confrontation. If the client decides to pursue confrontation of the abuser, refer her to an attorney who specializes in this type of work *before the confrontation takes place.* Explore all possible reactions and responses, and determine how and what she will do if she is not believed.

7. **Do not suggest that the survivor sue her abuser.** Let her make those decisions, but explore the pros and cons for pursuing litigation. Clinicians should *document everything.* The survivor needs to know that, if her case goes to court, the notes from psychotherapy can be subpoenaed. If this happens, copies will be given to the abuser's legal counsel.

8. **Get as much supervision as possible from those who work with abuse survivors.**

9. **Know that results from hypnosis are not admissible evidence in some states.** If the decision is made to use hypnosis, clinicians must have formal training and must have the client sign an informed consent form. (See the *APA Guidelines* for use of this type of treatment.)

10. **Remember that clinicians are not attorneys.** A therapist's job is to facilitate healing and the client's achieving of her goals.

11. **Establish a plan.** In the first few sessions, a treatment plan should be established with the client defining her struggles, her goals for therapy, and how she plans to reach those goals. This plan is not cast in stone and can be modified as treatment progresses.

12. **Be clear and consistent in maintaining boundaries.**

13. **Plan for times when the client is not in therapy and experiences a flashback.** Know how to ground her during a dissociative episode.

14. **Don't rush the process.** Recognize that memory work should not begin until trust has been established and support systems outside therapy are in place. Rushing the process is counteractive to the therapeutic process and may be harmful to the client.

15. **Know that each and every memory does not have to be accessed for healing to occur.**

16. **Never invalidate the survivor's experiences.** Be gentle.

Figure 3.2.   Memory Collage, by Juliann.

Figure 3.2. In this portrayal of memory, the woman has her fingers up to her lips and a puzzled expression on her face, representative of the confusion many individuals feel when amnesia occurs. The baby next to the brain indicates that some memories are stored in infancy, but these are preverbal memories or body memories. Clocks portray the passing of time, but not all are synchronized. The clock towers signify that, in many cases, abuse occurred at the hands of males as well as females. The mirror in the upper right-hand corner shows the reflection of a female; but another figure also is present in the mirror—an alter. A hand reaches from the mirror and touches the sleeping figure below, an attempt to convey that other parts of the self may be unaware of what happens when she sleeps and large blocks of time are unaccounted for.

17. **Know there is hope and healing for the survivor, but that the process can be arduous.**
18. **Document, document, document!**

REFERENCES

Barclay, C. R., & DeCooke, P. A. (1988). Ordinary everyday memory: Some of the things of which selves are made. In U. Neisser & E. Winograd (Eds.), *Remembering reconsidered: Ecological and traditional approaches to the study of memory* (Vol. 2, pp. 91-125). New York: Cambridge University Press.

Barclay, C. R., Pettito, A., Labrum, A. H., & Carter-Jessup, L. (1991). Mood-related self-schemata and mood-congruent effects in autobiographical memory: A study of women with premenstrual syndrome. *Applied Cognitive Psychology, 5,* 461-481.

Barclay, C. R., & Wellman, H. M. (1986). Accuracies and inaccuracies in auto-biographical memories. *Journal of Memory and Language, 25,* 93-103.

Benningfield, M. F. (1992). The use of hypnosis in the treatment of dissociative patients. *Journal of Child Sexual Abuse, 1*(2), 17-31.

Bjork, R. A. (1989). Retrieval inhibitions as an adaptive mechanism in human memory. In H. L. Roediger, & F. I. M. Craik (Eds.), *Varieties of memory and consciousness.* Hillsdale, NJ: Erlbaum.

Bloom, S. L. (1995). When good people do bad things: Meditations on the "backlash." *Journal of Psychohistory, 22*(3), 273-304.

Bower, G. H. (1987). Commentary on mood and memory. *Behavioural Research and Therapy, 25,* 443-455.

Brewer, W. F. (1988). Memory for randomly sampled autobiographical events. In U. Neisser & E. Winograd (Eds.), *Affect and accuracy in recall. The problem of flashbulb memory* (pp. 274-305). Cambridge, England: Cambridge University Press.

Brewer, W. F. (1994). Autobiographical memory and survey research. In N. Schwartz & S. Sudman (Eds.), *Autobiographical memory and the validity of retrospective reports* (pp. 11-20). New York: Springer-Verlag.

Brewer, W. F., & Nakamura, G. V. (1984). The nature and functions of schemas. In R. S. Wyer, Jr., & T. K. Srall (Eds.), *Handbook of social cognition* (Vol. 1, pp. 119-160). Hillsdale, NJ: Erlbaum.

Briere, J. (1992). *Child abuse trauma.* Newbury Park, CA: Sage.

Briere, J. (1995). *Manual for the* Trauma Symptom Inventory. Odessa, FL: Psychological Assessment Resources.

Briere, J., & Conte, J. (1989, August). *Amnesia in adults molested as children: Testing theories of repression.* Paper presented at the 97th Annual Convention of the American Psychological Association, New Orleans.

Brown, R., & Kulik, J. (1977). Flashbulb memories. *Cognition, 5,* 73-99.

Claridge, K. (1992). Reconstructing memories of abuse: A theory-based approach. *Psychotherapy, 29*(2), 243-252.

Cohen, B. (1990, August). Therapist's page. In Lynn W. (Ed.), *Many Voices.* Cincinnati: Many Voices Publications.

Cohen, N. J., & Squire, L. R. (1980). Preserved learning and retention of pattern analyzing skill in amnesia: Dissociation of knowing how and knowing what. *Science, 210,* 207-209.

Conway, M. A. (1995). *Flashbulb memories.* Hillsdale, NJ: Erlbaum

Courtois, C. A. (1992). The memory retrieval process in incest survivor therapy. *Journal of Child Sexual Abuse, 1*(1), 15-31.

Doe, J. (1991). How could this happen? Coping with false accusations of incest and rape. *Issues in Child Abuse Accusations, 3,* 154-165.

Dowling, G. (1985). A Piagetian critique. *Psychoanalytic Inquiry, 5,* 569-587.

Elliott, D. M. (1992). *Traumatic Events Survey.* Unpublished psychological test, University of California—Los Angeles.

Elliott, D. M., & Briere, J. (1995). Posttraumatic stress associated with delayed recall of sexual abuse: A general population study. *Journal of Traumatic Stress, 8*(4), 629-647.

Fivush, R., & Hudson, J. A. (1990). *Knowing and remembering in young children.* New York: Cambridge University Press.

Foulkes, D. (1993). Children's dreaming. In C. Cavallero & D. Foulkes (Eds.), *Dreaming as cognition.* London: Harvester Wheatshef.

Fowler, C. A. (1994). A pragmatic approach to early childhood memories: Shifting the focus from truth to clinical utility. *Psychotherapy, 31,* 676-686.

Foy, D., Sipprelle, R. C., Rueger, D. B., & Carroll, E. M. (1984). Etiology pre-military, and combat exposure influences. *Journal of Consulting and Clinical Psychology, 52,* 79-87.

Freud, S. (1923, 1959). The ego and the id. *Standard Edition, 19,* 12-66. London: Hogarth.

Freyd, J. (1993). Personal perspectives on the delayed memory debate. *Family Violence and Sexual Assault Bulletin, 9*(3), 28-33.

Ganaway, G. K. (1989). Historical versus narrative truth: Clarifying role of exogenous trauma in the etiology of MPD and its variants. *Dissociation, 2,* 205-220.

Gardner, R. A. (1992). *True and false accusations of child sexual abuse.* Cresskill, NJ: Creative Therapeutics.

Gardner, R. A. (1994). *Understanding children.* New York: Aronson.

Gil, E. (1988). Treatment of adult survivors of childhood abuse. Walnut Creek, CA: Launch Press.

Harvey, M. R. (1996). An ecological view of psychological trauma and trauma recovery. *Journal of Traumatic Stress, 9*(1), 3-23.

Herman, J. (1992). Trauma and recovery. New York: Basic Books.

Herman, J., & Schatzow, E. (1987). Recovery and verification of memories of childhood sexual trauma. *Psychoanalytic Psychology, 4,* 1-14.

Horowitz, M. J. (1986). *Stress response syndromes* (2nd ed.). Northvale, NJ: Aronson.

Horowitz, M., Wilner, N., & Alvarez, W. (1979). *Impact Of Event Scale*: A measure of subjective stress. *Psychosomatic Medicine, 41,* 209-218.

Janet, P. (1925). *Psychological healing.* New York: Macmillan.

Kihlstrom, J. F., & Barnhardt, T. M. (1993). The self-regulation of memory: For better and for worse, with and without hypnosis. In D. M. Wegner & J. W. Pennebaker (Eds.), *Handbook of mental control* (pp. 88-125). Englewood Cliffs, NJ: Prentice-Hall.

LeDoux, J. E. (1992). Emotion and memory: Anatomical systems underlying indelible neural traces. In S. A. Christianson (Ed.), *The handbook of emotion and memory: Research and theory* (pp. 269-288). Hillsdale, NJ: Erlbaum.

Livingston, R. B. (1967). Brain circuitry relating to complex behavior. In C. G. Quarton, T. Melnechuck, & F. O. Schmitt (Eds.), *The neurosciences: A study program* (pp. 499-514). New York: Rockefeller University Press.

Loftus, E. F., Polonsky, S., & Fullilove, M. T. (1994). Memories of childhood sexual abuse: Remembering and repressing. *Psychology of Women Quarterly, 18,* 67-84.

Mandler, J. M. (1990). Recall of events by preverbal children. In A. Diamond (Ed.), *The development and neural bases of higher cognitive functions* (pp. 485-516). New York: New York Academy of Science.

Mayman, M. (1968). Early memories and character structure. *Journal of Projective Techniques and Personality Assessment, 32,* 303-316.

McCann, L., & Pearlman, L. A. (1990). *Psychological trauma and the adult survivor: Theory, therapy, and transformation.* New York: Brunner/Mazel.

McGaugh, J. L. (1992). Affect, neuromodulatory systems, and memory storage. In S. A. Christianson (Ed.), *The handbook of emotion and memory: Research and theory* (pp. 245-268). Hillsdale, NJ: Erlbaum.

Myers, N., Clifton, R., & Clarkson, N. (1987). When they were very young: Threes remember two years ago. *Infant Behavior and Development, 10,* 123-132.

Nachman, P., & Stern, D. (1984). Affect retrieval: A form of recall memory in prelinguistic infants. In E. Galensoxx & J. Call (Eds.), *Frontiers of infant psychiatry, Vol. 2* (pp. 95-100). New York: Basic Books.

Nelson, K. (1993). The psychological and social origins of autobiographical memory. *Psychological Science, 2,* 1-8.

Piaget, J. (1969). *The theory of stages in cognitive development.* New York: Free Press.

Prince, M. (1995). Theory of memory as a process. *Treating Abuse Today, 5*(2), 29-30.

Richardson-Klaveien, A., & Bjork, R. A. (1988). Measures of memory. *Annual Review of Psychology, 34,* 475-543.

Rosenfeld, I. (1988). *The invention of memory.* New York: Basic Books.

Rubin, D. C., & Kozin, M. (1984). Vivid memories. *Cognition, 16,* 81.

Schacter, D. L. (1987). Implicit memory: History and current status. *Journal of Experimental Psycholpgy: Learning, Memory, and Cognition, 13,* 501-518.

Share, L. (1994). *If someone speaks, it gets lighter. Dreams and reconstruction of infant trauma.* Hillsdale, NJ: Erlbaum.

Spence, D. P. (1984). *Narrative truth and historical truth.* New York: Springer-Verlag.

Squire, L. R. (1987). *Memory and brain.* New York: Oxford University Press.

Squire, L. R. (1992). Declarative and non-declarative memory: Multiple brain systems support learning and memory. *Journal of Cognitive Neuroscience, 4,* 232-243.

Squire, L. R. (1994). Declarative and nondeclarative memory: Multiple brain systems supporting learning and memory. In D. L. Schacter & E. Tulving (Eds.), *Memory systems* (pp. 203-221). Cambridge: MIT Press.

Squire, L. R., Knowlton, B., & Musen, G. (1993). The structure and organization of memory. *Annual Review of Psychology, 44,* 453-495.

Squire, L. R. & Zola-Morgan, S. (1991). The medial temporal lobe memory system. *Science, 253,* 1380-1386.

Squire, L. R., Zola-Morgan, S., Cave, S. B. (1990). Memory organization of brain systems and cognition. *Cold Spring Harbor Symposia on Quantitative Biology*, 1007-1023.

Steinberg, M. (1993). *Interviewer's guide to the structured clinical interview for DSM-IV dissociative disorders (SCID-D)*. Washington, DC: American Psychiatric Press.

Steinberg, M. (1995). *Handbook for the assessment of dissociation: A clinician's guide*. Washington, DC: American Psychiatric Press.

Stern, D. (1985). *The interpersonal world of the infant*. New York: Basic Books.

Terr, L. (1979). Children of Chowchilla. *Psychoanalytic Study of the Child, 34*, 547-623.

Terr, L. (1983). Chowchilla revisited: The effects of psychic trauma four years after a school-bus kidnapping. *American Journal of Psychiatry, 140*, 1543-1550.

Terr, L. (1988). What happens to early memories of trauma? A study of 20 children under age five at the time of documented traumatic events. *Journal of the American Academy of Child and Adolescent Psychiatry, 27*, 96-104.

Usher, J. A., & Neisser, V. (1993). Childhood amnesia and the beginnings of memory for four early life events. *Journal of Experimental Psychology, 122*, 155-165.

van der Kolk, B. (Ed.). (1987). *Psychological trauma*. Washington, DC: American Psychiatric Press.

van der Kolk, B. (1988). The trauma spectrum: The interaction of biological and social events in the genesis of trauma response. *Journal of Traumatic Stress, 1*(3), 273-290.

van der Kolk, B. A., & Fisler, R. (1995). Dissociation and the exploratory study. *Journal of Traumatic Stress, 8*(4), 505-525.

Whitehouse, W. G., Orne, E. C., Orne, M. T., & Dinges, D. F. (1991). Distinguishing the source of memories reported during prior work and hypnotic recall attempts. *Applied Cognitive Psychology, 5*, 51-59.

Whitfield, C. (1995). *Memory and abuse.* Deerfield Beach, FL: Health Communications.

Williams, L. M. (1993). *Adult memories of child sexual abuse: Recent developments.* Paper presented at the 10th International Conference on Multiple Personality Dissociative States, Chicago.

Williams, L. M. (1994). Recall of childhood trauma: A prospective study of women's memories of childhood sexual abuse. *Journal of Clinical and Consulting Psychology, 62,* 1167-1176.

Williams, L. M. (1995). Recovered memories of abuse in women with documented child sexual victimization histories. *Journal of Traumatic Stress, 8*(4), 649-673.

Winnicott, D. W. (1971). *Playing and reality.* New York: Basic Books.

Winnicott, D. W. (1958). *The maturational process and the facilitating environment: Studies in the theory of emotional development.* New York: International Universities Press.

Wylie, M. S. (1993). The shadow of doubt. *Family Therapy Networker, 17,* 18-29, 70-73.

Zola-Morgan, S., & Squire, L. R. (1990). The primate hippocampal formation: Evidence for a time-limited role in memory storage. *Science, 250,* 288-290.

Chapter **4**

MUNCHAUSEN-BY-PROXY SYNDROME

Munchausen-by-Proxy Syndrome (MBPS) is a form of child abuse in which an adult—usually the child's biological mother (Yorker, 1994)—purposely makes the child sick (often using poison, suffocation, or starvation) or fabricates symptoms in order to get medical attention for her child, which gives the mother the appearance of a loving, caring parent (Bools, Neale, & Meadow, 1994; Feldman, 1994; Jones, 1994; Porter, Heitsch, & Miller, 1994; Schreier & Libow, 1993, 1994; Yorker, 1994). Although professional papers acknowledged the existence of MBPS as early as 1966 (Feldman, 1994), it was not until 1977 that the illness was named by Dr. Roy Meadow, an English pediatrician (Feldman, 1994; Plassmann, 1994; Schreier & Libow, 1993; Yorker, 1994).

Schreier and Libow (1994) and Yorker (1994) believe that MBPS is not as rare as it often has been considered. Yorker wrote, "gender bias tends to impede suspicion of abuse when the mother appears so competent and involved in her child's medical care" (1994, p. 38). Because the mother seems so devoted and concerned, doctors and hospital staff often do not suspect MBPS, and the child is made to endure extensive medical examinations (Schreier & Libow, 1993; Yorker, 1994).

Yorker (1994) listed some of the tests such a child might be subjected to:

> [B]lood tests (needle sticks in the veins or arteries), surgical biopsies involving general anesthesia, bronchoscopy (inserting a tube into the lungs), cystoscopy (inserting tubes through the urethra and into

the bladder), proctoscopy (inserting a tube into the rectum), and additional procedures that, under circumstances other than medical, would be considered child abuse of the most horrifying kind. (p. 35)

Some ways a mother might induce symptoms to maintain attention for a hospitalized child (and also sympathy for herself) would be to alter urine and blood specimens (Jones, 1994), to contaminate a child's IV (Schreier & Libow, 1993), or to cause heart block by rubbing the carotid artery (Porter et al., 1994). There is a great deal of deception and careful planning on the part of the perpetrator to gain the reaction she desires from the doctors (Jones, 1994). And, because doctors tend to accept statements on a patient's medical chart as facts, many fabricated illnesses are being treated several times (Schreier & Libow, 1993), causing the child to endure extreme and unnecessary pain (Bools et al., 1994).

Yorker (1994) listed some warning signs for a MBPS family:

1. An unexplained, prolonged, or recurrent illness in the child.
2. Discrepancies between history and clinical findings.
3. The signs and symptoms occur in the mother's presence and abate in her absence.
4. The mother appears very attached and attentive toward the child.
5. The mother "welcomes" invasive diagnostic procedures.
6. The mother has had some type of training in a medical field. (Approximately one-third of perpetrators have had such training, according to Rosenberg, 1987).
7. The mother has a history of unexplained illnesses or Munchausen Syndrome herself.
8. The father is distant, aloof, and unaware that the problems might be induced or fabricated (pp. 34-35).

THE PERPETRATORS

Mothers

MBPS mothers have an intense need to maintain a relationship with a doctor or to be in a hospital setting where the concern is caring for children (Schreier & Libow, 1993, 1994). The hospital becomes a "social circle" they are not easily weaned from (1993, p. 16).

There is no apparent benefit for a MBPS mother to induce or fabricate symptoms in her child, other than to maintain her relationship with the doctor.

She usually has a likable personality, which makes it difficult for a doctor to suspect MBPS or to confront her. Her child becomes an object she uses as part of her charade, and when she is confronted with her own behavior, a MBPS mother may lash out at the doctor—using her child to do so. At this point, she will attempt desperate measures to convince the doctor that her child actually is sick—and she may end up killing the child in the process (Schreier & Libow, 1993).

Schreier and Libow (1993) described three types of MBPS mothers. The first is the "help seeker." This is a mother who feels overwhelmed with her child-rearing responsibilities and is looking for help. The second type is the "doctor addict." These mothers fabricate histories or symptoms, but they rarely induce illnesses. The third type is the "active inducer." This mother will create extreme symptoms in her child. One might assume that the inducer is more psychologically disturbed than the fabricator, but that usually is not the case. "Distinctions such as . . . inducer versus fabricator, while useful for purposes of description and recognition, may not have heuristic value beyond these functions" (Schreier & Libow, 1993, p. 11).

Perhaps one of the most unsettling aspects of MBPS is that most perpetrators exhibit emotions that are not appropriate. Often they are calm and calculating when they are inflicting harm on their children (Schreier & Libow, 1993), or they smile when they hear that a child has to endure another round of tests. While they may be caring in front of others, MBPS mothers often become disinterested in their children when they think they are not being watched (Schreier & Libow, 1993, 1994). They may appear calm and unconcerned when their children are medically at their worst, and may even "exhibit gleeful excitement when the clinical catastrophe they have created causes both pain to their infants and confusion in the doctors" (1994, p. 904).

Although MBPS mothers are not psychotic at the time they are harming their children (Bools et al., 1994; Schreier & Libow, 1993, 1994), several researchers have discussed the possibility of personality disorders in MBPS mothers (Bools et al., 1994; Feldman, 1994; Plassmann, 1994; Yorker, 1994). When Bools, Neale, and Meadow interviewed 19 MBPS mothers, they found that 17 had avoidant, borderline, dependent, histrionic, or nonspecific personality disorders: "In this study there were few difficulties in making a clinical decision about the presence of a personality disorder. However, in many cases substantial difficulties were experienced in deciding what sort of personality disorder was predominant" (p. 783). Borderline and histrionic disorders were the most common for mothers who had induced illness in their children. Another finding was that MBPS mothers also tended to injure themselves (Bools et al., 1994; Plassmann, 1994).

MBPS mothers usually have a good knowledge of medical terminology. Many of them are in the medical field, often as nurses or orderlies (Schreier & Libow, 1993, 1994). However, some of them may have gained their knowledge from frequent childhood trips to the hospital with sick grandparents or parents (Porter et al., 1994; Schreier & Libow, 1993).

For some mothers, there also is a history of physical abuse (Bools et al., 1994; Plassmann, 1994; Porter et al., 1994). Plassmann had this to say about the adult survivor of abuse: "As adults these mothers appear to fend off psychotic and suicidal cries by acting out in a manner consistent with the Munchausen-by-proxy syndrome" (p. 10).

However, a history of emotional abuse, neglect, or isolation is more common (Bools et al., 1994; Schreier & Libow, 1993, 1994). Schreier and Libow (1994) wrote that, for a woman with a history of neglect, being pregnant and having a baby finally give her an avenue to be heard. "There is a chance that the doctor offers a second chance to attain a warm and nurturing relationship" (p. 904). Yorker (1994) suggested that the MBPS mother thrives on the attention she receives from a doctor—a highly respected person in our society. Also, a mother who was neglected as a child may distort the praise she now receives for being so caring to her children. She may come to feel that she must injure her children to keep that praise. These mothers put their own emotional needs—to be listened to and appreciated—above their children's health.

Fathers

Fathers usually are not the active perpetrators, although their role in this pattern of abuse is crucial. Because the father typically is passive and uninvolved (Schreier & Libow, 1993; Yorker, 1994), he may not even be aware that the abuse is occurring.

Given society's expectation that the mother is the primary caregiver, the hospital staff may not even question a father's absence from the scene. And in cases of MBPS, when the mother is so overly involved, it is easy to see why this type of father chooses to allow her to take care of things.

The husband of an MBPS mother typically is shocked and skeptical when his wife is confronted with the allegations. He may take some sort of action, but he rarely leaves her. If she threatens suicide, he may join in a united front with his wife against the doctors (Schreier & Libow, 1993).

Figure 4.1.   Quietly She Comes, by Jill. For me, Munchausen-by-Proxy Syndrome was one of the most disturbing kinds of abuse perpetrated by mothers. It was hard for me to understand how a mother could cause her child to endure so many invasive medical exams and procedures. This drawing represents one of the common forms of MBPS, a mother about to smother her child.

Doctors

Schreier and Libow (1993) found that, although both male and female physicians are involved with MBPS cases, about 75% of the time, the doctors are male. They give this explanation for their finding:

> Doctoring remains, by and large, a male-dominated profession in which a healthy dose of paternalism characterizes the doctor's attitude toward the passive patient. . . . Despite the need for a working partnership between pediatrician and parent in the healthy development and caretaking of the individual child, there is an enormous discrepancy between the prestige, power, and remuneration enjoyed by the professional baby doctor compared with that of the experienced mother-homemaker. (pp. 117-118)

Most of the actual abuse of the child in MBPS comes (unintentionally) at the hands of the doctor, through the course of various tests and procedures. Schreier and Libow (1994) stated, "There are more than 185 papers in the pediatric literature describing the severe physical and emotional suffering of children subjected to MBPS, suffering which, for the most part, is received at the hands of physicians" (p. 904).

When the child does not respond to treatment, the doctor may feel that he or she must try harder to help. He or she also may experience self-doubt. "These self-doubts in turn cause otherwise competent doctors to miss or misinterpret obvious clues concerning MBPS behavior" (Schreier & Libow, 1993, p. 131).

THE VICTIMS

The child victim of MBPS can be any age or either sex. There also seems to be no pattern relating to birth order as a determining factor (Schreier & Libow, 1993).

Infants are more likely to be subjected to inductions of illness than are children who can talk. The infant often has a strong bond with the mother. A child this young is not capable of understanding that her mother is the cause of her illness, especially when the symptoms are delayed. Instead, she views the mother as the doctors and nurses do—as a loving comforter and constant caregiver (Schreier & Libow, 1993).

However, Jones (1994) wrote, "We should not be misled into thinking that children's memory for traumatic events is nonexistent during the first years of life" (p. 770). Some children do show signs that they have been greatly traumatized after the abuse has ended. Jones (1994) noted a case in which a girl performed self-injury six years after she had been removed from her mother's care. Other authors related stories of children who had been smothered who later had panic attacks, fears of being in close spaces, and psychotic episodes after having lint balls blown in their faces (Porter et al., 1994; Schreier & Libow, 1993). In one case, a young victim of MBPS was later found smothering a foster sibling and sticking a wire in a pet's ear, punching it in the stomach, and trying to hang it by its leash. "These behaviors and his psychotic episodes certainly demonstrate that he did not escape his victimization with the emotional impunity of having been too young to remember" (Porter et al., 1994, p. 793).

The toddler often remains silent about abuse—even without being threatened—because, like the infant, he or she does not understand that someone as caring and loving as mother could be the cause of his or her pain. However, there are cases in which children know their mothers are doing something bad—and make comments about how they wish their mothers would stop doing the things that makes them sick (Schreier & Libow, 1993).

When MBPS abuse begins with an older child, the symptoms and medical histories usually have been fabricated. Extreme psychological damage is possible when the abuse begins at an older age. The child may "resists manipulation by the mother, which frequently leads to his or her withdrawal or even to profound psychological disturbance" (Schreier & Libow, 1993, p. 136).

An older child who has been abused in this manner for years may collude with the mother by actually fabricating symptoms or body responses (Schreier & Libow, 1993). A child may perform self-injury to maintain a strong bond with the mother. A child who is strongly bound to his or her mother often will resist intervention when the mother has been confronted (Schreier & Libow, 1993).

However, there have been few follow-up studies on the children of MBPS mothers. This, along with the unique aspects of each case, makes generalizations difficult (Schreier & Libow, 1993).

Shannan's Story

When Shannan was a child, her mother would inject salt into her veins in order to gain medical attention. Shannan's mother also was overly concerned with her bowel movements and used enemas and humiliation as part of her abuse. Shannan recalled, *"My abuse began with my mother treating me for constipation by sticking a thermometer in my anus to loosen my bowels. Supposedly this was doctor's advice."*

Shannan dealt with the abuse by dissociating or by telling herself that *"it was necessary medical stuff."* When she was in the hospital, her mother would bribe her with gifts to keep quiet.

As a child Shannan had boundary problems, was emotionally fragile, and had a low self-esteem. She also commented that she *"had a fear of being consumed"* by women.

While Shannan was growing up, her mother was *"angry and compulsive . . . . [She] wanted to live through me. [She was] obsessed with me, especially my body."* The rest of the family knew what was going on, but they considered it to be *"doctor's orders, not abuse."*

Shannan believes that her mother's addiction to the hospital setting stemmed from her mother's childhood: *"My grandfather was very interested in medical stuff. . . . My mother had scoliosis as a teenager, and my grandfather took her to numerous doctors. She repeated this trauma on me."*

As an adult, Shannan feels like an *"emotional hemophiliac—when I feel vulnerable [socially]."* She also has flashbacks of abuse during sexual intercourse.

Shannan's healing began when she found articles on MBPS, checked her medical records, and then got *"a good counselor."* She said that people who minimize MBPS or who do not understand it have been hurtful to her healing.

Shannan believes that if doctors had been more aware of MBPS, her abuse could have been stopped. She said, *"Sometimes profound abuse happens under the guise of medical necessity. I've seen many examples. We must try to enlighten the medical profession."*

FACTITIOUS DISORDER BY PROXY

The American Psychological Association (1994) included **factitious disorder by proxy** in Appendix B of the *DSM-IV*. This is not yet an actual diagnosis, so mothers who exhibit symptoms similar to MBPS currently are labeled as having a *factitious disorder not otherwise specified*. The criteria for a possible diagnosis of factitious disorder by proxy are as follow: A caretaker, motivated to "assume the sick role by proxy" (p. 727), will intentionally make the person in his or her care ill or will fabricate symptoms. The caretaker is not motivated by any external gains, and the behavior is not because of another mental disorder.

The person being "cared for" typically is a preschool-aged child (however, the child can be any age), and the abuser typically is the mother. An older child may collude with the mother. "The majority of induced and simulated conditions involve the gastrointestinal, the genitourinary, and the central nervous system" (APA, 1994, p. 725). It is rare for a mother to fabricate a mental disorder.

> This proposed disorder often coexists with factitious disorder, which is usually quiescent as long as the perpetrator can induce or simulate a factitious illness in the victim. (APA, 1994, p. 726)

Denial

The idea that a mother could harm her child often is met with disbelief in our society. No one wants to belief that a mother would intentionally subject her child to the torture of repeated medical procedures. Families often have a hard time believing this bizarre behavior takes place. Jones (1994) noted that most family members have an easier time believing physical or sexual abuse. Feldman (1994) suggested that an increase in media attention and publications on MBPS will help to reduce the denial.

Denial also usually comes from the mother when she is confronted. Feldman (1994) wrote that even when there is evidence of the mother's guilt, she almost always initially denies her involvement; and if the child is not legally bound to the hospital, the mother may immediately discharge the child and relocate, starting the cycle once again.

Another reason that a mother may deny her involvement is that, in attempting to deceive the doctors, she deceives herself into believing that her child actually needs medical attention. The mother also may project her "unconscious longings for nurturance" (Feldman, 1994, pp. 123-124) onto her child. If that is the case, she feels her child deserves the attention that she never got when she was younger.

In legal cases, the mother "may intensify the denial because the mother can find no way to 'save face'; she maintains her own version of events rather than be exposed as a 'liar' or viewed by the public as mentally ill" (Feldman, 1994, p. 125).

An MBPS mother is more likely to admit her guilt when the degree of abuse has been mild. Sometimes, a mother admits she has abused her child *this time* and "minimizes the seriousness of the possible consequences of the abuse" (Feldman, 1994, p. 123).

ENEMA ABUSE

Thirteen women in our study reported that their mothers or abusers had used enemas as part of their sexual abuse.

Treating Abuse Today did a survey of 46 adults (11 men and 35 women) who had been abused with enemas in childhood and found that this type of abuse is one of "the most serious forms of maltreatment" (Herman-Giddens & Berson, 1994, p. 48).

"There are few legitimate medical reasons for enemas" (Herman-Giddens & Berson, 1994, p. 49). Therefore, they can easily be experience by the child as either physical or sexual abuse. This kind of abuse clearly can be viewed as emotional abuse as well. The message it presents to the child is psychologically disturbing (Herman-Giddens & Berson, 1994). Many children view their enema experiences as humiliating, degrading, embarrassing, painful, forceful, aggressive, intrusive, and a violation of their boundaries (Herman-Giddens & Berson, 1994; Quintano, 1992).

It is not difficult to understand how one could view an enema as sexual because of the anal penetration involved in administering it (Herman-Giddens & Berson, 1994). This type of abuse seems to have a similar impact on the child's emotional and social development and functioning in adulthood as does sexual abuse (Quintano, 1992). Some abusers may be motivated to give the child an enema because they obtain sexual gratification from the process (Herman-Giddens & Berson, 1994). (It is interesting to note that most of the respondents in the *Treating Abuse Today* survey reported that their enemas were administered by their mothers or grandmothers.)

The survey on enema abuse revealed some of the most common reasons the perpetrators gave for administering enemas to children: "1) for constipation, 2) to clean them out, 3) because the doctor said to do it, 4) or for 'their own good'" (p. 46).

Respondents to the survey also revealed that as children and continuing into adulthood, they had trouble with toileting. They also had problems with eating, "gas and stomach aches, chronic constipation, social anxiety, relationship problems and trouble with authority figures" (Herman-Giddens & Berson, 1994, p. 46). Another notable finding garnered from the survey was that many of the female respondents who had been abused with enemas as children had been diagnosed as having PTSD, DID, or another dissociative disorder.

REFERENCES

American Psychological Association. (1994). *Diagnostic and statistics manual* (4th ed.). Washington, DC: Author.

Bools, C., Neale, B., & Meadow, R. (1994). Munchausen Syndrome by Proxy: A study of psychopathology. *Child Abuse & Neglect, 18*(9), 773-788.

Feldman, M. D. (1994). Denial in Munchausen Syndrome by Proxy: The consulting psychiatrist's dilemma. *International Journal of Psychiatry in Medicine, 24*(2), 121-128.

Jones, D. P. H. (1994). Editorial: The syndrome of Munchausen by Proxy. *Child Abuse & Neglect, 18*(9), 769-771.

Plassmann, R. (1994). Munchausen syndromes and factitious diseases. *Psychotherapy and Psychosomatics, 62*, 7-26.

Porter, G. E., Heitsch, G. M., & Miller, M. D. (1994). Munchausen Syndrome by Proxy: Unusual manifestations and disturbing sequelae. *Child Abuse & Neglect, 18*(9), 789-794.

Schreier, H. A., & Libow, J. A. (1993). *Hurting for love: Munchausen by Proxy Syndrome*. New York: Guilford.

Schreier, H. A., & Libow, J. A. (1994). Munchausen by Proxy Syndrome: A clinical fable for our times. *Journal of American Academic Child Adolescent Psychiatry, 33*(6), 904- 905.

Yorker, B. C. (1994). Munchausen Syndrome by Proxy as a form of family violence. *Research & Treatment, 10*(3-4), 34-39.

Chapter **5**

SELF-INJURY

Clients who self-injure can be confusing and troubling for therapists to deal with. Some persons self-injure in an attempt to fix an internal or external flaw they see in themselves (Favazza & Favazza, 1987). Self-injury usually is a private act (Courtois, 1988; Favazza & Favazza, 1987; Gil, 1988; Walsh & Rosen, 1988), and a survivor may be ashamed or afraid of her actions (Courtois, 1988). Briere (1992) contends that self-mutilating behaviors are cyclical for some survivors. Tension slowly builds until the survivor self-injures, and then the tension is reduced. The survivor feels a sense of calm for a period, then the tension begins to build again, and the pattern is repeated. Self-injury usually begins during childhood. "By adulthood, survivors often weave these behaviors into the fabric of their personalities" (Calof, 1995a, p.11).

One of the most common forms of self-injury is cutting (Plassmann, 1994; Favazza & Favazza, 1987). According to Calof (1995b), other common forms of self-injury are burning, lip and mouth biting, nail and cuticle mutilation, self-hitting, injurious masturbation, insertion of dangerous objects into body openings, and self-induction of pain without physical injury. More extreme forms include head-banging, applications of caustics and abrasives, scalding showers, swallowing foreign objects, hair-pulling, abrasive scratching, and aggravating chronic wounds. Self-surgery, self-suturing, and attempted removal or alteration of body parts (including clitoridectomy, castration, eye enucleation, and so on) are some of the most extreme forms (adapted from Calof, 1995b, p. 33).

Survivors in our study reported engaging in these types of self-injurious acts: cutting their breasts, inner thighs, and vaginas; burning their skin; performing injurious masturbation; and ignoring their health-care needs.

113

The Winter 1991 issue of *The Cutting Edge: A Newsletter for Women Living With Self-Inflicted Violence* listed some myths about self-injury:

1. Self-injurers are insane, psychotic, or hallucinating.
2. People self-injure for attention.
3. Self-injurers do not feel the pain.
4. People who self-injure enjoy the pain.
5. Self-injurers are addicted to the pain.

Although, some of these statements are true *for some survivors*, every self-injurer is unique, and these statements do not hold true for every survivor.

HISTORY OF A SELF-INJURER

Persons who self-injure may have histories of sexual abuse (Borden & LaTerz, 1993; Calof, 1995a, 1995b; Courtois, 1988; Favazza & Favazza, 1987; Hibbard, 1994; Plassmann, 1994; Trautmann & Connors, 1994; Zweig-Frank, Paris, & Guzder, 1994). Survivors may injure themselves as a way of expressing the rage they feel toward the perpetrator, which they were not allowed to express at the time of the abuse (Cauwels, 1992; Courtois, 1988). It is much easier to direct this rage inward at themselves. Other factors in their histories might be feelings of loss, poor health, physical abuse, a violent home life, or not being able to express anger (Calof, 1995s; Courtois, 1988; Favazza & Favazza, 1987; Trautmann & Connors, 1994).

Favazza and Favazza (1987) wrote, "the only physical contact they receive may be provided through beating and abuse; the stimulation achieved through abusive interactions might then reinforce further pain-seeking behaviors such as self-mutilation" (p. 202). Self-injury provides the survivor with a way to achieve the same results of the abuse by recreating it (Bass & Davis, 1992; Trautmann & Connors, 1994).

Because they were sexually abused at young ages, these survivors may associate pain with pleasure, and may self-injure to trigger sexual arousal (Calof, 1995b). Self-injury also can serve to make survivors feel ugly and unattractive, and therefore safe from further sexual assaults (Calof, 1995b; Courtois, 1988). Survivors sometimes think that if their sexual organs are removed, they will not be victimized again (Calof, 1995b).

Self-injury also may be a way to localize the badness they feel they have. Instead of believing they are all bad, these survivors focus on a specific body part (Favazza & Favazza, 1987). For example, a woman who has been sexually abused may localize her "badness" to her genitals. Also, if the survivor has dissociative identity disorder, a male alter of the woman might mutilate the genitals or breasts in an attempt to appear more masculine (Hocking et al., 1992).

Some persons who self-injure also have a history of eating disorders— anorexia nervosa or bulimia (Favazza & Favazza, 1987).

A most intriguing recent finding is that as many as 50 percent of female chronic self-mutilators have a history of anorexia nervosa or bulimia. . . . Anorexia, bulimia, and chronic self-mutilation probably are not merely associated with each other, but rather are differing manifestations of the same pathological process. (Favazza & Favazza, 1987, p. 206)

Favazza and Favazza (1987) suggested that *self-injury parallels anorexia*. Just as anorexia was viewed by professionals with skepticism for a time, no one wants to admit today that there are as many chronic self-injurers as there are.

Favazza and Favazza (1987) listed other factors that may be present in the histories of those who self-injure:

hypercritical or absent fathers, excessively protective and dominant mothers, loss of a parent either through divorce or death, stormy parental relations, and mental illness in family members, especially alcoholism. As children, self-mutilators often experience a sense of abandonment, of loneliness, and of unlovability, and they may carry these feelings into adolescence and adult life. (pp. 202-203)

EXPLORING ISSUES OF SELF-INJURY

Gil (1988) contended that, during assessment of self-injury, clinicians should questions that encourage disclosure of any information about the behavior. If the client is reluctant to disclose the information at this point, the questions can be used later in treatment, as long as the client is aware of the therapist's willingness to have an open discussion about the issue.

The following questions should be addressed once the client has acknowledged her actions of self-injury. They should be asked in a matter-or-fact, direct way. More specific information can be gained from the session once these questions have been answered:

- What type of self-injury do you engage in?
- What parts of your body do you injure?
- Does this require you to be hospitalized?
- What do you use to injure yourself (i.e., a razor or knife)?
- What time of the day do you injure yourself?
- What is the most extreme form of self-injury you have engaged in?
- Do any rituals or ceremonies accompany your self-injury?
- What problems does self-injury cause for you?
- Have you attempted to stop the self-injury? How?
- Who knows (or who knew in the past) about your self-injury?
- Is there anyone specific you would like to tell about it?
- Is there anyone specific you would be afraid to tell about it? What do you think about the self-injury?
- What do you believe others think about it?
- When did you begin to injure yourself?
- How many times a day, a week, or a month do you injure yourself?
- Do you medicate or treat the wounds or scars?
- Is there anything special you do or avoid doing after engaging in self-injury?
- Is there something you hope will happen after you have injured yourself (i.e., rescue fantasies)?
- What do you like about injuring yourself?
- What do you dislike about it?
- Do you wish to stop doing it, or to continue? In either case, why?
- What do you feel to be my [the therapist's] reaction to self-injury?
- Do you injure yourself while alone, or are there others present? (This includes pets.)
- Do you injure other people or pets?
- Do you seek others to injure you? (Adapted from Gil, 1988, p. 188-189.)

Hannah's Story

Hannah has mutilated herself since she was 11, when sexual abuse perpetrated against her by her mother, sister, and grandmother ended. She also was abused by her father and brother.

Hannah grew up on the West Coast in a suburban, upper-class family. She remembers her mother as having a *"'saintly' attitude to people outside the family."* Her father was often away from home. When he was there, her parents had violent arguments.

Hannah believes that her abuse began as physical violence before she was a year old. Her perpetrators threw her against walls, tried to drown her, and attempted to sew her mouth shut so she would not be able to cry or vomit while they abused her.

The sexual abuse began with enemas and led to a host of other horrors:

> *fingers inserted into rectum and vagina, crucifix inserted into vagina, "prepared" with Vaseline for genital sex with my father and brother, made to provide oral sex (to mother, father, and brother), made to stimulate perpetrators' genitals, genital rape, left in woods over night alone, tortured with snakes, hung up in a closet, observed mother and brother sexually active, also brother and sister.*

After the abuse ended, Hannah was depressed, *"introspective, shy, easily hurt—could not establish friendships, tended to be scapegoat at school."* She described her self-esteem as *"terrible."* Describing her relationship with other girls, she said, *"[I was] competitive (intellectually). [I] always felt like I was watching all other female peers—with envy—like I was the ugly duckling— wishing I was like them."*

Hannah has been diagnosed with Axis I major depression. She has periods of rage with violent impulses and had a problem in her 20s with acting out violently. Sexually, she has been celibate for the past five years. She is *"currently not dating or interested in relationships with either sex."* She still has low self-esteem: *"I feel as if I have to over-achieve to make up for intrusive 'badness,' as though I was created for serving others and have no rights to need [anything for] myself."*

When asked what might have stopped her abuse, Hannah responded, *"Probably nothing—I was abused young. However, I think that if people in my school system and church were more aware of symptoms of abuse, I might have been saved."* Therapy and journaling have helped Hannah some; she has not self-injured for the past year.

SELF-INJURY IS NOT A SUICIDE ATTEMPT

Although it may appear otherwise, in the case of the survivors of sexual abuse, self-injury usually is not an attempt to commit suicide (Calof, 1995a, 1995b; Courtois, 1988; Favazza & Favazza, 1987; Gil, 1988; Hibbard, 1994; Walsh & Rosen, 1988). Favazza and Favazza (1987) wrote that self-injury

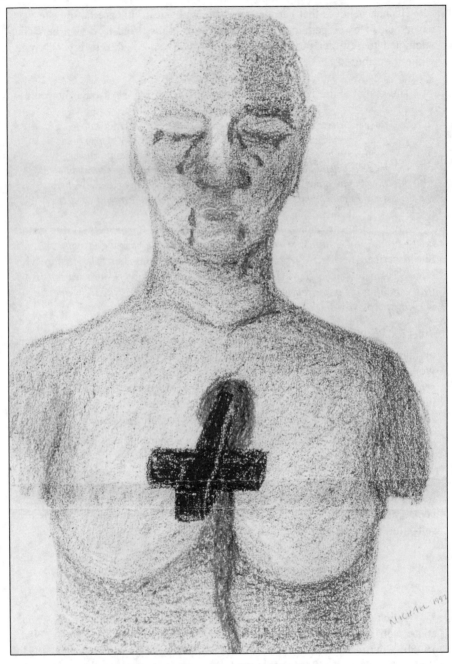

Figure 5.1.   Survivor's drawing.

actually prevents suicide, by "substituting the destruction of a body part for destruction of the whole body" (p. 196). And because it is a way for abuse survivors to manage their existence, they see self-injury as a prevention of worse harm (Calof, 1995a, 1995b). Hibbard (1994) suggested that, if the therapist continually misinterprets acts of self-injury as suicide attempts, treatment will be affected because the survivor will not be able to express and feel the emotions necessary to her healing. To ignore the real meaning behind the action may actually worsen the behavior of self-injury (Calof, 1995a).

Self-injury even can become a form of self-help (Plassmann, 1994). There is a survivor's mentality found in self-injury that is absent in suicide. The injurer wants to manage her life, not to end it.

> Of course we neither hope for nor encourage self-injury as a management tool for our clients, but in the context of the time-distorted, fragmented, information-deprived, and trance-logical realities of still-traumatized victims of abuse, self-injurious behaviors often become sane choices for survival. (Calof, 1995a, p. 12)

Motivations for Self-Injury

Blood-Letting. Some cutters gain relief from watching the blood drip from their wounds (Favazza & Favazza, 1987). "[I]n cutting their skin they provide an opening through which the tension and badness in their bodies rapidly escape" (Favazza & Favazza, 1987, p. 194). They begin to equate the release of tension with the sight of the blood. They also may feel they have to let the "bad blood" (i.e., between themselves and those with whom they have difficult relationships) leave their bodies (Favazza & Favazza, 1987, p. 194).

Some cutters keep the blood they shed in a jar or save the cloth used to stop the bleeding. They then use these items to comfort themselves during bad times. The scar or wound may also give the cutter comfort. Some cutters describe their wounds with great tenderness, almost as a mother would describe her child. Survivors may cut themselves because scar tissue is symbolic that healing has occurred (Favazza & Favazza, 1987; Trautmann & Connors, 1994). "Thus, with a few strokes of a razor the self-cutter may unleash a symbolic process in which the sickness within is removed and the stage is set for healing, as evidenced by a scar" (Favazza & Favazza, 1987, p. 195). Trautmann and Connors (1994) continued: "Some people self-injure because having a wound or scar that they can see validates their emotional pain, and makes it more 'real' to them. Other people watch the physical injury heal and then are able to feel hope for emotional healing" (p. 29).

Seeing the blood also helps those experiencing episodes of depersonalization (see Chapter 2) to feel that they are real or alive (Calof, 1995b; Favazza & Favazza, 1987).

Self-injurers who burn their skin instead of cutting it also feel a release of tension in the serous fluid that is caused by the burn. A blister filled with the fluid may be popped in a time of need, and the self-injurer watches the fluid leak from the body and feels relief (Favazza & Favazza, 1987).

Numbing. The act of self-injury may have a numbing effect on some (Calof, 1995b; Courtois, 1988; Favazza & Favazza, 1987; Trautmann & Connors, 1994). Courtois (1988) stated, "Often no pain accompanies these behaviors because they have formerly been used as anesthesia against the pain of the abuse" (p. 304).

Calof (1995b) agreed: "Survivors may use methodical self-injury as a means of inducing autohypnotic states that serve a number of purposes, including psychic and physical numbing, reduction of tension, and dissociation from ongoing experiences" (p. 31).

In a study of 250 self-injurers who cut or burned themselves, Favazza and Favazza (1987) found that 64% did not feel pain when they injured themselves. Favazza and Favazza referred to a controlled study in which 10 self-cutters were found to have increased plasma metenkephalin, "an opiate-like chemical produced by the body; it seems to mediate pain perception and emotional regulation" (Coid, Allolio, & Rees, 1983, p. 201).

Cauwels (1992) also discussed the possibility of raised levels of metenkephalin in those who self-injure, hypothesizing that self-injury may release neuropeptides (such as metenkephalin) that naturally dull the senses and relieve pain. However, Favazza and Favazza (1987) went on to warn that the idea of absence of pain in self-injurers should remain speculative. "Some self-mutilators may produce high levels of endogenous analgesic chemicals, and some may have neuro-anatomical flaws that diminish their perception of pain" (Favazza & Favazza, 1987, p. 201).

Establishing Control. Self-injury enables some survivors to achieve a sense of control (Bass & Davis, 1992; Calof, 1995b; Courtois, 1988; Favazza & Favazza, 1987). Cauwels (1992) contended, "Actually, *all* self-mutilation is to some extent a pathetic attempt to control somebody or something" (p. 129). Some survivors use self-injury to "mark out body ownership or boundaries" (Calof, 1995b, p. 34). Self-injury also allows some survivors control over "racing thoughts, rapidly fluctuating emotions, and an unstable environment" (Favazza & Favazza, 1987, p. 194).

Self-injury gives some people control over their emotions. They may feel lonely, helpless, or abandoned and use self-injury to release their anger or to ease their depression. They may suffer depression or feel guilt; many survivors of abuse feel they have done "something bad" or are to blame for their family's dysfunction. They mutilate themselves as a form of punishment (Favazza & Favazza, 1987).

Self-injurers also may be attempting to end the feelings associated with episodes of depersonalization (Calof, 1995b; Favazza & Favazza, 1987). Skin cutting can be an effective way to end such an episode (Favazza & Favazza, 1987). Self-injury proves to the survivor that she is real and capable of feeling (Hocking et al., 1992).

Feelings After Self-Injury. Survivors of traumatic sexual abuse learn to associate the period following abuse with a sense of safety. "In time, victims come to associate this 'safety' with an end-state that may include bleeding, body marks, various levels of residual pain, or unconsciousness" (Calof, 1995b, p. 34). Pain or stress can trigger a desire for survivors to achieve that end-state of safety, and they turn to self-injury (Calof, 1995b).

Survivors also may experience the feeling of overcoming assault when they survive their self-injury. Compared to the feelings of dread or fear they experience preceding the self-injury, the joy or excitement afterward may be like a euphoric state. This feeling of euphoria can become quite addictive (Calof, 1995b).

Some survivors feel they have achieved a release of pain after they self-injure (Bass & Davis, 1992; Hocking et al., 1992). They may not be able to understand the abuse they have experienced and the emotional pain caused by it. They can, however, understand self-inflicted pain because they can put a bandage on it and know that the wound will heal (Hocking et al., 1992).

Keeping Secrets. Many survivors of sexual abuse have been threatened by the abuser with extreme consequences if they tell anyone about the abuse. Self-injury gives these survivors a way to show exactly what has happened to them without actually breaking the promise to not tell (Calof, 1995a; Trautmann & Connors, 1994). Other survivors injure themselves because they are afraid their therapists will not be able to handle hearing about the extreme abuse they have endured. Self-injury may become a punishment for telling about the abuse that had been kept secret for so long (Calof, 1995a). Self-injury also may be a way for the survivor to ask for help without actually telling about the abuse (Courtois, 1988).

Trance Logic. Calof (1995b) defines *trance logic* as "the ability to freely mix perceptions derived from reality with those derived from imagined events" (p. 32). Some survivors are motivated by trance logic to injure themselves. Calof (1995b) gave some examples of this type of thought:

> *Hurting will relieve the pain or prevent worse pain. . . . I can't know I'm alive or real unless I hurt or bleed. . . . If I hurt myself, I'll become pure. . . . The misfortune happening to me is about me. . . . I'll hurt myself to make you stop. . . .Even if I can't make you stop, I'll hurt myself worse than you can hurt me. . . . I can survive your punishment because I can survive my own even worse punishment. . . . Since I'm going to be hurt anyway, let me take control of it and get it over with. . . . When I hurt myself, you'll feel the pain. (pp. 32-34)*

BORDERLINE PERSONALITY DISORDER AND SELF-INJURY

Although many researchers have noted a relationship between self-injury and borderline personality disorder (Favazza & Favazza, 1987; Hibbard, 1994; Zweig-Frank et al., 1994), some abuse survivors who injure themselves do not have a personality disorder (Favazza & Favazza, 1987).

Not all persons with BPD who injure themselves have experienced sexual trauma. Other factors may motivate their actions: They may be imitating something they have seen or be acting on their impulses (Zweig-Frank et al., 1994); they also may be motivated to injure themselves because they feel lonely or rejected by and separated from others (Favazza & Favazza, 1987). Self-injury relieves those feelings and other anxieties (Cauwels, 1992) and becomes an alternative to the emotional pain that the BPD person feels. She may use self-injury to control her "experience or to manage anger, abandonment, and loss of control" (Cauwels, 1992, p. 128).

Most frequently, persons with BPD self-injure by cutting or burning (Cauwels, 1992; Courtois, 1988). Courtois (1988) also found that persons with BPD frequently injury themselves by hitting or hurting themselves in a ritualistic manner. They also may have eating disorders (Cauwels, 1992; Courtois, 1988) or consume substances (i.e., drugs) that they know will make them sick (Courtois,

1988). Those who abuse drugs as a way to self-abuse are easily mistaken for addicts (Cauwels, 1992).

"However sick or disgusting it seems, self-mutilation performs the positive—if poorly chosen—purpose of helping the borderline cope" (Cauwels, 1992, p. 136).

TREATMENT FOR SELF-INJURY

Self-injury is a challenge to treat, and therapy can become trying for the therapist and the client (Favazza & Favazza, 1987; Walsh & Rosen, 1988). Some therapists are reluctant to address self-injury with clients because they are uncertain about treatment modalities or feel incompetent (Calof, 1995a). Therapists need to work out their feelings of uncertainty and frustration sparked by these acts (Favazza & Favazza, 1987), because *self-injury must be addressed whenever it appears* (Calof, 1995a). When self-injury is not addressed during treatment, the therapist is colluding with the client. However, it is important that the therapist's response to the client's injuries is therapeutic, not punitive, disgusted, or panicked (Courtois, 1988). Discussing self-injury behaviors helps to eliminate the secrecy surrounding them (Courtois, 1988). This is important, because if self-injury is kept secret, it may worsen. Self-injury needs to be talked about (Bass & Davis, 1992).

If a client seeks treatment for self-injury early on, the chances are greater that therapy will be effective. However, the act itself should not be the main focus of therapy; the underlying issues must be addressed (Courtois, 1988). Therapy often is a long-term process. Therefore, therapists must be committed to providing long-term treatment (Favazza & Favazza, 1987).

The therapist must assess the severity and risk of the self-injury (Courtois, 1988). Gil (1988) contended that it is best to approach therapy with a self-injurer matter-of-factly. How and why the client injures herself should be determined (Courtois, 1988; Gil, 1988). Once the goals of the self-injury are established, the therapist can discuss with the client healthier ways to meet her needs. The therapist should set limits with the client (Courtois, 1988), establish what triggers the injuries, and teach her methods to avoid these triggers. The therapist should have the client label areas where she often engages in self-injury as "high-risk areas" and help her to generate alternatives, but should not immediately ban the area—which may cause rebellion. It may also be useful for the client to keep a chart that shows the location and severity of each injury, the time of day the injury took place, and what the client was doing before and after the injury (Gil, 1988).

Figure 5.2. Collage, by Juliann. This collage is self-explanatory. The woman is cutting herself in an attempt to regulate her feelings. Bleeding helps her to feel real. The eyes have been cut out to signify her shame for her self-injurious behaviors.

Together a client and therapist should set goals, the first of which should be eliminating the possibility of accidental death. The therapist should generate suggestions on what decisions might help end the self-injurious behavior. Because most self-injury is done in private, the therapist should suggest that the client not isolate herself but spend the majority of her time in public places. She also should live with family or friends who are supportive of her receiving treatment, if possible. Then, when the client is having an episode of depersonalization, a friend or family member can hold her hand, rub her arm or back, and talk reassuringly to her (Favazza & Favazza, 1987). It may be helpful for the therapist to teach a client's support persons ways of dealing with episodes of depersonalization.

Having the client compare the short-term advantages of self-injury with the long-term consequences (i.e., scars, social morbidity, and accidental death) might be somewhat effective in reducing self-injurious acts. The therapist also should suggest to the client that, when she feels the need to injure herself, she should hold off for as long as possible. Other useful tactics include helping the client to identify what other alternatives she has; suggesting that she keep leather gloves on her hands to help her gain control; praising her for any success (no matter how small), because delaying the injury is the first step toward recovery (Favazza & Favazza, 1987); and empathizing with her. However, the therapist should avoid becoming a rescuer and should discourage rescue fantasies (Courtois, 1988).

Self-injury may become a way for survivors to "reenact" traumatic memories (Calof, 1995a, p. 12). These survivors often have split off and compartmentalized their traumatic experiences by dissociating during the abuse. Parts of the trauma may be triggered and reappear as partial flashbacks. If the frequency or severity of the client's injuries increase, it may mean she can no longer compartmentalize and contain her traumatic memories. When this is the case, the therapist should work on getting the client's ego strength developed, developing containment strategies, and dealing with external stressors. Once these issues have been addressed, depth work can begin. The client must learn to calm and soothe herself and to lessen her self-loathing. This (in conjunction with a support network of friends, family, and therapist) will enable her to resolve the traumatic memories. They will no longer appear as partial flashbacks, and self-injury will no longer be necessary (Calof, 1995a).

Therapists must help the sexual abuse survivor to stop associating pain with sexual pleasure. Calof (1995b) has found these questions to be helpful: "So, you say you liked it [the abuse]. Does this mean you would like the abuse to happen again?" (p. 32). The answer to this question usually is, "No." The next question would be, "'Well, then, why not?' The answer to this question leads to the aspects of the experience that the clients have learned to overlook, minimize, deny, or dissociate" (Calof, 1995b, p. 32).

Clients can use ideomotor (automatic writing or finger signaling), ideosensory (inner dialogue or imagery), or other techniques to reestablish the pain of their experiences. When the client can realize the pain of her experiences, she will be able to break the association between painful sexual abuse and pleasure. She will then experience the appropriate affects for her abuse memories. "Since this approach can trigger unexpected abreactions, clinicians must be judicious in its use, considering both pacing and containment issues" (Calof, 1995b, p. 32).

Clients also need to establish a sense of safety, ownership, and control over their bodies. Calof (1995b) suggested the client to use imagery to focus on physical experiences (such as quenching a thirst, yawning or sneezing, stretching, laughing, or scratching an itch) and how they made her feel. Clients also must be taught means to control tension—such as breathing exercises, bathing, or exercising—instead of turning to self-injury (Calof, 1995b). Physical activity also can be effective in giving the client a feeling of release (Bass & Davis, 1992). Imagery can be used to relieve anxiety (Courtois, 1988).

Finally, the client must learn to focus her anger where it belongs: at the perpetrator. This will help break the pattern of self-injury (Bass & Davis, 1992). A client who cuts herself may find some relief in cutting pictures and making collages. Gardening and pruning also are helpful to some survivors.

Deciding to treat self-injury on an outpatient basis depends on the seriousness of the client's behavior and her degree of impulsiveness and control (Courtois, 1988). If the patient's self-injurious behaviors continue to worsen, however, hospitalization may be necessary (Favazza & Favazza, 1987).

Many survivors of sexual abuse feel the need to injure themselves. This intentional bodily harm usually begins in childhood, continues until the survivor has sought help, and often thereafter as well. Ironically, it is not an attempt to destroy her life but is, in a way, an act of survival.

For each unique case of self-injury, there is an equally unique pain that lies behind it.

REFERENCES

Bass, E., & Davis, L. (1992). *The courage to heal: A guide for women survivors of child sexual abuse.* New York: HarperPerennial.

Borden, T. A., & LaTerz, J. D. (1993). Mother/daughter incest and ritual abuse: The ultimate taboos. *Treating Abuse Today, 3*(4), 5-8.

Briere, J. N. (1992). *Child abuse treatment: Theory and treatment of the lasting effects.* Newbury Park, CA: Sage.

Calof, D. L. (1995a). Chronic self-injury in adult survivors of childhood abuse: Sources, motivations, and functions of self-injury (Part I). *Treating Abuse Today, 5*(3), 11-17.

Calof, D. L. (1995b). Chronic self-injury in adult survivors of childhood abuse: Sources, motivations, and functions of self-injury (Part II). *Treating Abuse Today, 5*(4/5), 31-36.

Cauwels, J. M. (1992). *Imbroglio: Rising to the challenges of Borderline Personality Disorder.* New York: Norton.

Coid, J., Allolio, B., & Rees, C. H. (1983). Raised plasma metenkephalin in patients who habitually mutilate themselves. *Lancet, 9,* 545-546.

Courtois, C. A. (1988). *Healing the incest wound: Adult survivors in therapy.* New York: Norton.

The Cutting Edge: A Newsletter for Women Living with Self-Inflicted Violence. (1991). Volume 2(4). P.O. Box 20819, Cleveland, OH 44120.

Favazza, A. R., & Favazza, B. (1987). *Bodies under siege: Self-mutilation in culture and psychiatry.* Baltimore: John Hopkins University Press.

Gil, E. (1988). *Treatment of adult survivors of childhood abuse.* Walnut Creek, CA: Launch Press.

Hibbard, S. K. (1994). The mechanism and meaning of self-cutting. *Modern Psychoanalysis, 19*(1), 45-54.

Hocking, S. J., et al. (1992). *Living with your selves: A survival manual for people with multiple personalities.* Rockville, MD: Launch Press.

Trautmann, K., & Connors, R. (1994). *Understanding self-injury: A workbook for adults.* Pittsburgh, PA: Pittsburgh Action Against Rape.

Walsh, B. W., & Rosen, P. M. (1988). *Self-mutilation: Theory, research, and treatment.* New York: Guilford.

Zweig-Frank, H., Paris, J., & Guzder, J. (1994). Psychological risk factors for dissociation and self-mutilation in female patients with Borderline Personality Disorder. *Canadian Journal of Psychiatry 39*(6), 259-264.

Chapter 6

SURVIVORS' SEXUALITY AND IDENTITY DEVELOPMENT

IDENTITY DEVELOPMENT
AND THE SCARRED SURVIVOR

Identity Based on Appearance

In our society, girls (and not just abuse survivors) often are taught to play a submissive role to boys and to rely on their appearance to get approval from boys and men.

> [T]he crucial period for the development of women's appearance-based identity extends from the moment of birth, when it is physically based and preverbal, through adolescence, when it is taught and enforced by complex social forces including adults, peers, and society at large through books, magazines, the media, and even the responses of strangers in public. (Kaschak, 1992, p. 90)

Whereas little boys often play that they are "little boys," little girls play that they are women, dressing in their mother's clothes and wearing makeup (Kaschak, 1992). Kaschak (1992) stated, "Becoming a woman involves learning a part, complete with costumes, makeup, and lines" (p. 89).

Even in elementary school, girls know how important appearances are in our society. Young girls discuss the other girls, comparing one another and

129

deciding who is the prettiest girl in the class. By adolescence, a girl realizes that often her identity is directly related to her appearance. She also knows just how important a favorable appearance is in attracting the attention of boys. Whereas adolescence becomes a time of expanding and growing for boys, girls often are limited. They must act the part of the young ladies they are becoming (Kaschak, 1992). Kaschak (1992) suggested that, because girls and women in our society realize how important their appearances are, especially to attract men, many develop an external locus of control rather than an internal one.

A woman becomes her body and her face. She is judged for her size and shape—and whether they are pleasing in the eyes of men—rather than for her strength, health, or abilities (Kaschak, 1992). In light of this, it is easy to see why competition and envy are common between women (Miller, 1994). In spite of this sense of competition, however, women help one another enhance their appearances in order to attract men and boost one another with words of encouragement when men are not interested (Kaschak, 1992).

Developing a Sense of Self

In our culture, great emphasis is placed on a person's individuality. Our actions, values, and beliefs reflect the quality of our self or identity (Kaschak, 1992). However, an abuse survivor's sense of self probably was not fully developed before the abuse began (Blume, 1990). This has a direct influence on how she views herself and how she feels about her identity (Maltz, 1991). The victim of child sexual abuse learns that she must surrender to someone stronger than she. Eventually, she comes to believe that she does not have a self (Blume, 1990).

Miller (1994) commented that women in our culture do not have as strong a sense of self as do men: "Most women . . . feel that parts of themselves do not fit together" (p. 94). This is especially true for victims of child sexual abuse. It is not uncommon for the survivor to feel fragmented, as if she has a "good self" and a "bad self" (Miller, 1994).

Often, abuse goes along with poor nurturing by the parents. Jacobs (1994) said, "When the mother fails to merge with the child, fails to meet the infant's needs to the exclusion of all other concerns, the child is likely to develop a false self characterized by a splintering of the ego that interferes with emotional and interpersonal development" (p. 20).

Miller (1994) also addressed this issue, suggesting that an abused child develops a false self because of the repeated lies and broken promises she endures:

In less healthy families, the child learns to avoid needing what she cannot get from her parents. She develops a false self that obscures her real needs, desires, and experiences, even from herself. This restricted but adaptive self is what allows the child, and later the adult, to survive disappointments and violations. Because of the false self, the child can continue to function, but her capacity for attachment is seriously compromised. (p. 76)

Gender Identification

When a child has been abused, especially by the mother, she may have a difficult time developing her identity as a woman and relating to other women. Miller (1994) stated, "since her mother failed her as a role model, it is easy to see why she may automatically devalue other women" (p. 141). When a mother abuses a daughter (or a woman abuses a girl), it sends the child a contradictory message: To be a woman is to be submissive and powerful simultaneously (Sgroi & Sargent, 1993). Women who had been abused by females reported to Sgroi and Sargent (1993) that "they saw themselves and all other women as potential victims and abusers" (p. 24).

When a girl has been abused by her mother, she may grow up trying very hard to be as different from her mother as possible. However, a women abused by her mother also may feel that, to be a woman, she must be like her mother and take on her abusive characteristics (Miller, 1994).

If the adult survivor decides to reject the female role and take on an androgynous persona, she may be viewed by society as unnatural. This, along with her secret past, may cause her to feel like an outcast (Miller, 1994).

Abuse's Effect on Relationships

Because a victim of child sexual abuse is expected to meet the needs of her abusers and of anyone else who demands her to do so, and because she missed out on the nurturing she deserved, her sense of security and her relationship to the world and to others have been greatly corrupted (Blume, 1990). Maltz (1991) stated, "Some survivors may repeatedly sabotage their own best efforts to form close relationships" (p. 20).

Survivors struggle with the issue of trust. This is not surprising, considering that the survivor was repeatedly violated during her childhood by adults whom she should have been able to trust. For some survivors, it becomes easier to trust males than to trust females, perhaps because they were hurt more deeply by their mothers' abuse or lack of intervention than by their fathers' involvement in the abuse. "The intensity of her longing for a woman's love and loyalty makes her fear that any closeness to women will inevitably hurt" (Miller, 1994, p. 141).

Other issues survivors may struggle with are fear of abandonment (Miller, 1994) and lack of assertiveness (Blume, 1990).

An Identity Overshadowed by Shame

A child who has been sexually violated feels a great sense of guilt, not only for herself but also for the perpetrator. The child who is forced to engage in sexual activities at a young age becomes extremely confused about sexuality and loses the sense of boundary between her body and her perpetrator's. Because of this, she may learn to view her body and her developing identity with shame (Jacobs, 1994).

Her shame might be more intense if she felt pleasure from the abuse. "In part the shame of incest is the shame of experiencing pleasure at the will and domination of another. Just as the daughter's body has been taken from her, her sexuality is conditioned by the control of the more powerful other" (Jacobs, 1994, p. 125). She may feel that she was responsible for the abuse, in which case her shame will be accompanied by self-blame (Blume, 1990).

Miller (1994) theorized that the perpetrator's shame gets "split off" and located in the child, causing her to feel she is bad and filling her with shame. Borden and LaTerz (1993) suggested that, when the perpetrator is the mother, there is a greater sense of shame.

Sexual Identity

The victim of child sexual abuse is forced to be sexual long before she is ready for an adult sexual relationship. Blume (1990) stated, "Normally developing sexuality is of the child's choosing, and incestuous abuse is not. Therefore, the primary message incest sends is that the victim's sexual life is not her own" (p. 90).

If the survivor learned in childhood that sexual contact goes along with affection, she may sexualize all of her relationships. She cannot understand or make sense of relationships that do not contain sex: Sex makes the relationship real. Because sex and affection became enmeshed in the nurturing process, the survivor may not be able to distinguish when she desires one from the other (Blume, 1990). "In fact, many survivors 'sexualize' much of human experience: affection is sexualized. Anger is sexualized. Fear, need, trust, touch, and insecurity are all laminated with sexual feelings" (Blume, 1990, p. 90).

A survivor of child sexual abuse may learn to view herself as a sexual object. "Thus, as she begins to assess her self-worth in terms of her sexuality, the daughter may confuse perceptions of personal power with the reality of sexual objectification" (Jacobs, 1994, p. 120).

Her self-esteem becomes based on what she can do for someone else (Blume, 1990). This is because she learned at an early age that her sexuality *and her identity* were for another's pleasure. "The incest survivor grows up with sexual abuse a part of her development, and it becomes part of her view of herself" (Blume, 1990, p. 113). She may learn to feel that she is dirty in some way; but, at the same time, she does not understand exactly why or what caused her to feel this way (Blume, 1990).

To My Mother . . .
    by Elizabeth Ann

Where were you . . .
    that Christmas when I was four?
    those nights I cried?
I needed you but you didn't hear.
Where were you when I felt alone and cold,
    afraid to sleep,
    afraid of the assault of his fingers and penis inside me.
Where were you when I cried out for help?
    I found only a cold, bitter stone blaming me for it all.
Why did you blame me for so much?
    I was only a child.
    I could only learn what I was taught.
Yet still you searched for reasons to crucify me.
    Did you enjoy watching me suffer as the nails went in?
    I was only a child.
When I was nine . . .
    I remember.
You touched me and held me close,
    but your touch was like his,
    as you warmed your hands in my private place.

How could I know the difference?
　I craved closeness
　yet the only closeness I found
　came with lust and passion.
I was only a child.
　I loved you and him.
Why couldn't you hold me, and care about me?
Why didn't you teach me to love myself?
Why didn't you teach me that I was worthwhile?
Those are things I never learned from you
　and I only had you to teach me.
Perhaps because you did not know how.
　I was only twelve.
The night he died, I was sixteen.
　I reached out to you for comfort.
　And I found passion.
We became lovers.
We found a final unity, and total bonding of ourselves.
　Perhaps that was the only way you knew to comfort me,
　for me it was the only closeness I knew.
But now we were lovers.
I was your daughter; you were my mother,
　but we became one.
I learned to please you
　in the same way I learned to please him.
But he and I were never one.
　With him I remained a separate being,
　with you there were no boundaries.
I was just sixteen.
　I cried out from my loneliness,
　begging you to stay.
　But time and time again you left.
Cold, Bitter, Lonely,
　that is how I felt.
　That is how I feel.
Bitter; Oh so Bitter.
But now I am older. . .
　and you cry out in loneliness and despair.
It is you who cries for me to stay,
　but I won't.
I struggle to break the bonds that knit us together.
　Still I waiver, yearning for the closeness I never had. . .

and will never have from you.
But still I wish.
I also yearn to be free, to be separate, to be myself.
The warmth of your passion sickens me.
I am no longer a child.
I am angry.
And I am myself.

SEXUAL PREFERENCES OF SURVIVORS

Of the participants in our study (n = 80), 51% (n = 41) reported being heterosexual.[1] Another 4% (n = 3) responded that they *thought* they were heterosexual, but were not certain; and 4% (n = 3) were heterosexual with bisexual tendencies. Another 18% reported themselves to be homosexual (n = 14); and 11% (n = 9) considered themselves bisexual.

Three percent (n = 2) stated that their sexual preference varies with each alter; 1% (n = 1) reported being omnisexual; 3% (n = 2) responded "unknown"; 3% (n = 2) reported being nonsexual; and 4% (n = 3) did not respond.

Kinsey found that, among U.S. females, only 2% to 3% were "exclusively homosexual their entire lives" (Reinisch & Beasley, 1990, p. 140). Although the percentage of self-reported homosexuals in our study is higher than that in Kinsey's study of the general population, many of the women in our study who considered themselves homosexual reported having had sexual experiences with men at some point in their lives—unlike the exclusively homosexual women in Kinsey's study. However, Kinsey also found that about "half of college-educated women and approximately 20 percent of non-college-educated women had at least one same-sex erotic contact past puberty" (Reinisch & Beasley, 1990, p. 140). The combined percentage of homosexuals and bisexuals in our study is 33%: This represents women who have had (by choice) at least one same-sex sexual experience.

Ann's Story (Continued from Chapter 1)

Ann had some interesting points to make when she was asked how being abused as a child has affected her sexuality. Here is what she had to say:

---

1. All percentages are rounded to the nearest whole number.

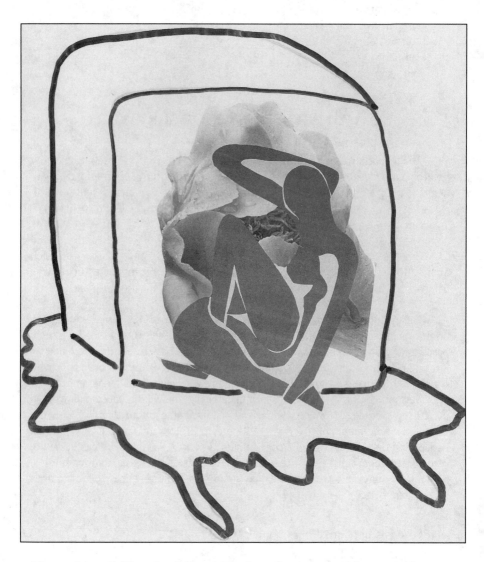

Figure 6.1.   Collage, by Juliann. The ice cube represents the woman's sexuality, which is frozen in time. Her figure is not well-defined in the center, signifying the confusion she often experiences around her sexuality.

Please be aware that this particular topic, I have never talked about in therapy—this particular piece of the questionnaire—my sexuality—is the most difficult. I am being gut-level honest about this and I'm glad for the opportunity, but there is a lot of fear of being judged and a lot of shame.

Because I was primarily sexually abused by my mother, and totally ignored or condemned by a father, who did not sexually abuse me, I have a longing to be sexually healed. . . .

At the present time, I am separated (about three years now). My marriage was always a mess sexually. My husband has always used pornography—in fact seems to need it to become sexually aroused. Early in our marriage, he would insist on going to hotels which ran X films in the room and would take me every Saturday night to X films in town. He would consistently talk about how attractive those women were and that he wished I were more like them. Thus, I felt used and rejected and unattractive and fearful of being abandoned. . . . So I have developed an incredible resentment at being sexually judged and yet an incredible longing to be judged as "good enough" to truly be recognized as a woman. . . . I was especially traumatized by X films which portrayed sex between women for male enjoyment.

At this point, what the abuse from my mother has precipitated is compulsive masturbation—to the point of exhaustion. I will start out with feeling rejected or insecure, and somehow I will begin fantasizing about being in a scenario where I am seen as attractive and respected by a "good man"—a man with no need for pornographic interaction. . . . However, the bottom line of this situation is that the fantasy, as I become aroused, leads to scenarios in which I am a "slave"—"sex slave"—being beaten and starved and made to overwork, kept nude, being forced to submit to frequent medical exams from males, gang raped in public with everyone laughing, and then finally being sentenced to death by beating. (After I finish, I am emotionally devastated and cry and hate myself.) The final scene of the scenario is always my dead body. In these fantasies, I start out trying to imagine how a good man would act, but he always turns into a sadist, and I turn into a pleading, frightened woman. . . .

Sometimes I wonder what I would need to be truly sexually healed. Is that possible? Sometimes I think that what would help me would be to become involved with a man who does not need pornography and who would be a real person in my life. I have never had a sexual experience which felt genuinely intimate and caring. Would this type of experience really help me? I don't know. At this point, I am committed to not looking to get involved. I don't trust myself or my judgment or other people.

When I engaged in sex with my husband, there would always be a point where I would dissociate and stop being present. . . . In all of my sexual experiences as an adult with men (not many), I always dissociated and felt like a doll throughout the interaction—an inanimate object.

I feel so incredibly ashamed about my mother sexually abusing me. This section was difficult to write. My mother, as she humiliated me, would tell me that someday I would "learn to like it and want it." My greatest fear is that another woman will someday force sex on me and make me be gay.

ISSUES INVOLVING SEXUALITY OF SURVIVORS

It is not surprising to find that many of the survivors in our study have issues with their sexuality as a result of the abuse they faced as children. One survivor commented, *"I am repelled by sex and attracted to it. I enjoy sex. I am hyper-aware of sex and sexuality. I feel controlled by my sexuality, victimized by it. I struggle to learn how to turn it off and on but it seems to control me."* Another survivor commented, *"All sorts of triggers—touches—make me numb. I dread intimacy."* Another participant said, *"Although I want to marry (for the companionship) and adopt kids, I never want to have sexual relations or bear children."* Another survivor said, *"I'm either celibate or acting out promiscuously. Most of the time I'm ashamed of my sexuality, and I'm ashamed of being a woman."*

Celibacy and Sexual Activity

In our study, the issue that affected more survivors than any other was whether or not to have sex. Almost half of the survivors (n = 30) said they do not desire sexual relations or they have gone through periods of celibacy. One survivor stated, *"I can go for months without sex, and without wanting to be sexual."* Another had this to say:

Sexually I choose to be celibate. Until I remembered being abused, I was very proud of being a virgin. I had not found anyone I loved enough to sleep with and was waiting until I had. When I remembered the abuse, I became very despondent and felt I was "spoiled goods." I have chosen to live my life as a celibate woman and am content this way.

Other survivors said they were sexually aggressive. One woman said, *"[I] could never get satisfied—never got enough sex."* Another said, *"I am sexually addicted. Sex and intimacy didn't go together for me."*

Other survivors in our study said they had alternated between periods of no sexual desire and periods of heightened desire. *"I go through long periods of being partnerless,"* one survivor stated. Another said, *"I get very freaked out and terrified with most women I date, so I'm essentially celibate except for brief relationships with men. It fluctuated though. Sometimes sex just terrifies me and sometimes it doesn't."*

Maltz (1991) wrote, "Some survivors may withdraw from sex, preventing any fresh discovery of healthy sex. Other survivors may become preoccupied and driven by sex" (p. 65). By avoiding sex, a survivor may feel she is protecting herself from being victimized again (Maltz, 1991). Or a survivor may engage in compulsive, dangerous sexual practices as an adult as an unconscious reenactment of the abuse (Dolan, 1991).

Miller (1994) stated that the survivor may act sexually aggressive because she wants to be in control:

> She may feel a sense of mastery or even revenge in choosing to be sexual with partners she does not really know or like, or in flaunting a provocative, flamboyant sexual lifestyle. She may feel that she is in the role of the aggressor, dominating her victim, and thus reversing the position forced on her as a child. (p. 136)

Intimacy

Another issue many survivors struggle with is intimacy. One woman in our study stated, *"I want to [have sex] sometimes, but once I realize what's going to happen, I panic and end up either crying or pushing him away, or just not remembering it at all. . . . I really need the closeness, yet it leaves me feeling alone."* Another commented, *"When I like someone physically, I turn on in my body but my mind spaces out. It's hard to have sex with someone I care about because I'm not used to having lust or sexual feelings."* When asked about the issue of intimacy, one woman stated, *"I just never wanted to get that close to anyone. I don't like to be touched, hugged, kissed. My husband fell in love with me, and I have found it difficult [to return his love]. But I would never let him know that (even after 45 years). I'm a good actress!"*

Sexual abuse can make it difficult for a survivor to form and maintain healthy sexual relationships (Maltz, 1991). A survivor of sexual abuse may be afraid of closeness and intimacy or not have the capacity to experience it. Like the survivor who commented that she has tried to return her husband's love and is a good actress, Maltz (1991) wrote that anxiety and stress caused by abuse may be present in adult sexual activity. This inhibits the survivor's satisfaction and interferes with the forming of intimate bonds. Also, the survivor may fear she cannot have intimacy without sexuality.

Sexual Preference

Several of the survivors in our study said that their abuse had caused them some confusion about their sexual preference. Some of the women who identified themselves as heterosexual reported that at times they find themselves attracted to women. One commented, *"At times I've felt attracted to women friends and they to me. But the thought of acting on those feelings terrified me. I never knew why before [I remembered the abuse]."* Another survivor said this:

> The abuse caused me to be curious about female homosexuality even though I never actually acted out on my fantasies. I did sometimes want (and still do want) the closeness and touch. It's less scary than heterosexuality. At the same time . . . it's morally wrong for me. I don't think I could have ever acted on my desires out of fear. I really do want to take care of myself and not add more shame and harm to my body and my life as a whole. This would do that; it's not worth it.

Another survivor said, *"I used to wonder if I was a lesbian."* Finally, one survivor in our study commented, *"I don't know what I am sexually. I know there were times when sex with my mother was enjoyed. Now the sex is a confusing issue."*

Sgroi and Sargent (1993) wrote, "same-sex sexual abuse tends to cause confusion and fears about homosexuality for many child victims" (p. 26). In this case, the victim fears that the same-sex abuser picked her because the abuser could tell she was homosexual; this adds to the child's trauma of being abused (Sgroi & Sargent, 1993). Harrison (1993) reported that many callers to a hotline in London for victims and survivors of sexual abuse said that their sexual orientation had been affected by the abuse. Specifically, one caller said that she must have been homosexual to have attracted a same-sex abuser. However, most researchers agree there is no connection between sexual abuse and sexual preference (Blume, 1990; Borden & LaTerz, 1993; Longdon, 1993; Young, 1993a, 1993b).

Impact on Sexual Activity

Another issue that affected survivors in our study was what occurred during sexual activity. Several commented on the fear they felt; dissociation or blacking out; sexual parts being numb; being unable to achieve orgasm or needing punishing fantasies to do so; pain; flashbacks; and alters emerging.

The first issue surrounding their sexual experience is their fear. Many survivors commented on how frightened or panicked they feel before or during intercourse. One survivor stated, *"I hate sex. I fear sex."* Another wrote, *"I'm afraid of intimacy with men. I've had only a few sexual relationships, nearly always with some built-in restrictions. [I'm] afraid of 'losing myself.' [I] don't want to bother dating anyone unless I know there's a real chance it will work out."*

In Westerlund's (1992) study of women's sexuality after they had been sexually abused, some participants reported a fear of sex often disguised as disgust or repulsion. Others reported a fear of the pain, both physical and emotional, that accompanied their sexual experiences. Westerlund commented, "Several respondents (14 percent) described an 'eerie' feeling of deja vu accompanied by 'intense' fear in association with specific sexual situations" (p. 82).

The second issue concerning the act of sex is dissociation. One survivor stated, *"[I] cannot make love without spacing into a fantasy situation. [I] love my husband, but sex is one of the losses of remembering. Even the urge is gone. Awful loss."* Another commented, *"Most times I black out during sex."*

Many survivors used dissociation to cope with their sexual abuse during childhood. They may continue the practice as adults (Jacobs, 1994; Miller, 1994). Dissociation also gives some survivors a sense of control (Westerlund, 1992).

A third issue that occurs during sex for some survivors is a numbing of their sexual parts. *"I usually go numb physically,"* one survivors said. Another woman made the comment that she was *"frozen"* sexually. This numbing of the genitals prohibited some of the women from experiencing orgasm. Others said they do not achieve orgasm without punishing fantasies. One woman said, *"[I am] unable to achieve orgasm. My sexual parts are usually numb."* Another stated, *"[I have a] hard time being orgasmic without punishing fantasies—turned out to be reenactment of abuses."*

If the survivor used numbing of the genitals to help her get through the sexual abuse she experienced as a child, she may feel that is the only way she can cope during sexual intercourse (Miller, 1994). This may cause her to be anxious and unable to experience orgasm. Westerlund (1992) also noted that some survivors in her study went numb during sex as a means of staying in control.

Because abuse often is associated with pornography or punishing fantasies, the survivor may feel she needs these later in life to become sexually aroused (Maltz, 1991). However, using pornography or punishing fantasies may make her feel disgusted with herself afterward.

> Relying on pornography and abusive fantasies may have evolved as a way survivors learned to avoid feeling powerless, threatened, and fearful. Survivors may have learned to use fantasy and pornography to dissociate and avoid focusing on their own emotions and sensations during a sexual experience. (Miller, 1994, p. 180)

A survivor also may use punishing fantasies or violent sexual activity as a way to recall "whatever excitement or pleasure—in addition to fear, pain, shame, anger, and revulsion—she may have experienced in her childhood sexual episodes. Another explanation is that she is attempting to master the childhood trauma by repeating it over and over" (Miller, 1994, p. 136).

While some survivors are sexually numb, others experience great pain during stimulation. One survivor commented, *"If I feel anything during sex, it's pain."* Another said this:

> *Sexuality and sexual pleasure are very important to me. Since I started being aware of the abuse, I have no orgasms. Sex became more frightening and complicated. When me and my lover make love there is always a stage when the good feelings of being stimulated cease. Shortly after I became aware of the abuse, the stimulation would suddenly turn into pain. . . . Sometimes I feel that my vagina is a wound.*

Some participants in Westerlund's (1992) study also reported experiencing pain during sexual activity. Some felt pain specifically during orgasm. Others experienced pain in their vaginas not specific to penetration or sexual activity.

Many survivors in our study also experienced flashbacks during sexual intimacy. One woman commented, *"There is much confusion, fear, and flashbacks with intercourse."* Another survivor stated, *"I am still afraid of sex and have flashbacks when I have intercourse. I avoid it."* Still another shared, *"I have experienced physical flashbacks."*

Dolan (1991), Maltz (1991), and Miller (1994) all commented on the fact that flashbacks often interfere with survivors' sexual activity and satisfaction. Westerlund (1992) had this to say about flashbacks:

> Many respondents (58 percent) experienced confusion between their partner and the offender when reliving the incest during flashbacks. It was not uncommon for women to scream in rage at partners during flashbacks. Some women "attacked" their partners at such moments and remained concerned thereafter that they would "overpower" or "abuse" them again. (p. 82)

Some survivors who have dissociative identity disorder have trouble with their alters emerging during sexual experiences. Others report deliberately switching to alters who can deal with intimacy. *"We have a very difficult time with flashbacks and some of the others come out,"* one woman stated. Another said, *"I hate sex unless there is a deliberate switch to an alter who can handle it, and then I am embarrassed and confused by my behavior in bed."*

The survivor learns young what helps her get through the abuse, and switching to alters may be one of those coping strategies. As an adult, she may intentionally or unintentionally continue this behavior when she engages in sexual activity (Miller, 1994).

Sex as an Obligation

Another concern several survivors reported was feeling obligated to have sex with their partners or husbands. One survivor said, *"I always felt like it was my job to provide sex for my husband. [I] never felt like I could say no."* Another stated, *"I allowed my first husband to rape me repeatedly, and acquaintances, such as lovers' brothers, to molest me."* One woman wrote, *"I feel obligated to have sex with my husband even if I'm physically hurting."*

Because the child is forced to engage in sexual activities against her will, she learns that sex is an obligation (Blume, 1990) or that she must take a submissive role in her adult sexual activity (Maltz, 1991). "The incest survivor often has an enormous problem seeing herself as a victim, damaged and struggling to heal; she can see only what she is doing to others, how she is not meeting their needs, especially sexually" (Blume, 1990, p. 223). Dolan (1991) emphasized that it is important for the survivor to realize that she does not have to have sexual relations if she is not ready. She is not obligated.

Masturbation

Several survivors in our study commented on the fact that they do not mas-turbate or touch their genitals in any way. When asked how the abuse had affected them sexually, many included the statement, *"I do not masturbate,"* somewhere in their response. One woman said, *"I can't do self-breast exams. I use thick wash cloths and toilet paper whenever I have to touch my genitals. I don't like looking at my body unclothed."* Another wrote this:

> I don't masturbate, and I think that's another side of the problem, another proof that I don't love myself enough, that I don't deserve it. I used to masturbate when I was a teenager, but I never had orgasms through masturbating and I always felt despicable because I masturbated.

It is natural for babies and young children to respond to stimulation and to explore "their bodies' sexual responses" (Blume, 1990, p. 204). The response of their parents, however, often makes them feel shame or guilt for doing so. "Our society struggles with its attitudes toward this natural experience, teaching embarrassment, guilt, and shame along with sexuality" (Blume, 1990, p. 204). Abuse survivors especially may be conditioned to believe that sex or sexual pleasure of any form is bad and wrong. Perhaps that is why several survivors in our study reported they do not masturbate, even though they were not specifi-cally asked about it.

Seduction

Many survivors in our study commented that they have tried to or do se-duce women. *"I seduced and left many women—used them as sex objects,"* one wrote. Another commented, *"I am only sexually attracted to women. When I meet a woman, I am always figuring out how to get her in bed, even though I am now faithful to my lover."* One survivor even admitted to sexually abusing her niece. She wrote, *"I feel that the abuse ENCOURAGED me toward bisexu-ality more than ever! I acted out on my niece with the same kind of behavior that was done to me as a child! I acted out with other women sexually—mutual agreement. It has affected my feelings toward sex with women!"*

Dolan (1991) suggested that, because the behavior was reinforced to her at a young age, the sexual abuse survivor may not be fully aware that she is being seductive in her adult sexual relationships: "[S]he may deliberately behave flir-tatiously because of the message she received through her victimization that her sexuality is all that she has to offer 'in exchange' for the potential nurturing of a relationship" (Dolan, 1991, p. 19).

Figure 6.2.   Box, by Jill. According to Sigmund Freud, any object that encloses a hollow space represents female sexuality, and the access to the enclosure represents the attitude toward the accessibility of the sexuality. I drew this box with an open lid because a child being sexually abused is not given the option of saying no to her perpetrator. The knives represent the objects that were forced into the child's vagina or anus.

Emotional Torment

Finally, survivors in our study reported experiencing a great deal of emotional torment in their sexual relationships as a result of their sexual abuse. One stated, *"It [being abused] has made it very difficult to be in a sexual relationship. I have to do a lot of talking to myself to realize my partner is not my mother. She won't hurt me, and she won't be mean after touching me sexually."* Another commented, *"I am shut down sexually. I feel guilty about this because my spouse is, rightfully, frustrated. But, sex torments me emotionally. This is a double-edged sword."*

Westerlund (1992) had this to say about her study's participants:

> An additional problem in relationships reported by over one-quarter of the respondents was an inability to integrate emotional intimacy and sexual intimacy. Thus, the development of erotic interest was accompanied by emotional detachment, and the development of emotional attachment was accompanied by erotic disinterest. This "split" was perceived as directly attributable to the incest experience. (pp. 50-51)

CONCLUSION

Because a survivor of sexual abuse struggles with several issues, such as trust and intimacy, her identity development is greatly affected. Often she struggles with boundary issues and is filled with shame.

This shame is carried over into her adult life and causes confusion around issues of sexuality.

REFERENCES

Blume, E. S. (1990). *Secret survivors: Uncovering incest and its aftereffects in women.* New York: Ballantine.

Borden, T. A., & LaTerz, J. D. (1993). Mother/daughter incest and ritual abuse: The ultimate taboos. *Treating Abuse Today, 3*(4), 5-8.

Dolan, Y. M. (1991). *Resolving sexual abuse: Solution-focused therapy and Ericksonian hypnosis for adult survivors.* New York: Norton.

Harrison, H. (1993). Female abusers—What children and young people have told ChildLine. In M. Elliott (Ed.), *Female sexual abuse of children* (pp. 89-92). New York: Guilford.

Jacobs, J. L. (1994). *Victimized daughters: Incest and the development of the female self.* New York: Routledge.

Kaschak, E. (1992). *Engendered lives: A new psychology of women's experience.* New York: Basic Books.

Longdon, C. (1993). A survivor and therapist's viewpoint. In M. Elliott (Ed.), *Female sexual abuse of children* (pp. 47-56). New York: Guilford.

Maltz, W. (1991). *The sexual healing journey: A guide for survivors of sexual abuse.* New York: HarperPerennial.

Miller, D. (1994). *Women who hurt themselves: A book of hope and understanding.* New York: Basic Books.

Reinisch, J. M., & Beasley, R. (1990). *The Kinsey Institute new report on sex: What you must know to be sexually literate.* New York: St. Martin's.

Sgroi, S. M., & Sargent, N. M. (1993). Impact and treatment issues for victims of childhood sexual abuse by female perpetrators. In M. Elliott (Ed.), *Female sexual abuse of children* (pp. 14-36). New York: Guilford.

Westerlund, E. (1992). *Women's sexuality after childhood incest.* New York: Norton.

Young, V. (1993a). Self-help for survivors. In M. Elliott (Ed.), *Female sexual abuse of children* (pp. 198-215). New York: Guilford.

Young, V. (1993b). Women abusers—A feminist view. In M. Elliott (Ed.), *Female sexual abuse of children* (pp. 100-112). New York: Guilford.

Chapter 7

FEMALE PERPETRATORS

Many sexual offenses perpetrated against children by women go unnoticed in our society because women are expected "to engage in a wide range of touching behaviors with children. . . . [W]omen clean children's genitals, breast feed for two to three years, and comfort, caress and cuddle their offspring" (Mayer, 1993, p. 21). Several other authors have commented on this fact, as well (Allen, 1990; Borden & LaTerz, 1993; Finkelhor & Russell, 1984; Roth, 1993). Roth (1993) had this to say:

> Women in this society are expected to be nurturant, affectionate, kind, and protective. Mothers are expected to be all these things to the nth degree. The brainwashing is so extensive that "inadequate" mothers feel guilty if they do not behave in all these loving ways, and children defend their inappropriate mothers. (p. 122)

Children tend not to report to other authority figures sexual abuse perpetrated by a parent upon whom they are dependent (Borden & LaTerz, 1993; Finkelhor & Russell, 1984). Perhaps that is why few studies have been devoted to women who sexually abuse children.

Many researchers have pointed out that female offenders seem to choose younger victims than do males (Faller, 1987; Fehrenbach & Monastersky, 1988; Finkelhor, 1984; Finkelhor, Williams, & Burns, 1988; Mayer, 1992; Rudin, Zalewski, & Bodmer-Turner, 1995). The could be because the female perpetrator needs to have a power differential between herself and her victim (Faller, 1987; Finkelhor & Russell, 1984). Rudin et al. (1995) suggested it was because young children are more easily coerced than older children; they are also not as likely to disclose the abuse.

The acts of sexual abuse perpetrated by mothers range from "voyeurism through kissing and fondling and mutual masturbation to digital exploration and penetration with objects" (Borden & LaTerz, 1993, pp. 5-6). Survivors from our study reported these kinds of abuse: digital penetration; inappropriate touching or fondling; objects inserted into the vagina or anus (e.g., bottle brushes, egg beaters, and broom handles); oral sex; enemas; kissing; being urinated or defecated upon; being forced to touch or engage in sexual activities with others; being tied or held down, locked in enclosed places, hung upside down, beaten, cut, drugged, or burned; cult activity or witchcraft; bestiality; pornography; douching; inappropriate conversations; overinvolvement in the child's sexual development (i.e., examining the vagina and breasts); exhibitionism; and abortions performed at home.

There seems to be an added sense of shame when the perpetrator is the same sex as the victim or when the perpetrator is a woman (Borden & LaTerz, 1993; Rudin et al., 1995). Borden and LaTerz (1993) had this to say:

> Many maternal incest survivors report an added feeling of shame about their abuse. They describe feeling an added stigma and isolation because others perceive their abuse to be out of the ordinary. . . . These survivors describe the betrayal they experienced by their mothers as more damaging than abuse by other perpetrators. (p. 6)

One survivor in our study stated, *"When I did briefly mention sexual abuse by the mother in a local support group, there was prolonged silence and discomfort, so I never mentioned it again. I got the feeling that it was a little too weird for people to deal with, so I dropped it."*

The female perpetrators in our study included mothers ($n = 67$), grandmothers ($n = 20$), family friends ($n = 18$), aunts ($n = 16$), baby-sitters ($n = 11$), neighbors ($n = 8$), cousins ($n = 7$), sisters ($n = 5$), and cult members ($n = 5$). Other abusers (reported by 3 or fewer survivors) included step-mothers, step-sisters, foster mothers, teachers, youth directors, Sunday School teachers, scout leaders, ministers, nuns, nurses, optometrists, therapists, and employees of family businesses.

Offenders rarely seek treatment for their abusive behaviors. The offenders who are in therapy usually have begun treatment to deal with their own issues of victimization. Other offenders are detected when their homes are investigated because of domestic violence or sexual abuse perpetrated by a male (Mayer, 1993).

APPEARANCE VERSES REALITY

Survivors in our study reported that the perpetrators who abused them had never been prosecuted for their crimes and often were pillars in their communities. No one suspected they could harm their children. In fact, many survivors said that people often commented to them how wonderful their mothers were. Rudin et al. (1995) noted that research studies devoted to perpetrators (usually incarcerated individuals) often yield different results from studies of survivors, whose perpetrators often are never caught or convicted.

Here is what some of these survivors had to say: *"She was very rigid, perfectionistic, unpredictable in her moods, and very mean. She was demanding. . . . I felt like I was her slave."*

Another survivor described her abuser this way:

> *She was a community activist, Sunday School teacher, PTA and Parliament leader. Always turning fun into learning activities. Dropped out from a brilliant Ph.D. program to marry Dad. . . . Often snapped unpredictably between rage and nurturing. She was a Frustrated Superwoman.*

Another stated, *"[I] remember her presenting a 'saintly' attitude to people outside the family and being very angry and overwhelmed when just with her children."*

One woman commented that no one believed that her mother abused her because she was *"an esteemed preschool director."* She later stated, *"She just had power because she was the mom. She performed crazy 'medical' things on me at her craziest."*

One survivor described the stepmother who abused her this way:

> *She was a very strong-willed dominating woman who was very two-faced. She would be very sweet to people to their faces and cut them to shreds behind their backs. She was very dirty, wore no underwear, and would go to the bathroom in the garden. She even chewed and spit.*

One woman in our study said about her mother, who was also her abuser, *"She* loved *having kids. Was the ultimate housewife (so it seemed): baking, playing with us, PTA, every year a school assistant, threw great birthday parties. She enthusiastically threw herself into our lives. Controlling."*

"She was a very strict disciplinarian and very active in religion. . . . She was emotionally distant and was typically unaccepting of me, i.e., always telling me what I did wrong or how I could do it better," another survivor stated.

One woman said that when her mother was drunk, she was a *"total raging maniac, very sexual and whorey,"* but when she was sober, she was *"kind most of the time."*

Another woman said, *"I felt I was the mother and she was the child, and I needed to care for and protect her."*

Another survivor described her abusing mother this way: *"Bitch. Negative. Needed a lot of attention. Hypochondriac. Wanted me to be her partner."*

Still another stated, *"[She was] cold, distant, hateful, and manipulative. She would throw things when angry. She wouldn't let us cry or laugh too loud."*

One survivor had this to say about her mother, who abused her:

> *As a small child I believed I had two mothers—a good mommy and an impostor mommy. The good mom was the public one—smiling, gentle, very well-mannered, pretty and proper. The impostor was vicious and ugly and violent, and she had a sickening sexual hunger that frightened and confused me. Above all, image was everything to mom. Our house was spotless. She was a "good wife," very solicitous to my father. In my father's presence she was Victorian in her attitudes towards sex—alone with me, and often my brother, she would parade around naked and liked to bend over a lot with great exaggeration. My mother rarely expressed affection except for "show" and criticized me constantly. I was shameful, bad, dirty. My mother was angry but denied her anger totally. She was bubbly and outgoing and involved in the community, but it always seemed forced and phony to me.*

One woman commented that her mother was *"cruel."* Another simply stated that her mother was *"a monster."*

Figure 7.1.   Duality, by Jill. This is my impression of the female perpetrator. She is part angel, part demon; loving in public, torturous in private. If you cover half of the drawing, you would not even guess the other could exist. That must be why there is so much denial about female abusers. People who see only the public side cannot begin to comprehend that there could be another, just as the daughter who is brutalized probably feels that the public mother must only be a dream.

OTHER STUDIES

Rudin et al. (1995) conducted a study of 211 victims between the ages of 1 and 18 from the Child Adolescent Sexual Abuse Resource Center in San Francisco (CASARC). Of the 253 lone perpetrators reported by the victims, there were 87 females: 60 adult and 27 juveniles. There were 31 cases of 73 co-perpetrators. The authors drew these four hypotheses from their findings.

1. That lone female abusers chose victims who were, on average, 3.3 years younger than victims chosen by lone male perpetrators.
2. That both female and male offenders chose more female victims; however, with female perpetrators, the difference between the number of girl victims verses boy victims was less than with the male perpetrators.
3. That "lone female perpetrators had a greater proportion of caretakers, while lone male perpetrators had a greater proportion of strangers" (Rudin et al., 1995, p. 968).
4. That, contrary to popular belief that male perpetrators are harsher in their abuse than female offenders, there was no difference in the level of severity of abuse among the lone females, lone males, and co-perpetrators (Rudin et al., 1995).

Rudin et al. (1995) had this to say about the study:

> This sample differs from studies that focused on child protective services (CPS) populations or offender populations and is reflective of a public health sample whose inclusion criteria were not limited to chargeable offenses, to the most severe cases, nor to intrafamilia abuse. Hence, it was likely that a wide continuum of cases regrading types of abuse, severity of abuse, and abusers who were nonfamilial would be represented. (p. 970)

According to Mayer (1992, 1993), female offenders fall into four categories: (1) mother-daughter; (2) mother-son; (3) triad (i.e., a mother, an adult male, and a child); and (4) sibling-sibling (i.e., a mother encouraging her children to engage in sex acts or prostitution). These offenses perpetrated by women can be "direct or indirect, involving verbal exploitation, voyeurism, and exhibitionism" (Mayer, 1993, p. 21).

In **mother-daughter incest**, the perpetrator often is viewed as possibly psychotic and disturbed with a background filled with abuse and neglect. These perpetrators have poor ego boundaries and turn to their children for emotional support instead of allowing the children to receive support from them. The perpetrators may come to feel that their daughters are extensions of themselves (Mayer, 1992).

In the **mother-son** group, the father usually is absent from the home, and the son is forced into a semi-spousal role for the emotional and sexual gratification of his mother (Mayer, 1992).

In the **triad** category, mothers either abuse or collude. "One type of mother allows abuse; the other participates in it" (Mayer, 1992, p. 26). Both types usually are dependent on their spouses and rationalize or deny the abuse. They often are addicted to alcohol or drugs. Through the abuse, they are seeking role reversals. The abusive mother seeks emotional warmth and affection, while the colluding mother seeks to place her daughter in the role of wife and parent. They often are operating from positions of learned helplessness (Mayer, 1992).

In the **sibling-sibling** group, "mothers derive vicarious or voyeuristic pleasure by coercing their children to engage in sibling incest" (Mayer, 1992, p. 20).

Mathews, Matthews, and Speltz (1989) studied 16 female sexual offenders, all of whom were adults when they began to abuse their victims. All but one had been sexually abused, and the abusive incidents happened anywhere from one to hundreds of times. Some behavioral traits and psychological features shared by many of the offenders were inertness, high reliance on males, low feelings of self-worth, substance abuse, underdeveloped social interaction skills, suicidal thoughts, humiliations, fear of rejection, anger, and indiscriminate sexual behaviors.

Of these 16 offenders, 14 either abused only female children or both males and females. The other two selected only male children to molest. The victims were 44 children and 1 adult. Sixty-four percent of the victims were female ($n = 26$), and 36% were male ($n = 16$). The types of abuse these offenders perpetrated ranged from sexual touching to intercourse (Mathews et al., 1989).

Mathews et al. (1989) divided the abusers into three groups: (1) teacher/lover, (2) intergenerationally predisposed, and (3) male-coerced.

With the **teacher/lover abuser**, the abuser's intent is not to be hurtful to the children with whom she is involved. Two women from the Mathews et al. study fit into this group. The authors wrote about one of these women:

This offender had a difficult time believing that her behavior was criminal because she had no malice for the children with whom she was involved. She taught children about sexuality in discussions and games, and she fell in love with an adolescent male who became her sexual partner. . . . She was not the victim of sexual abuse as a child but her background was fraught with severe emotional and verbal abuse. (Mathews et al., 1989, pp. 32-33)

Intergenerationally predisposed offenders typically have a history of sexual abuse in childhood, commonly beginning early in life and continuing until puberty. Frequently, multiple perpetrators abuse the offender during childhood. Seven women from the Mathews et al. (1989) study were identified as fitting into this group:

All the women in this group acted alone in initiating the sexual abuse. Their victims were family members, and with two exceptions they abused their own children. There are strong indicators that sexual abuse has been in their families for years. Other family members— aunts, uncles, siblings, cousins, parents, and grandparents—were also victims of sexual abuse. . . . These women report being sexually abused at a very early age, usually by more than one family member or entrusted caretaker. The abuse lasted until they were adolescents and usually involved more than one type of sexual abuse. (pp. 37-38)

Women in the **male-coerced category** often feel their husbands have "forced" them to participate in sexually abusive acts against their children. In addition to his abuse of the children, the male co-offender usually physically, psychologically, and sexually abuses the female offender. Every woman identified as being in this group in the Mathews et al. (1989) study had been sexually abused in childhood by a male:

The women in this category were passive and felt powerless in interpersonal relationships. They all endorsed, directly or indirectly, a traditional lifestyle with husband/father as the breadwinner and wife/ mother as the homemaker. . . . All reported that their relationships with men had never been good. All had been sexually abused by men in childhood. . . . In all of these cases the man was involved in sexual abuse first and brought the woman into it. (pp. 50-51)

Faller (1987) also studied 40 female perpetrators who had sexually abused 63 children. In her study, 85% ($n = 34$) were mothers to at least one of the children they abused. Another 55% ($n = 22$) were sexual only with their own children. And 30% ($n = 12$) molested their own children and also children outside the family system.

Faller (1987) determined five separate categories of female offenders: (1) polyincestuous abusers (*n* = 29), (2) single-parent abusers (*n* = 6), (3) psychotic abusers (*n* =3), (4) adolescent perpetrators (*n* = 3), and (5) noncustodial abusers (*n* = 1).

In the **polyincestuous abusers** category, there are at least two offenders and usually two or more children. There usually are several generations of sexual abuse and lateral sexual abuse in the extended family. Also, persons outside the household frequently are involved as both victims and abusers (Faller, 1987). "Such families are characterized by multiple sexually abusive relationships and group sex with children of both sexes" (p. 266).

Mother in the **single-parent abusers** group are not involved in relationships with men. In Faller's study, the mother was married to the victim's father in only two cases, and the mothers who had more than one child usually had different fathers for each. The victims of the single-parent abuser are both male and female. However, the oldest child typically is the one chosen for victimization and serves "as a surrogate partner for the mother, often having adult role responsibilities" (Faller, 1987, p. 267).

"When the offender is **psychotic**, she suffers from out-of-control libidinal impulses. In an effort to organize them she develops a delusional system that also provides justification for the sexually abusive behavior" (Faller, 1987, p. 267). These findings dispute the clinical assertion that most female abusers are highly disturbed and psychotic when they perpetrate sexual acts against children (Faller, 1987).

Adolescent abusers often have trouble relating to peers and do not have alternative sexual outlets. They typically gain access to their victims by playing with younger children or by baby-sitting. Their victimization usually is for their pleasure and not the children's (Faller, 1987).

A **noncustodial abuser** often has resisted the break-up with her spouse and is devastated by the loss and angry with him. The child becomes a source of emotional gratification for the mother and a vehicle for expressing her anger. Often, there is some indication during the marriage that the perpetrator is attracted to children (Faller, 1987).

McCarty (1986) reviewed 26 case records of incestuous mothers. She used three categories to classify these perpetrators: independent offenders, co-offenders, and accomplices.

McCarty found that over 75% of the **independent offenders** in her study had been sexually abused as children, most often by a brother. These women were of average intelligence, over half held steady jobs, almost half used or abused drugs, and at least half were determined to have serious emotional problems. In the independent offender group, 60% had sexually abused a daughter.

McCarty (1986) also found that the **co-offenders** in her study had been sexually abused as children. More than half of these women had less than average intelligence; the majority of them were homemakers. Each co-offender in the study had married as a teenager. Almost half of were in a second (44%) or a third (44%) marriage. Most often sons were the victims of these offenders.

All of the **accomplices** in McCarty's study worked outside the home. Over 75% of these women were of average intelligence. The majority of the accomplice offenders (over 75%) had abused a daughter.

ETIOLOGY AND MOTIVATIONS

Turner and Turner (1994) conducted a study of eight female adolescent perpetrators, all of whom had themselves been abused either sexually ($n = 6$) or emotionally ($n = 2$). The authors suggested that the acts of abuse on the part of these adolescents correlated to the relationships they had with their mothers, "who had never disclosed or resolved their own histories of sexual abuse before their daughters' acts of perpetration" (p. 7). Turner and Turner (1994) discussed several aspects of these dysfunctional mother-daughter relationships.

The first area the authors addressed was **attachment and attunement**. When the attachment between mother and daughter is healthy, the mother is able to be fully present in the relationship; healthy attunement is when the mother and daughter respond to each other mutually. When the mother has been abused herself, she cannot have a healthy attachment with her own child, possibly affecting all the child's future relationships. Attunement also is difficult if the mother has been abused. Because the mother never learned attunement as a child, she cannot provide it for her child:

> When the mother hesitates in caretaking, tenses, pulls away, acts short-tempered, is busy, or blames the child for being too needy, the daughter is likely to feel unworthy of being cared for. The mother's shame, whether from unresolved abuse, from a sense of inadequacy as a mother, or from society's denigration of women, becomes the daughter's shame. (Turner & Turner, 1994, p. 27)

The second area addressed by these authors was **enmeshment**. This occurs when boundaries are lacking between mother and daughter and there is no differentiation between generations (i.e., the mother turns to her daughter for guidance and understanding as often or more than the mother provides the same for the child). The mother feels that the daughter is an extension of herself, so when the daughter begins to differentiate herself (as is expected in healthy relationships), the mother feels threatened and abused by her daughter. Because they are enmeshed, the daughter absorbs her mother's victim dynamics. She views herself as bad, and her mother also sees her daughter as "an extension of her own 'bad,' disempowered self" (p. 27). The daughter feels she is not good enough to be an empowered individual, and she becomes vulnerable to abuse (Turner & Turner, 1994).

Enmeshed shame is the next area of the mother-daughter relationship discussed by Turner and Turner (1994). "Shame diminishes one's sense of self so thoroughly that the possibility of empathy becomes utterly distorted" (p. 28). The mothers of the adolescent abusers in this study had low self-esteem, reinforcing their shame. The majority of them had become pregnant at an early age in an attempt to escape the dysfunction in their families of origin. By having babies early, they may have been attempting to reenact their childhoods, trying to care for their babies as they never were cared for. However, they did not know how to do so. They often were abused or left by the fathers of their babies. These factors caused the women to turn to their daughters to meet their needs.

> In **malevolent enmeshed relationships**, the daughters become their mothers' caretakers in return for the limited caretaking and emotional support their mothers are able to provide. Childhood victimization prevented these mothers from having the experience of just "being children," so they do not know how to encourage or allow their daughters to be children. (Turner & Turner, 1994, pp. 28-29)

The next area discussed by Turner and Turner (1994) was **differentiation**. In healthy differentiation, the mother-daughter relationship evolves from a more dependent relationship to one in which there is room for the child to establish relationships outside the family system. Cyclic intergenerational abuse does not allow for the child to develop relationships outside the family system. Differentiation is what allows a person to empathize with herself and others. When the daughters in this study attempted to differentiate, the mothers felt they were losing parts of themselves. Because they had never been allowed to differentiate themselves, they would not tolerate the behavior in their own daughters (Turner & Turner, 1994).

The fifth aspect of the mother-daughter relationship was **malevolent attachment**. A mother who has a malevolent attachment with her daughter loves her; however, the love is overshadowed by distrust and anger. The mother believes the daughter is trying to hurt her intentionally. The mother may see her child as her own childhood self. "When her daughter fails to meet her expectations, the mother feels that it is deliberate, abusive, abandoning, and denigrating to their relationship" (Turner & Turner, 1994, p. 30).

A final aspect of the mother-daughter relationship Turner and Turner discussed was **abandonment**. Mothers in this study abandoned their daughters because they were not capable of coping with their daughters while trying to deal with the family situation. Mothers also abandoned their daughters when the daughters tried to differentiate themselves from their mothers (Turner & Turner, 1994).

Because the daughters in this study had these kinds of relationships with their own mothers, they were vulnerable to becoming abusers (Turner & Turner, 1994).

Roth (1993) had this to say about factors leading to sexual abuse:

> It occurs in the context of alcoholism, mental illness, chronic physical illness, severe loss, reenactment of the parents' pasts, or marital dysfunction. The abusive mother is struggling with her own psyche and past much as an abusive father is similarly disturbed. She is inappropriately and unconsciously acting out deep-seated problems. (p. 122)

According to Mayer (1993), there are four factors that might motive females to perpetrate sex acts on children. The first is **identification with the aggressor**. The female was abused in childhood, and as a way to deal with that trauma, she identified with and ultimately became the offender. Other studies have noted identification with the aggressor as a motivator for sexual abuse (Faller, 1987; Turner & Turner, 1994). In Faller's (1987) study, 19 of the 40 female perpetrators reported that they had been sexually abused in childhood.

A second motivator might be the female's **displaced anger**. Because she is unable to deal with her anger at being sexually abused in childhood, she displaces it onto a younger, powerless child (Mayer, 1993). Roth (1993) contends that if the mothers have not dealt with the issues of their own sexual abuse, they may recreate the abuse in the role of abuser. "Their children become the recipients of either their unresolved rage or their unmet needs" (pp. 122-123). Turner and Turner (1994) also believe that the abuse will be recreated, and the rage passed on to the child, if the mother does not address her own abuse.

A third motivator is **trauma mastery through reenactment**. In an unconscious attempt to master her early trauma and victimization, the perpetrator abuses her child in the same manner (Mayer, 1993).

The last motivation, according to Mayer (1993), is **unconscious patterning of family lifestyles**. Because the perpetrator's role models were abusive parents, she tries to recreate "an inter- and intra-generational family pattern of chaotic dysfunction and polymorphous abusive behaviors" (p. 22).

It is important for the therapist to consider these motivating factors during evaluation of the offender, because the treatment will vary depending on which category she falls into (Mayer, 1993).

Other Diagnoses of Female Perpetrators

Many female offenders are diagnosed with dissociative disorders or borderline personality disorders (Mayer, 1993). In Faller's study (1987), some other diagnoses of female perpetrators were mental retardation, brain damage, and psychosis. Also, 22 of the 40 female perpetrators in Faller's study reportedly were addicted to alcohol, drugs, or both.

CONFRONTATION

Should the Survivor Confront Her Abuser?

Survivors sometimes choose not to confront their abusers because the process involves a display of assertiveness they are not used to having with the perpetrator. Also, confrontations may be difficult because they break a denial that may have been in the family for years (Courtois, 1988). However, if the abuser is still in the survivor's life, the survivor may want to confront her in order to put the issue of the abuse to rest (Dolan, 1991).

Before any confrontation occurs, the desired or fantasized outcome should be explored, as well as what the survivor's response will be if the offender denies any accusations. Cameron (1994) discussed six reasons why a survivor should consider confronting her abuser:

1. It can empower her.
2. To "set the record straight," by specifically telling who, what, where, when, and how.
3. To provide closure by giving voice to what happened.
4. To help "clarify relationships." Cameron (1994) wrote, "Confronters can begin to understand what motivated the abuser to twist a relationship that was their birthright, they can recognize the responsibility of the offender and stop blaming themselves" (p. 19).
5. Confrontation helps the survivor recognize and express feelings such as grief and anger.
6. Finally, confronting an abuser will help the survivor begin to deal with the issue of forgiveness. Thus, the decision to confront or not must be explored in-depth with any survivor.

The decision to confront must be the survivor's. *She must feel that it is her choice* and not something that has been forced upon her (Agosta & Loring, 1988; Draucker, 1992). Even though a confrontation can be very helpful to and empowering for some survivors—because it gives them a chance to be assertive and to let the perpetrators know exactly how the abuse hurt them—it is not the right choice for others. It is not mandatory for healing. The survivor should understand that, and realize that it is an option she is entitled to choose if she wants to (Bass & Davis, 1992; Courtois, 1988; Draucker, 1992).

Courtois (1988) stated that when the survivor is considering this option, she should not immediately ask herself where and when and how the confrontation should take place. Rather she should ask herself *whether* she should confront at all. If the survivor chooses to confront, she needs to carefully prepare herself, "including an assessment of its [the confrontation's] potential for destruction and retraumatization, the survivor's ego strength, and her stage in her treatment process" (Courtois, 1988, pp. 333-334). Whitfield (1995) warned that if a survivor rushes too quickly into confrontation, it can be very damaging.

Preparing to Confront

Preparation is essential before a confrontation takes place, as impulsive confrontations often hurt the survivor (Draucker, 1992). Bass and Davis (1992) contend that the preparation is as important as the actual act of confronting the abuser. They suggest using role play to practice responding to different reactions from the abuser. They also recommend that the survivor write out what she wants to say so she will not forget the important points.

The survivor needs to plan for her safety at the confrontation (Bass & Davis, 1992; Courtois, 1988; Dolan, 1991). In cases where there is potential for danger or harm to herself, the survivor should meet the abuser in a public place, not give the abuser her address or telephone number (Bass & Davis, 1992), or take a supportive friend or family member with her (Bass & Davis, 1992; Dolan, 1991). Taking along a supporter also helps the survivor to stay in the present. Bass and Davis (1992) noted that taking a friend with her gives the survivor a "contemporary mirror" (pp. 138-139). The friend can remind the survivor of who she is *now* so that, in the face of her perpetrator, she does not fall back on who she was when she was abused.

Another way to ensure the survivor's safety is to have the perpetrator meet the survivor at the therapy session (Bass & Davis, 1992; Courtois, 1988; Dolan, 1991). Courtois said, "Although it is not always possible or desirable for a therapist to be involved, such involvement can assist the communication traumatization" (p. 338).

Another option for the survivor is to take along a sibling or another person who was also abused by the same perpetrator and have a joint confrontation. This gives each survivor a sense of support; she is not alone during the process. It also strengthens the case against the perpetrator (Courtois, 1988).

Yet another issue the survivor needs to think about before the confrontation is whether she wants to consider any harm (emotional or physical) the confrontation will do to other family members (Courtois, 1988). For example, if her perpetrator was her grandmother, she should consider how the confrontation will affect her mother or father. Are they in good health? Will she (the survivor) be able to handle their deaths? If a survivor decides to confront after considering the worst possible scenarios, she must be prepared to handle the outcome (Courtois, 1988).

Before confronting the perpetrator, the survivor must resolve many of the issues of guilt and self-blame. If the survivor is still blaming herself for the abuse, confrontation should be postponed, because "she is likely, as a consequence of her abuse, to consider the perpetrator's needs before her own" (Dolan, 1991, p. 64).She should have an understanding of how her abuse has affected her and her life (Courtois, 1988), and she should have developed a healthy sense of her self and her personal boundaries (Whitfield, 1995). She should be aware of what feelings the confrontation may cause in her (Draucker, 1992), and she should be able to use a negative response from her perpetrator to increase her self-understanding. She also should have enough ego strength to handle the stress the confrontation will probably hold (Courtois, 1988). A confrontation can cause "a return of trauma symptomatology" (Draucker, 1992, p. 75) for a survivor who has not prepared herself adequately.

Many survivors hope that if they confront their abusers, they will finally get the acknowledgment and apology they are entitled to (Bass & Davis, 1992; Draucker, 1992; Whitfield, 1995). However, the survivor should be aware that such hopes may not be realistic. The perpetrator will likely deny the allegations. Bass and Davis (1992) warned that the survivor *must be realistic and prepared for a negative response* so that she is not setting herself up for "another betrayal" (p. 135).

The survivor must prepare for these negative responses and for any other possible response she thinks the perpetrator may have. If she prepares herself for these and has thought about what her response will be to them, the confrontation—even if filled with negative comments from the perpetrator—can still be a positive experience for the survivor (Courtois, 1988). One survivor from our study shared a negative response from a confrontation, saying, *"My mother denied it and told me I was crazy."*

The survivor needs to prepare herself for the worst (Dolan, 1991). It is important for the survivor to be aware of what kinds of responses she may get from the abuser, remembering that this is someone who has abused her in the past. It is highly unlikely that the abuser will suddenly become sensitive to the survivor's needs (Bass & Davis, 1992). The survivor should be ready for any reaction and practice her response to whatever the perpetrator may say (Bass & Davis, 1992; Dolan, 1991). The survivor also must decide that she can live with any of the possible outcomes (Bass & Davis, 1992).

It is quite likely that the abuser will try to turn the confrontation around and blame the survivor for the abuse (Bass & Davis, 1992; Courtois, 1988; Dolan, 1991; Draucker, 1992; Whitfield, 1995). The survivor must be aware that the confrontation may actually reinforce the abuser's or the family's denial. She may feel pressured and tempted to regress to her childhood position of victim in the family (Courtois, 1988). However, Bass and Davis (1992) contend that while, as a child, the survivor did not have the means to protect herself against the abuse, *she should realize that she does not have to be vulnerable this time.*

Questions for the Survivor Before She Decides to Confront:

- Who do you want to talk to, and why?
- What do you want to gain as a result of the confrontation? Are you being realistic?

- What is motivating you to confront?
- Is there anyone who can give you the information you need?
- What could you gain as a result of the confrontation?
- What could you lose?
- Would you be risking losing something from the family (such as a job, etc.)?
- Can you live with being excluded from family functions?
- Do you want to risk losing contact with other members of your family who have not abused you?
- Will you be able to handle it if you are labeled "crazy?"
- Can you maintain your reality in the face of the perpetrator's denial?
- Can you withstand the anger you may face?
- Can you handle getting no reaction?
- Do you have a solid support system?
- Can you realistically imagine the worst and best outcomes that might result? And can you live with either one?
- Have you prepared for the confrontation? (Adapted from Bass & Davis, 1992, p. 134)

The Confrontation

The confrontation can be accomplished in a variety of ways: face to face, on the telephone, in a letter or telegram, or through an emissary (Bass & Davis, 1992; Draucker, 1992).

Bass and Davis (1992) contend that the confrontation is not a time for dialogue with the perpetrator or a time to listen to her side of the story; it is a time for the survivor to tell the perpetrator what she needs to say and then get out.

Some of the things a survivor might be looking for in the confrontation are acknowledgment; an opportunity to let the perpetrator know how much the abuse has affected her; an apology; payment for therapy; money for an education; prevention of further abuse by the perpetrator; a commitment from the perpetrator to seek therapy; to know the reasons and motives behind the abuse, and why the survivor was chosen; and revenge or to see the perpetrators suffer (Bass & Davis, 1992; Courtois, 1988; Dolan, 1991; Whitfield, 1995).

However, because it is not likely that a confrontation will cause the abuser to make major psychological changes, it may be more effective for the survivor to ask the perpetrator for specific changes in behavior (i.e., not to hug or kiss the survivor; Bass & Davis, 1992).

Some Advantages of Confronting. The act of confrontation can be traumatic for the survivor, but it also offers her some advantages. Through the act of a confrontation, the survivor can put the blame for the abuse on the perpetrator, letting herself know that she was not at fault—something she needed someone to do for her while the abuse was occurring (Dolan, 1991).

Confrontation also can be therapeutic, enabling the survivor to feel a sense of control and power over her life. She chooses to eliminate the denial around the abuse and to make the perpetrator be the one responsible for her actions (Courtois, 1988).

The Aftermath

Depending on how the confrontation went, the aftermath can be terrible, wonderful, or anywhere in between. It is normal for the survivor to feel a sense of relief because she no longer has to keep the secret or pretend the abuse did not happen. This also is when the survivor needs to decide if she wishes to continue or break contact with the perpetrator (Bass & Davis, 1992).

WHEN CONFRONTATION IS NOT AN OPTION

The survivor should not let others pressure her into a confrontation. Some survivors who have endured painful confrontations pressure other survivors to confront. According to Bass and Davis (1992), "Although some stages in the healing process are absolutely necessary, confronting abusers and telling family members are not" (p. 134). It is reasonable for the survivor to choose not to confront if the decision is made from strength instead of fear (Bass & Davis, 1992).

There are several reasons a survivor would choose not to confront her abuser. Some survivors do not have the support of friends or family (Bass & Davis, 1992); some will be in serious danger if they tell (Bass & Davis, 1992; Courtois, 1988); others do not want to break with their families (especially if the family is paying the survivor's tuition or the survivor is still living at home); some do not want to face the stress a confrontation will bring; and others have established their sense of reality and self without the confrontation (Bass & Davis, 1992).

Other survivors do not get the option of confronting. If the perpetrator was a stranger or the survivor has lost touch with her, a confrontation is not possible. Sometimes the abuser has died. These survivors may be extremely upset and feel they have no chance for reconciliation. One survivor from our study was tremendously angry with her mother because she died just when the survivor had gained the strength for a confrontation. However, some survivors feel a tremendous relief that they do not have to go through the whole ordeal. And even if a survivor does not have the option to confront, she still needs to resolve her feelings about the abuse (Bass & Davis, 1992).

Alternatives to Confrontation

Because most confrontations are met with negative responses, indirect methods of confrontation may be more positive experiences for the survivors (Courtois, 1988). Instead of directly confronting the perpetrator, the survivor might consider writing unmailed letters; role playing or psychodrama; visiting the perpetrator's grave site; drawing pictures or writing poems and having them published in a survivors' newsletter; making audio or video tapes; the empty chair technique; family sculpture; or donating money to an organization that helps survivors (Bass & Davis, 1992; Courtois, 1988; Dolan, 1991; Whitfield, 1995).

An option available to survivors who live in communities with ongoing treatment groups for perpetrators, survivors, and other family members is to go to one of the meetings and confront or discuss the reasons for the abuse with other perpetrators (Courtois, 1988).

GRIEVING THE LOSSES OF ABUSE

Reasons for Survivors to Grieve

When a survivor fails to grieve her losses, she perpetuates the traumatic reaction. However, many survivors are afraid of this task. A survivor may fear that once she begins grieving, she will not be able to stop. She may resist mourning out of pride or feel that if she mourns, the perpetrator has somehow won (Herman, 1992). However, Herman (1992) noted, "Mourning is the only way to give due honor to loss; there is no adequate compensation" (p. 190).

There are several reasons for survivors of child sexual abuse to grieve. Some of the things survivors grieve for are being abandoned, a loss of feelings, their pasts and presents, the damage they must now heal, the time and money it takes to heal, relationships that have been ruined, and the pleasures and

Figure 7.2.   Collage, by Juliann. The different faces of the women represent the many facets of the grieving process. No two women in the collage are the same, and no two grief experiences are the same—each is unique.

opportunities they missed out on while they were trying to deal with the abuse (Bass & Davis, 1992). Survivors may mourn because they feel that they have lost their moral integrity or because they cannot undo what has been done to them (Herman, 1992).

A survivor may grieve for her shattered image of the world as a safe place where children are loved and cared for and where people respect one another. Or she may grieve for the innocence she lost during the abuse (Bass & Davis, 1992) or for the childhood that was taken away from her (Herman, 1992). She may grieve for the part of herself that did not survive the abuse (Bass & Davis, 1992).

If a survivor was abused by family members, she may grieve for the fact that she does not have an extended family for her children (Bass & Davis, 1992). She may grieve for her loss of belief in good parenting and trust (Herman, 1992). Some survivors also need to grieve for inheritances they will not receive or for lost family roots (Bass & Davis, 1992).

Although survivors may feel they are foolish to cry over events that happened years ago, they need to express their feelings, to grieve their losses. If they do not do this, they will be limiting themselves and their capacity to love others (Bass & Davis, 1992).

Survivors need to take their grief seriously. Bass and Davis (1992) suggested that survivors should take a period of time to grieve and mourn, just as they would if someone close to them had died. They will not fully be able to grieve unless they allow themselves the time, space, and security to do so.

If a survivor does not grieve, she limits her "capacity for joy, for spontaneity, for life" (Bass & Davis, 1992, p. 119). When she was a child, she needed to suppress the feelings of fear and anger she felt during the abuse. Now these feelings must be dealt with so she can move forward with her life (Bass & Davis, 1992).

With the support of friends, survivors need to relive the abuse—secure in the fact that they now are adults. This time, however, they must allow themselves to grieve. They need to express the feelings they were not permitted to express at the time of the abuse. They need to know they are heard. They also need to be comforted and to learn to comfort themselves. Bass and Davis (1992) contend that survivors will be able to move beyond their grief once they have learned to comfort themselves. Herman (1992) noted that survivors often are amazed at how little concern they feel for the perpetrators' fates once they have mourned the abuse.

Deep Within
Anonymous

From deep within me a sadness came,
All consuming and replacing the pain.
It spread through my bones,
     It spread through my heart,
It spread through my soul,
     It touched every part.
Sadness for what can never be,
Sadness for you and sadness for me.
There's a longing I have,
     There's a hole in me still,
That I'm looking for someone
     Or something to fill.
I've begun to grieve, to grieve for the past,
I'm trying to let go of my pain, at last.
Oh why can't she see the things that she did
Were meant for adults, and not for a kid.
My tears fall down
     Off my cheeks they run.
I'm crying again
     And I've only begun,
To see the truth, the truth at last;
It's all about my distant past.
Past into present,
     Oh Lord, show me how,
Past into present,
     Let go of it *now*!
Lord, please tell me why can't she see,
The things she's done, they were done to *me*!
She took so much from me that day,
When she claimed my innocence,
     I still want her to pay!
She claimed my childhood
     And with it my peace,
And left uncertainty,
     When will it cease?
The peace of knowing who I really am,
The peace of knowing where I've really been.
But, I'm making an effort to sift through this trash,
To look at my life, but not in a flash.

Patience I'll need to do this job right,
For it's going to take time,
    Peace won't come overnight.
I've asked for help from the One up above,
To send down some help like he sent the white dove.
Please take all the pain
    The rage and torment,
To be filled with God's Grace
    And be freed from imprisonment.

The Tasks of Mourning

Worden (1991) contended that certain tasks must be accomplished in order to complete the process of mourning. If these tasks are not completed, further growth and development are impaired.

The first of the tasks is for the griever to **accept the reality of the loss** (Worden, 1991). Survivors must overcome their denial about the abuse. They need to realize that the abuse happened, that it was not their fault, and that they could not have prevented it. They also must stop denying that the abuse had an effect on them. Worden (1991) commented, "Belief and disbelief are intermittent while grappling with this task" (p. 12).

The second task of mourning is for the griever to **work through to the pain of grief**. Worden (1991) suggested the German word *Schmerz* as useful for talking about pain. Here is what he had to say about it:

> [I]ts broader definition includes the literal physical pain that many people experience and the emotional and behavioral pain associated with loss. It is necessary to acknowledge and work through this pain or it will manifest itself through some symptoms or other form of aberrant behavior. (p. 13)

Society may feel uncomfortable with the survivor's pain and pressure her to get over the abuse and put it behind her. This may cause the survivor to deny that she needs to grieve.

Survivors may try to bypass the second task by cutting off their feelings or denying their pain. Others use alcohol or drugs to keep from feeling the pain.

The third task of mourning is to **adjust to the current environment** (Worden, 1991). For the survivor, this could be a world in which the perpetrator no longer plays a key role. The survivor must adjust to her new role; she needs to adjust to her sense of self and to her sense of the world.

The fourth task of mourning is to **put the trauma behind and move on with life**. "For many people, Task IV is the most difficult one to accomplish. They get stuck at this point in their grieving and later realize that their life in some way stopped at the point the loss occurred" (Worden, 1991). This task is hindered if a survivor tries to hold onto the past. She may feel she never wants to trust another person again because the loss from her abuse was too painful.

The Processes of Mourning

While acknowledging that Worden's tasks of mourning are useful, Rando (1993) believed that mourning is better discussed in terms of processes, for three reasons.

1. One does not know until the end of the task if it has been completed successfully. At that time, the mourner has to readdress the task if the specific desired outcome has not been accomplished. When mourning is viewed as a process, it allows for more immediate feedback and for those around the mourner to focus on what she is currently experiencing (Rando, 1993).
2. Processes can be checked up on and evaluated throughout the mourning experience. The processes become the focus, not the outcome, thus enhancing the "chance that any necessary intervention will be timely and effective" (Rando, 1993, p. 43).
3. "[P]rocesses provide a useful checklist for evaluating the precise status of the mourner and addressing grief and mourning" (Rando, 1993, p. 43). When those around the mourner focus on where she is in the process, they can evaluate when she is stuck *before she has reached the end of a task and failed* (Rando, 1993).

Rando (1993) established the "six R processes" of mourning. These are interrelated and build upon each other; however, some may occur at the same time. Also, the subprocesses of mourning may appear in more than one process, and the course of the mourning can fluctuate, taking the individual back and forth through the processes (Rando, 1993).

The first process of mourning is for the mourner to **recognize the loss** (Rando, 1993). The survivor of sexual abuse needs to acknowledge that the abuse has occurred and try to understand the reasons for it.

There are two subprocesses to this first phase. The first is for the mourner to **acknowledge the death** (Rando, 1993). Rando was speaking specifically about mourning death; abuse survivors instead must acknowledge with the sexual abuse or any of the losses they experienced because of it. If the survivor has not acknowledged the fact that she was sexually abused in childhood, she has no need to grieve. By not admitting how much the abuse has affected her, she fools herself into thinking she does not need to heal and readapt her life.

The second subprocess in this first phase is for the mourner to **understand the death** (Rando, 1993). (Again, survivors should substitute "the abuse" for "death.") The survivor needs not only to acknowledge the abuse but to understand some of the reasons for it—what contributed to the abuse and the circumstances surrounding it. The survivor should not use these reasons to justify her abuse. She just need to understand them.

The second process of mourning, according to Rando (1993), is for the mourner to **react to the separation**. Once she has accepted that she was abused, the survivor must focus on how this changes her relationship with the perpetrator. Healthy mourning will be promoted if the survivor allows herself to express all the emotions and reactions she is feeling.

There are three subprocesses to this phase. The first is to **experience the pain** (Rando, 1993). The survivor must experience the pain and her feelings about the abuse. She also must experience the pain of losing her mother or the pain of trying to understand how a parent could abuse a child.

> Like acute grief, pain may be experienced across all dimensions of human functioning: the psychological (including the spiritual), behavioral, social, and physical. The type, intensity, and duration of that pain will be different for each individual, determined by the unique constellation of factors associated with the mourner and the loss. (Rando, 1993, p. 47)

The second subprocess of this phase is to **feel, identify, accept, and give some form of expression to all the psychological reactions to the loss** (Rando, 1993). The survivor needs to "overcome personal, social, cultural, ethnic, or religious resistances to the processing of all of the psychological reactions to the loss and its implications" (Rando, 1993, p. 47). Three steps will help with this:

1. The survivor must consciously cope with all the emotions—positive or negative—that accompany the loss.

2. The survivor should identify, label, and differentiate these emotional responses (so that painful emotions can become more bearable) in order to gain control over them.
3. The survivor must find spoken or unspoken expressions that are appropriate and personally comfortable for her (Rando, 1993).

The last subprocess in this second phase is to **identify and mourn secondary losses** (Rando, 1993). The survivor will have to mourn the secondary losses of the abuse (several are listed in the section of this chapter titled "Reasons for Survivors to Grieve").

The third process of mourning is to **recollect and reexperience the deceased and the relationship** (Rando, 1993). (Again, the "deceased" should be replaced with the "perpetrator" here.) The survivor will have to decide what type of relationship she wants to have with the perpetrator. In this process, the survivor may need to identify any unfinished business she has with the perpetrator and find a way to achieve some sort of closure. A confrontation may help the survivor to achieve some closure; however, as mentioned before, whether or not to confront should be her choice, not one forced on her.

There are two subprocess to the third process. The first is to **review and remember realistically** (Rando, 1993). The survivor needs to remember all the positive and negative aspects of her relationship with the abuser. Here is what Rando (1993) had to say:

> The mourner must repeatedly review the entire relationship, the expectations and needs that initially formed it, its ups and downs, its course and development, its crises and joys—all elements of it throughout the years. As these events and features of the relationship unfold, the mourner can examine associated feelings and thoughts: negative ones, such as anxiety, ambivalence, and guilt, as well as more positive ones, such as satisfaction, happiness, and meaning. (p. 49)

The second subprocess is to **revive and reexperience the feelings** (Rando, 1993). The survivor must undo the ties that bind her to the perpetrator and memories of the abuse. This does not mean that she is expected to forget about the abuse and what was done to her; rather, she should understand that she cannot change the past and that she could not have prevented the abuse.

The fourth process of mourning is to **relinquish the old attachments to the deceased [or the perpetrator] and the old assumptive world** (Rando, 1993). The assumptive world is an organized schema in which, based on her previous experiences, a person assumes certain things to be true about the world and herself. "[T]he assumptive world is viewed as being fueled by the individual's experiences, memories, and needs, and confirmed through experiences, behavior and interaction patterns, and role relationships" (Rando, 1993, p. 50). If the survivor repressed the abuse and remembered it years later, the fact that she was abused may not fit in with her **global assumptions** (i.e., those pertaining to the world; Rando, 1993). If the survivor's mother was the perpetrator, this may interfere with her **specific assumptions** about her mother (i.e., she was caring, loving, and protecting).

According to Rando (1993), the fifth process of mourning is to **readjust to move adaptively into the new world without forgetting the old**. After releasing the attachment to the old assumptive world and to the perpetrator, the survivor is able to establish new connections that are appropriate with the changes that have taken place. The word "move" denotes action and suggests that the survivor will be able to progress to a place where she can function. The word "adaptively" suggests that the survivor will be able to adjust and adapt to the change.

There are four subprocesses to this phase of mourning. The first is to **revise the assumptive world** (Rando, 1993). The survivor needs to modify her assumptive world, which was violated with the knowledge of her abuse. The extent to which she needs to do this depends on six things:

1. the perpetrator's importance and centrality to the survivor's life;
2. the types and number of roles the perpetrator played in the survivor's life;
3. the meaning the perpetrator gave to the survivor;
4. the pattern of interaction the survivor had established with the perpetrator;
5. the type of abuse perpetrated and the degree to which it violated "other needs, feelings, thoughts, behavior and interaction patterns, hopes, wishes, fantasies, dreams, assumptions, expectations, and beliefs" (Rando, 1993, p. 52); and
6. "the number, type, and quality of secondary losses" (pp. 52-53).

The more numerous or important to the survivor the violations were, the more she will need to reconstruct her assumptive world.

The second subprocess to the fifth phase of mourning is to **develop a new relationship with the deceased [perpetrator]** (Rando, 1993). The survivor must decide what kind of relationship she wants to have with the perpetrator, or if she wants to have one at all. However, it is important for someone who was sexually abused to have at least one positive memory of the abuser.

The third subprocess is to **adopt new ways of being in the world** (Rando, 1993). In order for the survivor to be healthy in her mourning process, she cannot pretend that the abuse did not occur or has not affected her in some way. She may have to take on new roles, learn some new skills, change some behaviors, and establish new relationships.

The fourth subprocess is to **form a new identity.** "With a new assumptive world, a new relationship with the deceased [perpetrator], and the acquisition of new skills, behaviors, roles, and relationships, the mourner is no longer the same person she used to be" (Rando, 1993, p. 59). She needs to change her image of herself to reflect this new reality. The part of herself that was victim should no longer define her sense of self and identity. She may feel she is losing a part of herself and need to mourn that. However, in the case of sexual abuse, the part she loses is the **victim self,** which is replace by a more positive sense of herself as a **survivor.**

The sixth and final process in Rando's (1993) "six R processes of mourning" is for the survivor to **reinvest.** The energy once invested in the relationship with the perpetrator and in dealing with the issues of the abuse must be reinvested into something more healthy, something that benefits the survivor by giving her a sense of satisfaction. For example, she can do volunteer work with sexually abused children; she can establish a healthy relationship with someone who will not abuse her in any way, letting her know she is worthy of love; or she can return to school and get or finish a degree.

Common Behaviors Associated with Grief

According to Worden (1991), many people who experience acute grief reactions exhibit some of the same behaviors. He broke the behaviors into four categories: feelings, physical sensations, cognitions, and behaviors.

Feelings. Some feelings commonly associated with the process of grieving are sadness, anger, guilt and self-reproach, anxiety, loneliness, fatigue, helplessness, shock, yearning, emancipation, relief, and numbness (Worden, 1991).

These are all normal reactions and should not be considered pathological. However, it they last for extended periods of time, the grief may be considered complicated (Worden, 1991).

Figure 7.3. Angry Tears, a survivor's drawing.

Physical Sensations. Worden (1991) noted that the physical sensations surrounding grief are often overlooked, even though they are important during grieving. The physical sensations Worden listed include hollowness in the stomach, tightness in the chest or throat, oversensitivity to noise, a sense of depersonalization, breathlessness or feeling short of breath, muscle weakness, lack of energy, and dry mouth (adapted from p. 25).

Cognitions. Worden (1991) listed five cognitions that commonly accompany the grieving process: disbelief, confusion, preoccupation, sense of presence, and hallucinations.

Behaviors. Worden (1991) listed several behaviors often reported by those who are grieving. Following is a list of those common among survivors grieving issues of abuse: sleep disturbances, appetite disturbances, absent-minded behavior, social withdrawal, sighing, restless overactivity, and crying. Survivors may experience any or all of these behaviors.

CONCLUSION

Women in our society often are seen as nurturers. But, as we have seen, that is not always the case.

Survivors of abuse often struggle with whether or not to confront the perpetrator. While confrontation is not always necessary or an option, a survivor will always need to deal with and resolve the losses of her abuse.

REFERENCES

Agosta, C., & Loring, M. (1988). Understanding and treating the adult retrospective victim of child sexual abuse. In S. M. Sgroi (Ed.), *Vulnerable populations: Vol. 1. Evaluation and treatment of sexually abused children and adult survivors* (pp. 115-136). Lexington, MA: Lexington Books.

Allen, C. M. (1990). Women as perpetrators of child sexual abuse: Recognition barriers. In A. L. Horton, B. L. Johnson, L. M. Roundy, & D. Williams (Eds.), *The incest perpetrator: A family member no one wants to treat* (pp. 108-125). Newbury Park, CA: Sage.

Bass, E., & Davis, L. (1992). *The courage to heal: A guide for women survivors of child sexual abuse.* New York: HarperPerennial.

Cameron, C. (1994). Women survivors confronting their abusers: Issues, decisions, and outcomes. *Journal of Child Sexual Abuse, 3*(1), 7-35.

Courtois, C. A. (1988). *Healing the incest wound: Adult survivors in therapy.* New York: Norton.

Dolan, Y. M. (1991). *Resolving sexual abuse: Solution-focused therapy and Ericksonian hypnosis for adult survivors.* New York: Norton.

Draucker, C. B. (1992). *Counseling survivors of childhood sexual abuse.* Newbury Park, CA: Sage.

Faller, K. C. (1987). Women who sexually abuse children. *Violence and Victims, 2*(4), 263-276.

Fehrenbach, P. A., & Monastersky, C. (1988). Characteristics of female adolescent sexual offenders. *American Journal of Orthopsychiatry, 58*(1), 148-151.

Finkelhor, D. (1984). Boys as victims. In D. Finkelhor (Ed.), *Child sexual abuse: New theory and research* (pp. 150-170). New York: Free Press.

Finkelhor, D., & Russell, D. (1984). Women as perpetrators. In D. Finkelhor (Ed.), *Child sexual abuse: New theory and research* (pp. 171-185). New York: Free Press.

Finkelhor, D., Williams, L., & Burns, N. (1988). *Nursery crimes: Sexual abuse in day care.* Newbury Park, CA: Sage.

Herman, J. L. (1992). *Trauma and recovery: The aftermath of violence—from domestic abuse to political terror.* New York: Basic Books.

Herman-Giddens, M. E., & Berson, N. L. (1994). Enema abuse in childhood: Report from a survey. *Treating Abuse Today, 4*(4), 45-49.

Mathews, R., Matthews, J. K., & Speltz, K. (1989). *Female sexual offenders: An exploratory study.* Orwell, VT: Safer Society Press.

Mayer, A. (1992). *Women sex offenders: Treatment and dynamics.* Holmes Beach, FL: Learning Publications.

Mayer, A. (1993). Adult female incest offenders: Treatment considerations. *Treating Abuse Today, 3*(6), 21-26.

McCarty, L. (1986). Mother-child incest: Characteristics of the offender. *Child Welfare, 65*(5), 447-458.

Quintano, J. H. (1992). Case profiles of early childhood enema abuse. *Treating Abuse Today, 2*(5), 11-13.

Rando, T. A. (1993). *Treatment of complicated mourning.* Champaign, IL: Research Press.

Roth, N. (1993). *Integrating the shattered self: Psychotherapy with adult incest survivors.* Northvale, NJ: Jason Aronson.

Rudin, M. M., Zalewski, C., & Bodmer-Turner, J. (1995). Characteristics of child sexual abuse victims according to perpetrator gender. *Child Abuse & Neglect, 19*(8), 963-973.

Turner, T. T., & Turner, T. N. (1994). *Female adolescent sexual abusers: An exploratory study of mother-daughter dynamics with implications for treatment.* Brandon, VT: Safer Society Press.

Whitfield, C. L. (1995). *Memory and abuse: Remembering and healing the effects of trauma.* Deerfield Beach, FL: Health Communications.

Worden, J. W. (1991). *Grief counseling & grief therapy: A handbook for the mental health practitioner.* New York: Springer.

Chapter **8**

VERBAL TREATMENT MODALITIES: GIVING VOICE TO THE TRAUMA

Psychotherapy is a form of treatment in which time and space are redefined for an hour a week. During this sacred hour, boundaries are honored, certain rituals are maintained, everything else is shut out, and another world exists outside the door of the therapist's office. It is a place where what the survivor has lived through is honored and respected. Dolan (1992) discussed the process of healing:

> Sexual abuse is a veritable baptism by fire. If survivors don't let it destroy them—and every person has to find his or her own way to accomplish this—the inevitable work required to overcome the effects of abuse will make them exceptional people. Some clients of mine have compared recovery to a shamanic journey. In the shamanic tradition, a person suffers a terrible trauma, gathers up every bit of inner strength he or she has and survives. After the trauma has occurred, the act of moving beyond it—coming to terms with it and then healing—is the vehicle for becoming personally gifted and exceptional. This is the role of Shaman or Healer. Sexual abuse survivors are healers of themselves and hence, Shamans. . . . Enduring is perhaps the most crucial condition for moving beyond the abuse and fulfilling hope in creating or reclaiming a life worth living, something to treasure. (pp. 23-24)

Herman (1992) identified three phases in working with trauma survivors. The first is for the therapist to develop a trusting relationship with the survivor

Figure 8.1.   Journey Collage, by Juliann.

Figure 8.1. The curled-up figure in the bottom right-hand corner represents the survivor coming into treatment, ashamed and unable to maintain eye contact. The face of the small child represents the inner child who lives within the survivor. Next to her are the eyes of a much older woman, signifying how the sexual abuse aged her. The fingers and feet are pressed against a red door, behind which is a volcano, signifying the survivor's attempts to stop eruptions of thoughts and feelings. In the center of the collage, a road leads to a ladder that climbs a mountain. The road to healing is long and arduous. At the top of the mountain there is a butterfly to signify freedom and a rainbow to signify hope. The figure of the woman leaning toward the sun represents warmth and healing. Although the journey is long there, is light and warmth at the end. She no longer needs to be silent or ashamed, for her resiliency has manifested itself again and again throughout the journey.

and to work on issues involved with safety. The second is for the survivor to remember and mourn her losses. And the third is reconnection. Each phase involves certain tasks, which are discussed in the following sections.

SAFETY: THE FIRST PHASE OF TREATMENT

During the first phase of treatment it is essential that trust be established and the survivor's safety ensured. This is no easy task when trauma has violated one's core beliefs about the world. Healthy core beliefs are include these: "I am invincible" (physical and psychological belief about safety); "I am worthy and have value because I am alive" (moral belief about worthiness); "I am entitled to good things happening to me" (belief about justice); and "The world I live in is fair, controlled, and logical" (belief about fairness) (Janoff-Bulman, 1985).

Epstein (1991) listed these four basic worldviews that are altered by trauma: (1) the world is a place filled with certainty and security; (2) the world is understandable, fair, and stable; (3) the self is deserving of good things and is capable and respectable; and (4) people can be trusted, and there is value in being connected to others. A survivor comes to therapy believing that none of these are true.

She knows the world is not a safe place. But it is not only the world that's unsafe, the survivor often feels unsafe in her own body. Young (1992) described the phenomenon this way:

> How do I live with (but not in?) a dangerous, damaged, or dead body? In addition, how do I continue to live in "the body" of a family or a world that is equally dangerous, damaged, or dead? So a child experiencing severe sexual abuse, seemingly faced with physical and psychological annihilation, may abandon the body, make it "outside me," pretend it doesn't exist or turn on it in anger and confusion. . . . To physically challenge or compromise my boundaries threatens me, as living organism, with annihilation; what is "outside me" has now seemingly entered me, occupied me, reshaped and redefined me, made me foreign to myself by confronting and confusing inside me with outside me. (pp. 90-91)

Based on Young's description, one can see why dissociation is a useful survival mechanism for the survivor of severe abuse: It enables her to survive in an otherwise intolerable situation and one in which she believes she has a defective body.

Several researchers have documented that the most harmful long-term consequences follow from intrusive forms of sexual abuse that involve oral, anal, or vaginal penetration; abuse that is savage and sadistic; abuse that is prolonged over many years; and abuse that is perpetrated by a parent, step-parent, or other caregiver (Browne & Finkelhor, 1986; Courtois, 1988; Herman, Russell, & Trocki, 1986; Russell, 1986).

Over 80% of the survivors in our study were subjected to all of the phenomena described in the last paragraph. One survivor described the following abuse by her mother: *"She used a toothbrush, bottle brush, nutcracker, long crochet needles, very bad sharp things,"* all of which were thrust into the daughter's vagina and anus. Another woman described her abuse this way:

> *Fingers fondling me to orgasm or slapping my crotch to orgasm, fingers penetrating me, pencils in my rectum to keep quiet, objects inserted (yeast suppositories, knife handle, floral tape, turkey baster, plunger handle, clitoris hit or pinched, candles and matches burning my crotch.*

Given the horror she has lived through, a survivor needs to know what to expect in the healing relationship. Herman (1992) suggested using the analogy of running a marathon to describe what the treatment process will entail. Salter (1995) noted, "To some extent what makes the therapist's office safe is that it embodies all the things that are lost in a trauma-based world-view: meaning, efficacy, and benevolence" (p. 260).

Safety begins when the survivor starts to gain some control over her bodily symptoms of intrusion and hyperarousal. To do this, she needs to establish some reassuring, calming messages for herself. Williams (1995) suggested using "safety notes"—sayings or drawings written on paper that represent safety and include empowering symbols such as rainbows, trees, or flowers. Helping the client to identify and determine which behaviors help her to feel safe or unsafe is part of this process as well.

The therapist should have the survivor describe and define a safe place, if there ever was such a thing for her. Steele and Colrain (1991) identified this as the client's "spot of safety" (as referenced by Williams, 1994). Identification of a safe place at work also is important. The client should identify triggers in the home and work environments that cause her to feel unsafe. Abuse survivors often have unclear boundaries with everyone in their lives. Learning to establish clearer boundaries is part of the therapeutic work they must do. Clear boundaries will help them feel safe. Survivors often carry objects that symbolize safety, such as a medallion, a cross, or Kachinas. Therapists should honor and encourage this practice.

Family members who are supportive of the survivor can be involved in part of the treatment process. These persons can be made aware of behaviors or expressions that may trigger flashbacks. Family members can be educated on how to cope with and express their own frustrations and other feelings, both positive and negative, that are associated with the survivor.

Additional steps to establishing trust include assessment, formulating the treatment plan, establishing goals, fostering development of coping skills, and using support systems.

When asked what had been healing to her, one survivor in our study had this to say about trust and therapy:

> *Finding (after years of attempts at therapy and a bunch of misdiag-noses, etc.) a therapist who could gain enough of my trust (and earned it) to work through a lot of resistance from me and my thick defenses and proved safe in all ways to literally get me to risk my life by revealing those dark secrets.*

Another survivor revealed the following:

> *Therapy with a woman I trusted. Revealing the whole truth in intimate detail was the greatest cure. Her continual support and trust of my perceptions helped me to believe my own memories. Writing and painting and doing volunteer work (helping others) has also been helpful to me.*

This survivor found someone she could trust. But it took a long time, and she felt as if she was risking her life to tell the secret. She revealed that, when she was a child, her perpetrator had threatened her life if she told anyone about the abuse. For her to "tell the tale" was a monumental achievement (Salter, 1995).

Another survivor said this:

> *The most beneficial part of my healing has been the relationship with my therapist. Her openness, acceptance, and listening has helped, far more than skills or techniques. I have been self-motivated to learn and to work to heal. I have journaled extensively, written poetry and prose, put together artistic collages, put together and taught training materials for graduate students in counseling about helping*

sexually abused clients, read extensively on the subject in at least 30 books, attended an Ellen Bass workshop on abuse, participated in group therapy, shared with my sister. My therapist is still the only one who knows how bad the abuse was (very violent, sadistic, and torturous).

Another survivor had this advice for therapists:

Don't force the trust issue. Don't overuse the psyche terms if they (the survivors) don't like them. Don't force them into recollection. Don't push hypnosis. Go at their pace, not yours. Show them you are human and you make mistakes. Don't be or act Godlike. Don't forget confrontations or forgiveness. If they decide to do either, support and help them.

Each client must make a commitment to the therapeutic process and take an active role if the therapy is to be successful. In other words, she must be committed to her own healing. The clinician's role during this first phase is to educate the survivor about both the short- and the long-term implications of being abused.

Yet another survivor, when asked what has helped her heal, had this to say:

Moving far enough away from my family so the abuse couldn't continue. Soothing music and environmental tapes. My therapist had two ground rules when we first met: We'd both be as honest as possible, and I wasn't to do anything to hurt myself or anyone else. Then she added a third one just for me: Coming to therapy wasn't optional. There were many times I didn't want to go, but I was usually glad I had been there after 20 or 30 minutes and we'd work through the difficulty. Journaling, although I've never been able to do it consistently. . . . A brief phone call to my therapist on a daily basis alleviated many difficulties for me and made the therapy hour more productive. Before we instituted this arrangement, many times neither of us had any idea what had transpired over the past week because I'd split so much. . . . Connecting daily was like catching a fire while it was still contained in a trash can rather than waiting until the entire building was engulfed in flames before trying to bring it under control.

Trust Between Therapist and Survivor

Commenting on the issue of trust between therapist and survivor, Briere (1989) had this to say:

> Psychotherapy, in some ways, represents a paradox for the sexual
> abuse survivor: on the one hand, she has been victimized and exploited
> in the context of an inter-personal relationship, yet on the other it is
> suggested that her best chance for recovery may be to engage in a
> similar situation where, she is told, she should 'trust' that further
> abuse will not occur. (p. 111)

Briere draws our attention to the similarities between abusive relationships
and psychotherapy. A close relationship exists between the survivor and the
individual in a position of authority. Throughout the course of therapy, the survivor is "expected to be" vulnerable and able to tolerate uncomfortable emotions and feelings. If the survivor used dissociation to cope with the ongoing
and repeated trauma of being sexually abused, during the treatment process she
may engage in the same coping mechanisms as a form of survival.

It is the clinician's responsibility to be on time for sessions, to maintain
appropriate boundaries, to keep the sessions focused, to pace the sessions, and
to move at the client's pace. No single event denotes a conclusion to the first
stage; it is a gradual process.

Finally, current family relationships should be explored. The clinician should
have the survivor identify who in her life is protective of her and who provides support and help. The survivor also should identify who is hurtful, toxic,
and dangerous in her family. Use of an extended genogram is helpful for the
therapist to gain a better understanding of who is who in the family. A genogram also is useful for identifying patterns and signifying those persons who
are safe and supportive as well as those who are hurtful and damaging to the
client. It also provides a more organized, comprehensive framework of the survivor's family system.

REMEMBERING AND MOURNING:
THE SECOND PHASE OF TREATMENT

During the second stage of treatment, the survivor verbalizes the traumatic
events. She narrates the tales in detail. It is common for a survivor to do this
without much feeling in the initial stages of therapy. The clinician may need to
ask what kinds of body sensations she is experiencing as she is talking.

McCann and Pearlman (1990) recommend asking these questions:

- When you remember what happened, do you see any pictures in your
  mind?

- Can you see colors?
- Can you see what you were wearing?
- Are you aware of any smells, sounds, or bodily sensations? (p. 205).

In sharing the traumatic events, the survivor struggles to make sense of what and why these events happened. Herman (1992) wrote,

> Psychotherapy does not get rid of the trauma. The goal of recounting the trauma story is integration not exorcism. In the process of reconstruction, the trauma story does undergo a transformation, but only in the sense of becoming more present and more real. The fundamental premise of the psychotherapeutic work is a belief in the restorative power of truth-telling. (p. 181)

If the survivor is able to verbalize the trauma, the reality of the atrocities committed against her body, soul, and spirit begin to become real, and she can feel overwhelmed and flooded. For years she may have believed she was bad and that what she experienced as a child was her fault. Now she finds herself reliving those feelings all over again:

> *I'm f---ed up. I can't handle feeling my own feelings. They always feel like they* [her feelings] *will kill me, or I feel crazy from them. I don't trust. I'm scared all the time. I hate myself. My emotions are things I have to learn about still. All I ever feel is fear and deep emotional pain. . . . I hate me. I'm scum. I'm dirt. I should have died!*

When the survivor is in therapy, there are always at least three persons in the session: the client, the therapist, and the perpetrator(s). Salter (1995) described these perpetrators in the following way,

> Such figures are introjects, part of the internal landscape for the client. They are part of who she thinks she is. She has internalized what she believes to be their goodness; their approval of her—however tainted to the outside eye—looked like sweet water at the time. To say that nothing was as it seemed is to raise the question of whether the same is not true of her as well. . . . Remind the client of the good, as well as the negative parts of the figure. (p. 266)

The survivor must deal with a profound sense of loss and mourning that seems to have no limits. This intense grief can be overwhelming. (For more on grieving, see Chapter 6). She may refuse to mourn because it seems like "giving in" to the perpetrator. Reframing her grief reaction as an act of courage rather than surrender may be helpful.

The second phase of therapy also involves a reclamation of the self. Reclaiming the self means experiencing many different feelings, one of which is mourning. "Mourning is the only way to give due honor to loss; there is not adequate compensation" (Herman, 1992, p. 190). Part of this phase involves the survivor's struggles with issues surrounding retribution, absolution, and remuneration.

As a clinician it is painful to watch the survivor struggle, but she is done a grave injustice if the clinician attempts to rescue her. To rescue assumes that she is not capable of helping herself. Rescuing does not empower the survivor. It makes her dependent, and here recovery is her responsibility. It is a collaborative approach between therapist and survivor, but ultimately the work is done by the survivor. One survivor in our study said,

> We are special people, with many strengths and special skills. We are also very fragile, need a lot of respect, encouragement, empathy, and unconditional acceptance. We hold no responsibility for our victimization and deserve full credit for our survival. We need to know that we are responsible for our lives now. Recovery is our choice, and its speed is to be determined by us.

Another echoed this idea: *"We need caring and compassion as a person. Don't turn us into a "number." Also we don't need sympathy. Sympathy develops a "poor me" attitude leading to victim mentality. We need honest evaluation to grow and expand ourselves."*

Affects

Some of the affects experienced by sexual abuse survivors include rage, helplessness, fear, loss, shame, and guilt. The meanings ascribed to the sexual abuse by the survivor are self-blame and inability to trust.

Cognitive schema play a critical role in the recovery process (Epstein, 1991; Horowitz, 1986; Janoff-Bulman, 1985; McCann, Sakheim, & Abrahamson, 1988). These schema are the way the survivor organizes her internal world, but they are based on external events.

Traumatic events cause the survivor to question her core beliefs about herself, other persons, and the world. She is compelled to search for a complete meaning to life. One survivor said,

> I am in Hell. I hear and read that peace and recovery are there in my future, but the agony now is unbearable. I live with fear, and

mistrust almost everyone (myself included) in one way or another. The few "intimate" or close relationships I've had in my adult years have mostly been abusive and or ended in tragedy. I have sharp instincts but find the desire for caring with another human being so strong that even abusive relationships are very difficult to avoid (or) to end by my leaving.

Another survivor stated, *"I am so tired of hurting. I feel ripped off. I am so lost. I hope she didn't kill my soul."*

Work of the second stage is finished when the client begins to reconnect with herself and others and feels as if the future holds some promise. "The reconstruction of the trauma is never entirely complete; new conflicts and challenges at each stage of the life cycle will inevitably reawaken the trauma and bring some new aspect of the experience to light" (Herman, 1992, p. 195).

RECONNECTION: THE THIRD PHASE OF TREATMENT

During the third stage of recovery, Herman (1992) likened the survivor to an immigrant. She literally must rebuild her life in a culture quite foreign to what she encountered as a child. Survivor issues during this phase center around intimacy and identity. One survivor shared this:

The fact that the therapist has lasted through all of my stages so far [has been helpful]. I am running out of ways to get rid of him. He has lasted longer than anyone and I am now on unknown territory with him. I can no longer predict my own behavior. It feels funny, but I like it. The second thing [that has helped my healing] is the warm physical feelings I get in the pit of my stomach where the "hole" used to be. I love that feeling when I am in pain and after there is a flow of circulation to where I hurt, and I love my 12 Step friends and the no cross-talk idea.

This survivor also had some advice for mental health professionals:

We need to talk. We have been silenced for so long. Sometimes if there are long silences it is because we are trying to put words (which we don't have) to our feelings (which we have never felt before). We do not need the air filled with psychological euphemisms. Don't be afraid to wait in the silence for our words to come out. . . . . It is only relevant to say how much the therapy works and how important it is for the therapist to stick with it even if we sit there and tell you it's a bunch of baloney. We need a chance to be wrong once in awhile without being punished. If I doubted my mother in any way, I was punished so severely you could not even imagine how hard it is for me to doubt (and voice my doubts). Indeed just voicing them helps me change them myself.

As survivors move into this third phase, they may feel more ready to explore and understand their relationships with others; they also may begin to feel as if they want to have a healthy relationship with someone significant. Sheehan (1994) identified five basic fears of intimacy: fear of merger, fear of abandonment, fear of exposure, fear of attack, and fear of one's own destructive impulses.

- **Fear of merger** involves losing one's self and control. Sexual abuse survivors know what it feels like to lose control over their bodies and their lives. For some survivors, their sense of self was violated on a daily basis. It is difficult for survivors to know where their boundaries end and someone else's begin. "Sexually abused people usually have associated sex, merging, and abuse with each other, resulting in powerful, conflicting feelings" (Sheehan, 1994, p. 99).
- **Fear of abandonment** involves loss of protection from significant others in childhood. Survivors may struggle to come to grips with why the nonoffending parent did not protect them. They don't see the world as a safe place, and may feel that they have been abandoned by God. "Some vow that no one will ever do that to them again. They avoid sexual relationships or become very promiscuous, avoiding emotional involvement" (Sheehan, 1994, p. 96).
- **Fear of exposure** is the fear of being known and understood for what one really is. Its roots are based in feelings of shame. "Victims of sexual and physical abuse feel shame because they tend to believe they did something to deserve the abuse. They also see themselves as damaged and undesirable" (Sheehan, 1994, p. 99).

One survivor recounted such feelings:

One of the times I was hospitalized for suicide, I was telling a tech about a time when Mom had used a rake handle on me. He said, "You mean she raped you?" For the first time I had something to call it. My therapist has actually touched me on the head or hand after telling him about a circumstance. He told me it wasn't my fault. He's explained that it was survival. It helped a little to feel less dirty.

When asked what she wanted mental health professionals to know, this same survivor answered:

We aren't looking for pity. We are trying to reach back to the beginning of our trauma, so we talk about the abuse, trying to sort out our feelings, guilt, shame, anger, etc. Asking how we feel sometimes helps us to sort out those emotions. It also helps if they use certain words or phrases, etc., to help us begin to seek deeper into our memories for answers to our feelings.

- **Fear of attack** is the fear of experiencing emotional or physical assault, both of which are quite common in families where sexual molestation occurs (Sheehan, 1994).
- The last fear discussed by Sheehan (1994) is **fear of one's own destructive impulses.** This involves anger or rage and the survivor's fear of hurting someone else. Victims of abuse have a great deal of anger and rage, and often fear being out of control and harmful to others. They also frequently associate these angry feelings with their abusers and fear they will be like the abusers if they let themselves feel angry (Sheehan, 1994, p. 100).

One survivor had this to say about this kind of fear:

I'm sober 12 years. AA lectured me that I couldn't afford a resentment, much less rage! As time went by, I used to wonder what in the world I was doing wrong. I couldn't get into the 12 steps for long and I couldn't even fathom forgiving certain people (i.e., husbands). I really began to question my innermost being. When I began to read (Survivors Anonymous) literature, I felt such an enormous relief that I wasn't crazy, that it was okay . . . and perfectly natural to feel rage. I almost cried from relief. I'm normal for what happened to me.

Sheehan (1994) suggested using metaphors (see Stephen & Carol Lankton's work; Lee Wallis's books) and bibliotherapy (*The Velveteen Rabbit* by Margery Williams [1969]; *The Missing Piece Meets The Big O* by Shel Silverstein [1981]) to facilitate the healing process.

Dysmorphobia

Stone (1989) noted that incest survivors often have a fear of being ugly. This is called **dysmorphobia**. Sometimes this sense of ugliness is present because the survivor was part of "dirty" or "unacceptable" sexual activities. Or she may have been called ugly by the perpetrator and made to believe she was so ugly that no one would ever want her except her molesters. Stone (1989) suggested that one of the underlying phenomena in dysmorphobia could be "A conviction of ugliness as a kind of amulet against predatory adults. . . . Besides these fear-motivated aspects of the dysmorphobic symptoms, there is often another component, having to do with the very human wish to be loved for some reasons unrelated to physical attractiveness" (p. 245). The survivors in our study said again and again how ugly they felt. It was a pervasive theme throughout their responses.

HAIL VALIANT WOMEN

Together valiant women
We came together in the cold.
Searching, learning, longing
To mend our wounded souls.
Listening, singing, weeping,
Sometimes laughing through our tears,
We learned to start believing,
While pushing through our fears.

Eyes closed, valiant women,
Created boundaries clear
Designed to keep us safe
When we don't want someone near.
We gently touched our bodies;
Tears fell from my eyes.
I felt a raging hatred;
I'd believed my mother's lies.

She told me I was ugly,
That only in the dark,
Could somebody love me,
And the pain raged through my heart.
My throat became constricted.
The sharp pain startled me.
The horror of the oral rape
that began when I was three!

Another valiant woman
Held me close and tight.

And told me I was beautiful
And rocked away my fright.

Led by valiant women
We began to see
That healing souls was possible,
That we might one day feel free.
Of secrets that still haunt us
And scars so old and deep,
That now affect relationships
And interfere with sleep.

Valiant women formed a circle,
Standing tall and proud,
Affirming selves and others,
We sound our strength out loud!
"I AM WOMAN . . . HAIL VALIANT WOMEN"

TECHNIQUES TO HELP CLIENTS COPE WITH TRAUMATIC ISSUES

1. **Dose the pain.** When asked what she thought would be helpful for mental health professionals to know about working with the survivors, one survivor replied, *"We are telling the truth. The recovery work is very draining emotionally, and sometimes I wonder what they think we do to cope between sessions (or right after a session that is very intense)."*

2. **Teach the client self-soothing statements.** Together, client and therapist should generate examples of what is consoling and comforting to the client. Salter (1995) wrote,

   The most important aspect of any self-soothing exercise lies in the term "self." When the client leaves the office, the means of soothing need to leave with him. . . . Soothing that stems only from the therapist will increase the client's distress. He must then stay in the therapist's presence and/or stay connected to him in order to feel safe. The client must either please the therapist or control him. (p. 291)

3. **Teach the client to access available support systems.** Teach her to image or visualize those persons who have been supportive of her in the past but who might not be readily available in a time of distress.

4. **Educate yourself about how abuse survivors test a therapist's ability to accept the details of the abuse.** Pearlman and McCann (1994) suggest addressing this issue directly. This can be accomplished by saying,

> You may be thinking about whether I will have the ability to comprehend and grasp and accept all of your thoughts, feelings, and details about your life. You may wonder if I will be disgusted or unable to accept what you share, perhaps because certain people have not been able to hear you. Let me reassure you that what you have to share is okay. (p. 88)

5. **Tread lightly.** I tell my clients if they want me to hold their hands, they need to tell me. A person who has been severely traumatized has undoubtedly had his or her boundaries violated. The therapist should not reinforce this issue by assuming he or she knows what the client needs.

6. **Be aware of gender issues.** This may be a sensitive issue, especially if the client was sexually abused by a female and the therapist is female. In such cases, it is not uncommon for the client to have underlying concerns about being revictimized. She may attempt to sexualize the relationship in order to "reenact the trauma," as a way to test the limits of the therapy. The client's concerns also may focus on beliefs that the therapist will condemn her as guilty and deserving of any punishment. It is the therapist's responsibility to set and maintain clear boundaries.

7. **Identify and access inner thoughts and dialogues the client is having with herself.**

8. **Discuss the fact that change is not a linear process.** More often than not, it is change followed by plateau, then change followed by plateau, and so on.

9. **Gently challenge and negate the survivor's blaming of herself.** The clinician should continually reframe the survivor's symptoms as survival mechanisms—normal ways of responding to the abusive situation. Therapy should be consistent in appropriately and gently challenging the client's negative comments about herself. **Inappropriate therapeutic responses** would be, "I can't believe you are still blaming yourself for what happened in the past" or "You continue to be so negative." A more helpful comment would be, "It seems when you talk about the abuse you often say something negative and blaming about yourself."

10. **Do not pathologize what the survivor has experienced.** Briere (1992, p. 127) suggested following up a flashback with the suggestion "that such experiences represent the mind's attempt to heal itself" because the survivor breaks the memories down into small parts, which is what a flashback is composed of—pieces of parts of the traumatic experience.

For flashbacks that occur outside the sessions, ask the survivor to record the date, time, and place in addition to her thoughts and feelings. As repressed memories coming to the surface create intense feelings of helplessness and despair, clients should be forewarned that these reactions may occur. A plan should be developed for effectively dealing with the flashbacks and the accompanying symptoms.

DEALING WITH THE FEELINGS

Bergart (1986) defined a number of strategies for working with child sexual abuse survivors. She suggested having clients begin by distinguishing the feelings they are experiencing: In this method, the clinician provides the client with a "feeling chart" and asks her to circle or check the feelings that best match her own. The client then rates the intensity of her feelings from 1 to 10, with 10 being the most intense and 1 indicating that she is experiencing the feeling only slightly. The clinician asks the client to do this outside of session two or three times a day, suggesting that she date the chart and note what she is doing at the time. A pattern will emerge which the client can use to intervene before her symptoms escalate to an incident of dissociation: When symptoms of anger, sadness, or rage rate 5 or above, she needs to take steps to prevent emotional flooding.

Together client and therapist should list interventions the client can use to prevent her from feeling out of control. She can journal, draw, paint, talk to a friend, or look at favorite art books. All of these need to be written down in a place available to the client. Additionally, the therapist needs to keep a copy of the coping interventions in the client's file.

The survivor also needs to realize that it is normal to experience a number of different feelings toward the perpetrator. Feeling both love and anger toward an abuser may create confusion and a sense of discomfort. Additionally, she should be aware that family members often react negatively when a survivor discloses that she was abused. They might accuse the survivor of lying and not corroborate that the abuse took place. Finally, the survivor needs to know that it is *never* her fault. One survivor in our study wrote, *"Sometimes we need a break in remembering if we've blocked it out. We need to hear over and over, 'It was NOT our fault.'"*

The survivor may be horrified or filled with shame if part of the abuse was pleasurable. The therapist and client need to explore together what the perpetrator told the survivor. *Responsibility for the abuse always belongs to the perpetrator.*

The therapist should also remember that a survivor may equate experiencing emotions with losing control, which is frightening for her. One way of handling this is to ask the client to draw what she is feeling at the beginning of the session and then again at the close of the session.

Grounding Techniques

It is not uncommon for a trauma survivor to assume body postures she finds comforting. These body postures often include a fetal position or one in which her knees are pulled close to her body with her feet not touching the floor. Although this stance may provide comfort for her, it will not help her become grounded to the present. Placing her feet on the floor may feel unnatural, because the survivor is convinced that this increases her vulnerability. Maintaining eye contact might be difficult as well. She should be gently encouraged to assume these postures, which enhance being grounded.

Grounding is a method survivors can use to reduce or mitigate depersonalization episodes, overpowering fury, intense emotions, and recurrent flashbacks (Blake-White & Kline, 1985). The object of grounding is to facilitate and enhance the survivor's connection to the present and her sense of being in control. An example of a grounding script might be, "My name is Sally. I am at home. I am an adult. I exist and am here in this blue chair. I can feel my feet on the floor." The survivor should focus on specific items around her and sense her feet on the floor.

Distraction is another technique that helps in the grounding process. Activities such as reading, drawing, or watching television can be used for distraction. Briere (1992) called grounding an "interruption of the fragmentary processes" (p. 119).

It is critical that the clinician understand and use grounding techniques. Benham (1995) made these suggestions:

> We tell the patient where she is and what month, day, and year it is. We repeat this information over and over in reassuring tones. . . . We illuminate the area by turning on the lights, or opening the drapes, we ask the patient to open her eyes if they are closed, so that the patient can see where she is and who we are. We also ask the patient to try to move her eyes so as not to be in a daze; as this seems to

keep patients locked into a dissociative state or flashback. . . . We ask her to identify our eye color. (p. 33)

Here are some more techniques to help in the grounding process:

- Reassure the client that she is safe: "I know you may be frightened right now, but you are here (define the place), and you are safe."
- Ask her to describe what she sees around her: the color of the carpet, the chair she is sitting in, and her clothing.
- Do not encourage the client to go deeper into the dissociative state. This is very counterproductive.
- Encourage her to feel her body weight: "Can you feel your feet on the floor? Your back resting against the chair cushion?" Benham even suggested asking the client to get up from the chair and walk around.
- Have the client identify a safe place in her home—the place where she feels the safest and can go when she thinks she is going to dissociate. Some clients identify closets as safe places, because they provide a containing environment. Pillows, favorite blankets, cassette tapes, and any other objects that represent safety and healing can be placed in the safe place.
- Identify persons who can be called upon for support, and keep a list of telephone numbers in a safe place with a cellular or cordless phone if possible.

Shame

Shame is variable for each individual: What is shameful for one person is only slightly embarrassing for someone else. A gesture, such as turning away from others or hiding one's face, can characterize shame. Wurmser (1981) said that at the core of shame is the individual experiencing the sense of being unloved and unlovable. Two factors inherent in the internal experience of shame are exposure and defectiveness (Wurmser, 1981).

Shame can be experienced in front of others, as a form of exposure, or singularly, as a sense of having failed oneself. Both situations evoke intense feelings of helplessness, frailty, and powerlessness. The masks of shame include anger or rage, depression, envy, perfectionism, body loathing, and repression.

Kaufman (1985) suggested that shame begins on an interpersonal level within the context of a relationship with a significant other: For example, when the infant's primary caregiver fails to respond in an appropriate manner to the infant's needs, the infant learns the beginnings of shame. Some of the most injurious kinds of shaming include belittling, mocking, denigration, shifting of blame, or completely ignoring the needs of the other person.

Kaufman identified this bonding of trust between two persons as their "interpersonal bridge." He contended that shame is stimulated when this "bridge" is disconnected. If an individual is shamed for long periods of time, the shame becomes internalized and he or she may experience a sense of shame almost constantly.

We develop our sense of ourselves from what significant others verbally convey to us about ourselves; from how we learn to fit in first with our families and then with others, such as peer groups and social groups; and from how we are treated by others who are important to us. For example, when we are hurt, do they attempt to comfort us, or are we shamed with accusations? "What's wrong with you? Stop crying. You are acting like a baby. It's all your fault anyway!"

Nathanson (1992) had this to say about about emotion: "An affect lasts but a few seconds, a feeling only long enough for us to make the flash of recognition, and an emotion as long as we keep finding memories that continue to trigger that affect. Often an emotion lasts quite awhile" (p. 51). An emotion such as shame may last for years.

Shame is a layered emotion (Wurmser, 1981). Nathanson (1992) suggested that individuals have four major patterns of reacting and responding to shame. He identified this as the "compass of shame," which is composed of withdrawal, attack of the self, attack of the other, or avoidance. "In each, shame affect is experienced differently" (Nathanson, 1992, p. 312).

Individuals who **withdraw** frequently encounter physical symptoms of shame and the thoughts that accompany the shame experience. Needing to escape is paramount for these individuals, as are feelings of distress and fear. Psychotherapy and treatment of the withdrawal reaction involves the therapist providing empathic responses, recognizing the interactions that are shaming, and communicating that it is possible to reclaim and redeem the self. Nathanson (1992) said, "Therapeutic passivity—the decision to remain silent in the face of a humiliated, withdrawn patient—will always magnify shame because it confirms the patient's affect-driven belief that isolation is justified" (p. 325).

Avoidance is another point on the compass of shame, and can be seen in several approaches: by never doing anything of which one is ashamed, by directing attention away from the self, by openness, or by acquiring expensive possessions that catch the attention of others.

Another kind of shame avoidance behavior can be seen in the individual who is driven to succeed—the workaholic who becomes wealthy and powerful as a way to cover up internal shame. Persons who deal with shame in this manner often employ a variety of techniques to reduce the shame: substance abuse or addiction; cosmetic surgery, and a constant, unrelenting pursuit of pleasure. "Those who suffer the most from chronic shame are the most likely to be seen as 'narcissistic' because of their constant attention to anything and everything that might produce even more shame" (Nathanson, 1992, p. 313).

Nathanson (1992) discussed how children deal with growing up in a home where they are not loved or protected: "To grow up in a dangerous home implies nearness to death and an atmosphere or terror, while to grow up believing one is a defective child in a good home implies a life of shame rather than peril" (p. 341). Thus, it is far easier for the child to say "I am bad" than to admit, "My parents were incompetent and uncaring."

An effective way to work with individuals who avoid shame through substance use is to define and describe shame in detail. The therapist should give concrete examples of the painfulness of shame and state that everyone experiences shame—including the therapist.

Attacking of the self is the third category identified by Nathanson (1992). The feelings most frequently experienced by persons in this category are self-disgust and self-dissmell. Nathanson (1992) defined dissmell this way:

> a primitive mechanism by which we keep something at a distance from us, something or someone we define as too awful or foul to get near. Whenever one person decides that another person is unacceptable at the level of dissmell, it is very difficult (if not impossible) to get them together. (p. 124)

Persons who attack themselves want to avoid feelings of fear, animation, and pleasure. Nathanson (1992) noted:

> Central to this therapeutic work is the attempt to determine the nature of the relationship within which the patient learned the definition of self that is so connected with shame. Giving up chronic masochism means giving up the shaming parent, which implies abandonment unless the patient feels safe within the therapeutic relationship. (p. 33)

Attacking of the self is challenging to treat because it is the final product of repeated endeavors to mitigate deep levels of shame. Together client and therapist should explore why attacking the self is more positive than someone else shaming the client. Nathanson (1992) cautioned, "it is not uncommon for these individuals to believe that they do not have the right to get better" (p. 334). The goal of attacking the self is to stay connected to others, regardless of the cost.

Attacking others is Nathanson's fourth compass point. The most frequently experienced feeling here is anger. The propensity to attack others occurs when the survivor experiences "something that makes us feel like a child in danger, one who cannot expect protection from a loving other, and one who must mount a solitary defense against increasing peril" (Nathanson, 1992, p. 364). Individuals who operate from this mode are inclined to externalize, blame, and be suspicious of others. Nathanson described how such an attack might play out. The survivor tells someone else that he or she smells bad, then acts disgusted so that the other person feels less than, helpless, or alienated. So anger, dissmell, and disgust are affects related to the other style of shaming.

Jacobs (1996) described shame, guilt, and fear like this: "These are 'feelings about feelings,' the boundary keepers, the affects that color our lives like a background wash on canvas, lending a faint or intense hue to whatever other thoughts and feelings may be occurring" (p. 298). The majority of the survivors in our study had intense background colors of shame.

Jacobs also discussed what the therapist can do to facilitate the lessening of shame:

> Although there is not much a therapist can directly offer a patient, she can offer a patient permission, that permission is the permission to be himself. I think that patients are constantly assessing our interventions for whether or not we offer permission to have the feelings, aims, and needs they have. They note our positive tone of voice, and choice of words. And when they do not find permission, they often assume . . . that they do not belong in human company anymore. This is a fundamental shame self-statement, "I am not fit for human belonging." (p. 312)

UNDERSTANDING THE SURVIVOR

McCann and Pearlman (1990) suggested asking the following questions of the survivor:

- What is the first thing you remember about what happened?
- What happened next?
- What is the last thing you remember happening?
- Can you clearly remember the sequence of events or the time frame?

Because the clinician's office is a safe place, processing the memories over and over in this environment helps build the survivor's tolerance for intense emotions. Briere (1992) characterized this phenomenon as "process desensitization" (p. 139).

Anger

Rage is an extreme angry response to a situation that is viewed as one in which pain, fear, or frustration is likely to occur. Calof (1996) wrote about rage: "To unearth, reshape, and set aside traumatic rage, we must first understand the nature of the clay" (p. 62). Rage falls at one end of the continuum of angry responses, with minor irritations at the other.

It is important to allow the client to proceed at her own pace with regard to expressing anger. She may fear the anger or rage that is within her. It may signify being out of control. It may be consuming, and a strong desire to punish may be present, as well as feelings of helplessness.

Simonds (1994) wrote:

A safe physical release of anger involves control over three components: (1) the capacity to direct the anger at a safe object (connectedness); (2) the ability to regulate the intensity of strength used (modulation); (3) the mastery required to end the activity (sequencing). (p. 137)

In the beginning, anger work should focus on containment. The release of anger can be structured through physical activities. Expression of anger is best left to the middle and later phases of therapy.

The first phase in anger work is identifying the triggers and feelings associated with being angry. Defining anger, providing information on the physiology of anger, and normalizing angry feelings are appropriate during this phase.

Wanting to attack the perpetrator can be defined as an option for staying alive instead of living with a sense of internal deadness caused by the abuse. The therapist should help identify how anger at the perpetrator might be disguised as other feelings, such as anxiety and depression.

Figure 8.2.   Healing and Wholeness Collage, by Juliann.

Figure 8.2.   The circles at the bottom of the page signify healing and wholeness, as does the egg. At the lower right-hand corner, a butterfly is in a cocoon, much like the survivor when she first begins treatment. At the top of the page, the butterfly has emerged and is free, as is the survivor who completes her treatment. Echoes Salter (1995):

> And so the quilt takes shape. There are those who would argue for the simplicity of a woven piece—something in the evenness of a fabric that has never been cut and stitched. But quilts came originally not from worn-out clothes, as some think, but from the leftover, the hidden, the seemingly flawed, the crumpled up and thrown away— and in the teeth of trauma, stitch by stitch, session by session, stubbornly put together not just a pleasing pattern but one that comforts and warms in a way few woven pieces can. (p. 299)

The therapist should help the survivor recognize the anger, label it as anger, divide it into parts, trace its roots, and learn to express it in a number of different ways.

After some of the anger work has been done, the therapist should ask the client these questions:

- What do you want to do with the anger?
- What do you need to do with it?
- What can you allow yourself to do with it (Rando, 1993, p. 467)?

It may be helpful to the survivor to do memory work before beginning anger work. Otherwise she may be unable to connect current feelings of anger to past events. Together therapist and survivor should determine if the survivor needs to focus on learning to contain her anger or on releasing her anger. During certain times she may need containment strategies for her anger, and at other times she may need to learn to release it.

Asking the survivor to define anger is a place to begin. Simonds (1994) identified a number of questions that relate to anger:

- When you are angry what happens? What do you do?
- Have you ever lost control when angry?
- Do you recognize anger when you are feeling it?
- How did family members express their anger when you were growing up (p. 161)?

Before beginning anger work, Simonds (1994) recommended having the client designate a nonverbal signal (e.g., raising a hand) to let the therapist know she is beginning to feel overwhelmed and out of control. At this point, containment exercises should be employed.

One survivor in our survey had this to say when she was asked how she felt about what had happened to her as a child:

> *Angry. I feel as if I've been cheated out of a hell of a lot. I sometimes wonder what type of person I would've turned out to be without the incest. I feel as if I was robbed of a childhood and that I was forced to be a woman while still a child. Now I'm a woman but part child and I'm angry about it.*

Another replied this way: *"Extreme anger, frustration, rage. Like a carefully controlled time bomb waiting to explode and hoping somehow I can find safe ways to release these feelings."*

Nightmares

Nightmares are terrifying dreams from which the survivor often wakes during Rapid Eye Movement sleep. Nightmares can be composed of actual events, completely fabricated events, or a combination of the two. Nightmares produce great amounts of stress for the individual, and she may express anxiety about going to sleep for fear of experiencing them.

Freud (1920) believed nightmares were a "repetition compulsion." Trauma is experienced and then reexperienced again and again through nightmares. One of my clients reported having a recurrent nightmare about tidal waves. In every nightmare, she could taste the salt water, feel the coldness of the water wash over her, and feel objects hit her legs while she was floating.

Dreams that recur often are given titles by the dreamer: for example, "My Ultimate Destruction" or "Nightmare on 35 Broad Street." Coalson (1995) called these "ghost titles" (p. 315)—powerful negative labels survivors ascribe to their nightmares.

These negative labels need to be eliminated. The process begins by having the survivor alter one small detail in the dream (for example, enlarging a small circle of light or changing the color). Being able to do this provides the client with some control, and usually the intensity of the dream diminishes when she begins to visualize changes in it. Another technique I have used is to ask the survivor to draw the nightmare and change something in the drawing (such as the color of an object).

Nightmares are vivid and clear, seemingly just like real life. It is not uncommon for nightmares to include experiences involving all the senses. Terr (1990) suggested four different kinds of nightmares related to traumatic events: "exact repetitions, modified repetitions, deeply disguised dreams, and terror dreams" (p. 240). In terror dreams, the survivor awakens with her heart beating rapidly; she may be crying or feel intense fear but be unable to remember what the dream was about.

Nightmares may begin soon after the traumatic event or not occur until months or even years later. It is not uncommon for survivors to experience a resurgence of nightmares around an anniversary date.

Nightmares produce feelings of anxiety because the dreamer believes she is not in control. The dream seems real and often has horrific qualities, and the dreamer is aware that there is a significance to it all (Halliday, 1987).

Halliday (1987) advocated a three-pronged intervention approach. The first step is to discuss the meanings the nightmare has for the individual, identify its impact on her life, and list factors that may lead to the situation. Discussing the nightmare is not enough to resolve its recurrence for long periods of time, but it can be quite therapeutic for the survivor in the beginning stages of treatment. It is most helpful to allow the client to interpret the symbolic meaning of her dreams.

Altering the scenes and encouraging face-to-face encounters constitute the second step advocated by Halliday (1987). The dreamer is instructed to visualize a new beginning and ending and to change some small detail in the nightmare, or to confront the chaser, killer, monster, or other adversary in the dream. However, if she is going to confront the monster in the nightmare, she needs to prepare herself before she goes to sleep by planning what she wants to say to him or her.

The third step of treatment focuses on the unresolved issues in the survivor's life (Halliday, 1987). These clinical issues have been identified together by client and therapist.

Recurring nightmares are a classic symptom of post-traumatic stress disorder and often can be linked to a traumatic event in the survivor's past. Survivors need the chance to discuss and explore the meanings of these dreams. Each client should be encouraged to decode her own dreams. A survivor can be asked to give the dream a title and to consciously change some small detail in it. Halliday (1987) identified this as "story line alterations." The goal is to reduce or eliminate the nightmares and to provide the survivor with an opportunity to establish some control over the dreams.

Cognitive Distortions

It is impossible to refute a cognitive distortion if it is not recognized as such. Thus, these internal voices need to be divided and identified before they can be confronted. These confrontations must occur on an internal level between the different voices of the client. One of the voices the survivor often hears is that of an internal perpetrator. This voice is blaming, shaming, controlling, and cruel. Another internal voice that often coexists with the perpetrator is the protector. Part of the therapist's job is to help the survivor delineate between these different voices.

Salter (1995) suggested the following in working with a client who has these issues:

Direct confrontation is appropriate, shaming or humiliation never are. Even with confrontation, the therapist must be careful to confront only part of the client which she then specifically labels as a derivative internalization of the perpetrator. If she generalizes it to the client herself, she simply continues the cognitive distortions of the perpetrator. (p. 277)

Identifying these thoughts as belonging to the perpetrator makes it easier for the survivor to come between herself and the internalized perpetrator. Differentiating between the client's own internal voice and that of the perpetrator helps the survivor to begin to think differently. This differentiation can be facilitated by asking the client to visualize confrontations between the different internal voices.

Salter (1995) advocated setting up an exercise so that the abused child is given a voice to share her fears, her confusions, and her deep sense of being wounded. This makes it hard for the child to be further victimized verbally by the internalized perpetrator. If she is unable to identify as yet with her internal child voice, the therapist should ask the survivor if she would blame her favorite child in the family for being molested. The survivor typically will be highly incensed that the child is blamed. Salter (1995) has called this technique, "going outward in order to go inward" (p. 280).

Briere (1989) advocated using "tape recognition" to deal with the survivor's intrusive thoughts, which are similar to auditory hallucinations but are not psychotic symptoms. The "tapes" are the recurrent thoughts the survivor experiences related to the abusive incidents. These cognitions often are connected to abusive episodes. Briere has identified three stages of treatment: "a) recognition, b) identification, and c) disattention" (p. 97). First, the client learns to **observe** her cognitive processes. She begins to understand that some of these thoughts are "learned." Second, the client learns to **identify** when these tapes are playing in her head. Third, the client learns to **respond** to the tapes, label them as intrusive thoughts, and refute them:

When the old messages play in the survivor's head, the therapist should ask her to visualize taking the old negative tape out of the recorder and replacing it with positive affirmations by actually pushing the play button in the mental image. An actual cassette tape can be made using the client's or the therapist's voice. The tape can include soft, healing music and positive affirmations that the client and therapist generate together. Briere (1989) recommended using the voice of the second person in refuting cognitive distortions.

Examples of Cognitive Distortions.

1. **All-or-nothing thinking.** Everything is black or white, all good or all bad, with no shades of gray. For example, "Thinking about me makes me feel selfish and not worth anything."

   Rational response: "Sometimes you focus on your own needs, but that doesn't mean you are worthless."

2. **Overgeneralization.** Thinking is extrapolated from one situation to cover all situations. For example, "I was abused by a woman. This means all women will abuse me and are untrustworthy."

   Rational response: "You were abused by a baby-sitter who was female. Some women and some baby-sitters are abusive and not to be trusted, but some women are trustworthy.

3. **Mislabeling.** The survivor identifies one negative aspect of herself and interprets it to mean that she is defective. For example, "I am too lazy to make any changes."

   Rational response: "You are brave. It took a great deal of courage to come to therapy. You continue with it even though it is scary."

4. **Mental filter.** The survivor focuses only on the negative aspects and filters out the positive aspects of a situation. For example, "I am a failure."

   Rational response: "You are not a failure. You have attained a number of things to be proud of in your life. You am working toward a college degree and work part-time."

5. **Disqualifying the positive.** Negative beliefs are paramount because anything positive is radically minimized. For example, "I am so lucky to have aced my SATs. The scorers probably felt bad for me and gave me some extra points."

   Rational response: "You *earned* high scores. You studied hard and took an extra study course."

6. **Jumping to conclusions.** The survivor comes to a negative conclusion regardless of the situation. For example, "All my family and friends are going to disown me for telling about the abuse."

Rational response: "Some of your family and friends are going to be surprised by these revelations on your part. Those who really care for you will try to understand."

7. **Magnification.** Errors are amplified and overstated. Positive or self-enhancing factors are downplayed. For example, "I am a freak. I am scarred forever because of this abuse."

   Rational response. "The sexual abuse happened, but there is healing. You will not allow your past to hold you prisoner."

8. **Minimization.** The survivor negates or completely denies the impact the abuse has had on her life. For example, "The abuse has affected me but I'm working toward healing."

   Rational response. "The abuse has made an impact on you, and it is important that you discover just how and learn to put it in the past."

9. **Emotional reasoning.** Feelings are not viewed as contorted or skewed. The voice of the internal perpetrator likely is the cause of these distortions. For example, "It was my fault. I should have just said, 'No, I won't let you touch me.'"

   Rational response: "She told me I asked for it, and that has caused me to feel badly. But I am not responsible for what she did to me."

One survivor shared how she has challenged these internal negative messages:

Verbally reminding myself, "It didn't happen because I was a bad girl, it wasn't my fault." They were sick and responsible for their own actions. I am a lovable person. I am good. But getting past the anger is hard.

10. **Shoulds.** Survivors are replete with "should haves." Inability to live up to such standards may result in the survivor feeling angry, being guilt-ridden, and experiencing a real loss of self-esteem. For example, "I should have just screamed every time she came near me."

    Rational response: "Even if you had screamed, no one would have heard you. She did threaten to kill you if you told anyone or made a sound."

11. **Personalization.** The survivor believes she is responsible for the abuse. For example, "I was responsible for what happened because I had orgasms. I must have liked it for my body to respond like that. That's what she told me."

Rational response: "Your physical response was normal. This does not mean that you liked it or that you are to blame."

SURVIVORS SPEAK

The recovery process begins when the survivor begins to grasp the emotional effects of the trauma, and her thoughts are not distracted and absorbed by these feelings. One survivor said, *"I feel the most important aspect of healing/recovery is to break through the walls of isolation created by the abuse/abusers and society as a whole. We are continually made to feel it was 'our fault.'"*

When asked what was important for clinicians to know when working with women who had been sexually abused by other women, one survivor in our study responded this way: *"Being compassionate, patient, flexible, and very open and human are essential elements if therapy is to be productive and effective. It is also imperative that the survivor is believed."*

Responding to the question of what had helped in her healing, another survivor wrote:

> *My faith in God; the WONDERFUL, TERRIFIC counselor at my local women's shelter; Laura Davis's Courage to Heal; my spiritual family's support and prayer; my husband's support; my terrific support group for survivors of sexual assault. My internal drive to get behind the masks I had been wearing. I read. I researched. I cried, raged, screamed, and cried some more with my support system. I gave full attention to my pain the first 6 months. I dropped out of all extra activities. I also had an article I had written on child sexual abuse accepted for publication by a woman's magazine—that really boosted my self-esteem. After I remembered the abuse by my mother, I went to the neighboring town and bought a postcard. I wrote on it, "Dear Mom, I remembered and I told. . . . Love, your daughter." I took it to group and asked those there to sign it. I never sent it—I just hung it above my desk—it was very empowering.*
>
> *Teaching Sunday school, etc. so I could stop running and focus. The aerobics class I joined, at the urging of my counselor, was*

terrific for venting my rage. I journaled everyday the first few months; that really helped me to believe me. I know that without the support group, I would have moved much slower and been more afraid; they have accepted me and my pain, validated me, and let me know I wasn't alone. The women's shelter let me sit in the shelter and cry when I was remembering. The staff and volunteers there are very supportive and willing to listen anytime, day or night. Behind all this was a verse a friend had shared with me along ago—it helped me to stop terrorizing myself and put the responsibility for the abuse where it belonged. Proverbs 17:15: "He that justifies the wicked, and condemns the righteous, both alike are an abomination to God."

When asked what has been helpful in the healing process, another survivor identified many different things:

The counselor who is doing the group and one on one by asking the right questions to help me focus and dig up the answer for myself. Helping and nudging me to accept my memories. Helping me understand how coping behaviors have affected my life and helping me to find healthier ways. Group for providing a safe place to work through memories. They provide acceptance, support, shared feelings, and safety. My husband for loving me no matter what I say, do, or feel. Being strong when I am weak. My children for giving me a reason to go on. My faith in God for providing hope in despair. My intellect for grasping difficult concepts and ideas. Oddly enough, my MPD for providing relief from my horror to recover and rest.

Several survivors in our study listed their faith in God or spiritual practices as healing and a source of comfort. One woman wrote,

My spiritual practice has been invaluable. It feels right and true, these beliefs, real deep down. It reinforces me, helps to strengthen me, gets me to trust myself. Helps me to listen to my intuition and trust it, even when I can't explain it. Helps me focus on what I need from myself. Not what everybody else needs. There have been moments of deep healing, deep shifts. I went to a 3-day workshop called "A Full-Bodied Woman," where we worked on alters created to represent the various aspects of being a woman. Some real healing occurred there. . . . Both the facilitator at that workshop and my therapist have helped a lot, with their love, guidance, and acceptance. My therapist also has some shamanic training. She performed an extraction and soul retrieval for me. These were important to my understanding and healing. Being accepted by friends, being held by them, really feeling loved, S.O.F.I.E., reading all the stories from others like me [in survivor newsletters], feeling understood and not so alone.

Another survivor wrote, "I'm still healing. A lot of crying, a lot of therapy, female groups, self-care, self-pampering . . . . Reading my Bible daily works well, praying also, writing, lots & lots of writing."

What the client internalizes about the therapist's beliefs about her is one of the most important phenomena in the treatment process (Salter, 1995). One survivor said that mental health professionals need:

> *To be patient and very good listeners. Many times there were only fragments, pieces, a sentence I would say—things would not seem relevant—then weeks later my therapist would reintroduce these as I was talking—like pieces of puzzles—and I was able to delve deeper with these new pieces to join the old. I find it hard to explain this process.*

Another added:

> *Even though we appear to have it all together, at times we really hurt a lot inside. Please don't give up on us. We've given up on ourselves too much so we don't need others doing it too. We need constant encouragement. And don't compare us with your other clients. We need to be reminded at times that we are survivors, and even though it may not seem like it at times, we really can heal if we keep working.*

Again, responding to the question of what mental health professionals should know, one survivor said,

> *Be really, really gentle. Believe us. I've spent my life not being listened to. Totally take cues from where we are at, what we are dealing with, what we can deal with at any one time. Don't push or jump ahead. Validate our stories, validate our feelings. It's so terrifying a process to go through. Absolutely terrifying, remember that. Keep bringing us back to figure out what we need.*

After many years of individual therapy and a 12-step recovery program (Incest Anonymous), another survivor reported how she felt about herself: *"I'm incredibly brave and a talented woman who can credit a little 10-year-old child for saving my life."* The person to whom she is referring is her inner child.

These messages are clear for treatment providers: listen; reflect at appropriate times; allow the survivor to proceed at her own pace; facilitate the integration process, but have the survivor draw her own conclusions; know that survivors put up good fronts; and communicate over and over again the belief that healing is possible. All of this confirms Salter's (1995) contentions on the significance of the therapeutic relationship.

Finally, one survivor put it all in perspective for clinicians:

> *You are our teachers about life, feelings, and maybe even behaviors. We are frightened, hurt, non-trusting, self-hating people. We need/ want you to try to understand that this recovery work is just as traumatic as it is healing, and that you must be willing to walk what you talk. We are honoring ourselves by healing and . . . we are allowing you the privilege to share in our healing.*

There is nothing we can add to what she so eloquently says other than this: The resiliency of the human spirit is amazing!

REFERENCES

Bergart, A. M. (1986, May). Isolation to intimacy: Incest survivors in group therapy. *Social Casework, 266-275.*

Blake-White, J., & Kline, C. M. (1985). Treating the dissociative process in adult victims of childhood incest. *Social Casework: The Journal of Contemporary Social Work, 66,* 394-402.

Briere, J. (1989). *Therapy for adults molested as children: Beyond survival.* New York: Springer.

Briere, J. (1992). *Child abuse trauma: Theory and treatment of the lasting effects.* Newbury Park, CA: Sage.

Browne, A., & Finkelhor, D. (1986). Impact of child sexual abuse: A review of the research. *Psychological Bulletin, 99,* 66-77.

Calof, D. L. (1996). Chronic self-injury in adult survivors of childhood abuse. *Treating Abuse Today, 5*(6)/*6*(1), 61-67.

Coalson, B. (1995). Nightmare help. Treatment of trauma survivors with PTSD. *Psychotherapy, 32*(3), 381-388.

Courtois, C. A. (1988). *Healing the incest wound.* New York: Norton.

Courtois, C. A. (1991). Theory, sequencing, and strategy in treating adult survivors. In J. Briere (Ed.), *Treating victims of sexual abuse*. San Francisco: Jossey-Bass.

Dolan, Y. (1992). A message from the other end of the tunnel: Reflections on hope. *Treating Abuse Today, 2*(4), 23-24.

Epstein, S. (1991). The self concept, the traumatic neurosis, and the structure of personality. In D. Ozer, J. M. Healy, Jr., & R.A.J. Stewart (Eds.), *Perspectives on personality* (Vol. 3). Greenwich, CN: JAI Press.

Freud, S. (1920, 1953). Beyond the pleasure principle. In *Complete Psychological Works, Standard Edition, Vol. 18.* London: Hogarth Press.

Gil, E. (1988). *Treatment of adult survivors of childhood abuse.* Walnut Creek, CA: Laurel Press.

Halliday, G. (1987). Direct psychological therapies for nightmares: A review. *Clinical Psychology Review, 7,* 501-523.

Herman, J. (1992). *Trauma and recovery.* New York: Basic Books.

Herman, J., Russell, D., & Trocki, K. (1986). Long-term effects of incestuous abuse in childhood. *American Journal of Psychiatry, 143,* 1293-1296.

Horowitz, M. (1986). *Stress response syndrome.* New York: Basic Books.

Jacobs, L. (1996). Shame in the therapeutic dialogue. In R. G. Ice & G. Wheeler (Eds.), *The voice of shame: Silence and connection in psychotherapy* (pp. 297-314). San Francisco: Jossey-Bass.

Janoff-Bulman, R. (1985). The aftermath of victimization: Rebuilding shattered assumptions. In C. R. Figley (Ed.), *Trauma and its wake* (pp. 15-35). New York: Brunner/Mazel.

Kaufman, G. (1985). *Shame: The power of caring.* Cambridge, MA: Schenkman Books.

McCann, I., Sakheim, D. K., & Abrahamson, P. A. (1988). Trauma and victimization: A model of psychological adaptation. *Counseling Psychologist, 16,* 531-594.

McCann, I. L., & Pearlman, L. A. (1990). *Psychological trauma and the adult survivor: Theory, therapy, and transformation.* New York: Brunner/Mazel.

Nathanson, D. L. (1992). *Shame and pride: Affect, sex, and the birth of the self.* New York: Norton.

Pearlman, L. A., & McCann, I. L. (1994). Integrating structured and unstructured approaches to taking a trauma history. In M. B. Williams & J. F. Sommer, Jr. (Eds.), *Handbook of post-traumatic therapy* (pp. 38-48). Westport, CT: Greenwood Press.

Rando, T. A. (1993). *Treatment of complicated mourning.* Champaign, IL: Research Press.

Russell, D. (1986). *The secret trauma: Incest in the lives of girls and women.* New York: Basic Books.

Salter, A. C. (1995). *Transforming trauma: A guide to understanding and treating adult survivors of child sexual abuse.* Thousand Oaks, CA: Sage.

Sheehan, P. L. (1994). Treating intimacy issues of traumatized people. In M. B. Williams & J. F. Sommers, Jr. (Eds.), *Handbook of post-traumatic therapy* (pp. 94-105). Westport, CT: Greenwood Press.

Silverstein, S. (1981). *The missing piece meets the big O.* New York: Harper-Collins.

Simonds, S. (1994). *Bridging the silence.* New York: Norton.

Steele, K., & Colrain, J. (1991). Abreactive work with sexual abuse survivors: Concepts and techniques. In M. Hunter (Ed.), *The sexually abused male: Application of treatment strategies* (pp. 1-55). Lexington, MA: D.C. Heath.

Stone, M. H. (1989). Individual psychotherapy with victims of incest. *Psychiatric Clinics of North America, 12*(2), 237-255.

Terr, L. (1990). *Too scared to cry.* New York: Harper & Row.

Williams, L. M. (1994). Amnesia for childhood trauma: A prospective study of women's memories of childhood sexual abuse. *Journal of Consulting and Clinical Psychology, 62,* 1167-1176.

Williams, L. M. (1995). Recovered memories of abuse in women with documented child sexual victimization histories. *Journal of Traumatic Stress, 8*(4), 649-673.

Williams, M. (1969). *The velveteen rabbit.* New York: HarBrace.

Wurmser, L. (1981). *The mask of shame.* Baltimore, MD: John Hopkins University.

Young, L. (1992). Sexual abuse and the problem of embodiment. *Child Abuse & Neglect, 16*, 89-100.

Chapter **9**

NONVERBAL TREATMENT MODALITIES: GIVING FORM TO THE TRAUMA

Nonverbal techniques used appropriately as treatment modalities do several things: They facilitate an emotional release; tap into unresolved feelings; strengthen a sense of self; help teach about controlling impulses; are guilt-reducing; provide a vehicle for synthesis of self; promote an awareness of understanding and acceptance of self; and help the survivor find new ways of expressing herself.

NONVERBAL BEHAVIORS

In the initial stages of treatment, a survivor may be unable to make eye contact with the clinician. This lack of eye contact may denote fear of rejection, a learned way of responding, or a dissociative episode. As therapy progresses and the survivor begins to trust the therapist and feel safer, she will begin to engage in more and more eye contact.

Clinicians need to be aware of and pay attention to where and how the client positions herself in the room—for example, close to or removed from the therapist. Issues of self-injury and how the client responds to and treats her own body should be explored. The therapist should pay attention to the client's upper- and lower-body postures and determine if her postures are closed or open and whether she assumes a grounded posture (i.e., feet on the floor, elbows on the armrests, back against the chair).

If the client is fragile, the therapist should ask her to postpone drawing until she is more secure. If she feels overwhelmed, as if her life is being disrupted by drawing, the clinician should not encourage her to engage in the activity. At a later point in time it may be much more tolerable and appropriate for her.

Simonds (1994) suggested three goals for nonverbal interventions: containment, exploration, and expression. During the early phases of treatment, techniques representing containment may be the most appropriate, especially for clients in states of crisis.

The second phase of trauma work centers on exploring traumatic mem-ories and connecting feelings to those memories. Expressive techniques may be more appropriate during this phase. Feelings of rage and grief are common. If the feelings become too intense or overwhelming, use of containment exercises should be employed. New insights are gained about the abusive incidents during this second phase of treatment. The survivor needs to come to the understanding that she was not to blame for the abuse. It was not her fault; she had no choice.

Struggling to come to terms with these issues may produce intense grief. A sense of empowerment can be facilitated by asking the survivor to create a picture in which she says "no" to someone to whom she was never able to say "no" in the past. This second phase of treatment is completed when the survivor can "(1) manage PTSD symptoms when they arise; (2) . . . discuss the trauma with affect that is neither unendurably intense nor completely absent; (3) . . . respond to present events without confusing them with the past, or she can readily identify such confusion; and (4) . . . recognizes that she was not to blame" (Simonds, 1994, p. 15).

The third and final phase of treatment may involve career definitions or changes in career plans. The client can begin to engage in healthier patterns of living and knows how to engage in self-soothing activities. Issues of termination are a part of this phase. However, during this phase the survivor may regress from time to time.

A number of treatment specialists have suggested that art therapy is an appropriate adjunct to talk therapy in clinical work with trauma survivors (Anderson, 1995; Howard, 1990, Johnson, 1987; Walker, 1992). Anderson (1995) discussed the importance of nonverbal techniques: "The power of art media to evoke emotional rather than intellectual responses is at the core of the basics of the usefulness of art as a therapeutic medium" (p. 414).

Anderson also suggested that talk therapy allows the client to stay in the intellectual mode, which permits her to stay disconnected from her feelings. Using art as a medium facilitates an affective response by the client and enables her to have a tangible acknowledgment of the traumatic events (Lemon, 1984); it also externalizes sexual abuse (Carozza, Heirsteiner, & Young, 1983). It does not support her maintaining the split between thinking and feeling.

Art often is created outside the session and brought in for the clinician to see. Sometimes art-making activities can be initiated by the therapist and engaged in during the session. Art-making activities should never be suggested by the therapist without first exploring the survivor's thoughts and feelings about using the medium. She should be instructed to stop immediately if she becomes overwhelmed and flooded emotionally.

One of the most freeing aspects of art materials is the choice the client is given (Landgarten & Lubbers, 1991) of "the color, the medium, the line, the form, the space, and the style" (Ellingson, 1991, p. 8). She had no choice as a child. (Simond [1994] cautioned, however, that clay and finger-paints can produce regressive behaviors in clients. She recommends the non-art therapist use chalk, crayons, oil pastels, markers, and charcoal pencils.)

How and where the artwork is to be stored is an issue to be decided by clinician and survivor. Using a sketch pad is a good option. It keeps the artwork together and is easily stored. It also enables the survivor to have a visual record of her work and progress. Themes may become obvious as the treatment progresses.

GROUP WORK

Group therapy has been suggested as appropriate treatment for survivors of sexual abuse (Alexander & Follette, 1987; Courtois, 1988). First, discussing the abuse in a group refutes the family's denial of the problem. It challenges the family edict of, "Don't talk, don't trust, and don't tell." Second, it helps the survivor experience an environment in which clear boundaries are established and maintained. There is a clear beginning and ending in the group meeting each week. Third, a group experience helps to decrease the sense of isolation and the feelings of being different often experienced by abuse survivors.

As a cautionary note, group work with trauma survivors should not be undertaken unless the therapist has been trained to work with individuals in a group setting.

One particularly effective technique in group work is to have two therapists, whose personalities and styles complement one another, work as co-facilitators.

Groups provide several advantages for survivors: they provide support; they lessen the sense of isolation survivors often feel; they provide a chance for members to learn and grow from one another and to try out new behaviors in a safe, supportive environment; and they provide a different type of group experience than that which the survivor was exposed to in the original family group.

While there are many positive aspects to therapy groups, some negatives do exist: a difficulty with confidentiality outside the group setting; less individualized attention; and the possibility that the group can be hurtful if it is not facilitated by experienced group leaders.

Yalom (1995) listed 11 primary factors related to the process of change in the group: "(1) instillation of hope; (2) universality; (3) imparting information; (4) altruism; (5) the corrective recapitulation of the primary family group; (6) development of socializing techniques; (7) imitative behavior; (8) interpersonal learning; (9) group cohesiveness; (10) catharsis; (11) existential factors" (p. 1).

He noted,

> The distinctions among these factors are arbitrary; though I discuss them singly, they are interdependent and neither occur nor function separately. Moreover, these factors may represent different parts of the change process: some factors (for example, universality) refer to something the patient learns; some (for example, development of socializing techniques) refer to changes in behavior; others (for example, cohesiveness) may be more accurately described as preconditions for change. Though the same therapeutic factors operate in every type of therapy group, this interplay and differential importance can vary widely from group to group. Furthermore, patients in the same group may benefit from widely differing clusters of therapeutic factors. (Yalom, 1995, p. 2)

Groups function best if they include between 6 and 12 persons. Before beginning a group, the therapist must consider these steps:

1. **Define a target population.** The clinician must determine how group members will be selected and screened. Individuals who are suicidal or psychotic are not good candidates for group work.
2. **Determine group dynamics.** For example, can a group of female survi-

vors who have been abused by males be mixed with females who have been abused by females? Will the group dynamics be different? Other factors to be considered here include open versus closed group meetings; structured versus unstructured; and process versus content groups.

3. **Define the goals of the group.** Facilitators should define the goals of the group experience and delineate the goals for each session before beginning the first group.

4. **Set the time and length of group meetings.** Facilitators should determine the meeting time, day of the week, and length of time the group will meet. Most groups meet between 1½ and 3 hours.

5. **Establish a meeting format.** Facilitators should determine the format and establish a consistent pattern for each group meeting: for example, introduction of group members or topic for the evening; icebreaker (in initial group meetings); group rules (about confidentiality, missed sessions, and so on); introduction of the theme or topic for the evening (if a structured group); decisions on how to process the experience and facilitate discussion and sharing among group members; rules for giving another member feedback; ending the meeting; and homework.

6. **Determine how group progress will be evaluated.**

7. **Develop plans for dealing with potential problems** and define different roles individuals often assume in group settings.

8. **Determine the number of sessions and how to prepare for termination.**

The next section discusses several different types of group experiences for survivors of sexual abuse.

A Healing Celebration Group

Yamamoto-Nading and Stringer (1991) created a group experience for women survivors of childhood sexual abuse. Their manual, *A Healing Celebration,* is quite comprehensive in dealing with the issues these women struggle with.

Each group meeting begins and ends with the same ceremony or ritual. After the beginning ritual, group leaders present any business items and then move to "check-in" time. This time is allotted to group members who want to discuss anything that has been a problem for them since the last group meeting. "Celebrating Ourselves" is the next step. Each week group participants have opportunity to relate anything positive that has happened since the last meeting.

At most meetings participants are asked to write or draw. A homework assignment is given at the close of each meeting, and there are two parts to the closing. First, group members state what they plan to do for themselves during the week that is nurturing. Second, they identify anything they need from other group members after leaving.

The manual lists problems that could be encountered, based on the subject matter being discussed. A sample screening questionnaire is included, as is a brief discussion by the authors on how to deal with a situation in which the interviewee would not benefit from the group (Yamamoto-Nading & Stringer, 1991).

The following paragraphs give some brief information about each of the sessions.

- **Session 1** focuses on **"Breaking the Silence."** This session is designed to facilitate the sharing of each participant's story. One of the facilitators begins by holding a rock and telling a story about it. After the story, the rock is passed to the next group member who is going to share her story. Each time a new member shares her story she is handed the rock.
- **Session 2** centers on **"Celebrating Healing."** This meeting focuses on the different stages of healing. Group members are given a piece of rope and told a story about the rope and how it related to their journey of healing.
- **Session 3** focuses on survivors **becoming visible**. This involves group members defining and discussing coping strategies for dissociation, amnesia, and other symptoms.
- **Session 4** focuses on **"Truth Telling About the Abuse."** Each group member is asked to write about being sexually abused as a child. The writing is to be completed in the voice of the third person, or the "she voice." Guidelines are give for this exercise and group members are asked to write down the answers to a number of different questions: "Where is she? What can she hear? What is she thinking?" (Yamamoto-Nading & Stringer, 1991, pp. 82-83).
- **Session 5** deals with the **strategies abusers used to keep group members silent** (tricks, keeping secrets, threats, etc.).
- **Session 6** centers on the survivor **getting to know her child self**. This is a guided imagery exercise. After participating in the exercise, each member is asked to construct and create the child who appeared in the visualization.
- **Session 7, "Feelings and the Child,"** is another guided imagery exercise. After the visualization exercise, participants are invited to "use construction paper, crayons, markers, pastels, etc., to create the image of the child figure" (Yamamoto-Nading & Stringer, 1991, p. 112).

- **Session 8** deals with **connecting the past and the present.** The authors wrote,

> The goal of this exercise is to discover how some of the needs, present both in childhood and in the adult, can be met today. The discussion, progressively adding information about losses and needs, culminates in a brainstorming activity about ways to meet those needs which can be met. What will become apparent is that there are some needs, particularly of the child, which cannot be met. It is these which can be grieved. (Yamamoto-Nading & Stringer, 1991, p. 117)

- **Session 9** centers around **anger.** Group participants are asked to engage in a guided imagery exercise, and then to draw their anger in the shape of an animal. Additionally, members are asked to keep a journal of their anger for a week. Other activities during this session include each survivor writing down her description of anger and brainstorming as many different reactions to anger as possible, with the responses then divided into two separate parts—restrained and unrestrained. Feelings connected with both these kinds of responses are discussed, as are the consequences for each kind of response.
- **Session 10** is defined as an **open discussion.** Time is spent identifying further needs of the group members. Topics most frequently encountered are relationship issues, assertiveness, and trust. Group members are reminded of the number of sessions remaining. It is not uncommon for group members to struggle with the knowledge that the group is coming to an end, and some members may attempt to negotiate an extension. Group members also may discuss their own disappointment in not being "cured" after this group experience.
- **Session 11** centers on **building relationships** and group members' expectations of others. Members then discuss if these expectations are reasonable or unreasonable.
- **Session 12** involves **trust** and defining the characteristics of a trustworthy person. This is then related to the survivors' own lives, and how trusting or not trusting has had an impact on them.
- **Session 13** explores **assertiveness.** Group members are invited to explore and discuss their present behaviors and patterned ways of responding. Assertive, aggressive, and passive types of behaviors are identified and described.
- **Session 14** is the **celebration.** The authors wrote,

> We usually give a symbolic gift which is meaningful to this particular group—every group is unique and takes on its own personality. Some groups are very nurturing to their inner child, so we have

honored them with a small toy. One group had a very difficult time believing in the process and always wanted a magic cure. We made magic wands to give them. In addition, we always think of three characteristics of each individual that we have valued in our time together. We write them down on a Celebration Certificate which we distribute at the last session as a reminder of their progress and participation. (Yamamoto-Nading & Stringer, 1991, p. 164)

Termination and Closure

Lubbers (1991) provided some directions for facilitating closure and separation in a group setting. Although these exercises originally were developed or evolved out of her work with eating-disordered clients, they are appropriate for other groups too. She discussed the importance of recognizing relationships that have developed as a result of the group experience.

First, the therapist creates a "good-bye gift box" for each group member. A large gift box is drawn on a sheet of paper. "Then each member is asked to place a symbol within a box of something you would like to give or communicate to the departing member. It can be a symbol of your feelings for the person who is leaving" (Lubbers, 1991, p. 80).

The next exercise is designed to facilitate the memory of being connected to each other in the group. The members are to "(1) Draw and cut out the shape of their hand and, (2) to decorate the cutout with a symbol representing themselves. One of the ways we stay connected to others is through our hands. Afterwards they are to put their paper hands on a large sheet of paper that has been placed in the center of the table" (Lubbers, 1991, pp. 80-81). This is followed by processing the representations of their selves and why they placed their hands on the paper as they did.

Bussard and Kleinman (1991) ask group members to draw about saying good-bye. Drawing enables individuals to give symbolic representation to their feelings. Drawing also makes the feelings and experience of saying goodbye more concrete. Sometimes what a survivor cannot verbalize she is able to convey through a different medium, such as drawing. Drawing releases the feelings and thoughts related to termination. It also helps to contain them, with the paper being the container.

Brende's 12-Theme Educational Group

Brende (1994) developed a 12-theme psycho-educational group experience for survivors.

- **Theme 1** focused on **power versus victimization**. Both positive (asking for help) and negative (using force) aspects of power were defined by the facilitator, listed on a blackboard, and discussed by group members. Members were asked how they would use power in a positive way in the coming weeks.
- **Theme 2** focused on **seeking meaning**. Survivors were asked to discuss how they had responded to and survived traumatic events in their lives (by dissociation, numbing, etc.). Prior to this, group members had been asked to read Frankl's (1984) *Man's Search for Meaning* or to view a video on these issues.
- **Theme 3** involved issues of **trust, shame, and doubt**. Definitions for each of these topics were discussed, focusing on how group members experienced them. Ways to build trust were explored and discussed. In the last hour of this meeting, participants participated in trust exercises, such as a trust walk.
- **Theme 4** involved a **self-inventory**. Group discussion centered on truth versus secrecy. Included in this discussion were memories, nightmares, withdrawal, and secrecy. Participants were asked to share what was healing rather than retraumatizing. The second part of this session involved each member being asked to "Draw the most significant traumatic experience that has happened to you. Then, on a separate sheet of paper, list every traumatic experience you have had, the date on which it happened, and the symptoms or other affects since it occurred" (Brende, 1994, p. 427). Pictures were then discussed, with an emphasis on the positive aspects of what was shared.
- **Theme 5** centered around issues of **anger**—both its destructive and its constructive elements. Group facilitators explored how anger is related to grief, fear, and guilt. Both physical and emotional components of anger were explored and discussed. Examples of hidden anger were generated (teeth grinding, sadistic sarcasm, etc). In the last hour of this meeting, members discussed being assertive and their rights. Brende (1994) suggested using an assertiveness exercise to illustrate the point.
- **Theme 6** involved **fear**, symptoms and behaviors related to fear, and how fear could be a positive and a negative force in life. Group participants were asked to draw their "Most frightening memories and their most common responses to fear" (Brende, 1994, p. 429). Members then were divided into pairs (not self-selected) and asked to draw how they could be helpful to one another in coming to terms with fears.
- **Theme 7** focused on **guilt**. Members discussed both positive and negative aspects of guilt and how unresolved guilt could manifest itself in their lives. Participants were asked to draw a memory related to guilt (Brende, 1994, p. 429). Again, groups member were paired and each

member drew how she would try to be helpful in her partner's struggles with guilt.

- **Theme 8** focused on **grief**. Participants were given information on grief, including definitions, phases of grief, the impact of unresolved grief, and how it relates to feelings of isolation and abandonment. Participants were asked to draw a memory related to their own feelings of unresolved grief. Drawings were shared and discussed in the group. Group members then were asked to identify how they could come to terms with their own destructive grief.

- **Theme 9** involved **life versus death** issues. Self-destructive tendencies (e.g., abuse of food or alcohol) were identified, explored, and discussed. Group members were encouraged to share their thoughts and fantasies about suicide and asked to draw their self-destructive thoughts. Group members selected a partner and identified how they could be helpful to that person.

- **Theme 10** involved **differentiating acts of justice and acts of revenge**. Participants were asked to verbally describe definitions of both and to include personal examples, if they felt comfortable doing so. Brende (1994) also asked members to make a list of persons they needed to forgive.

- **Theme 11** focused on **finding a purpose in life**. Group members were asked to discuss what "having a purpose" meant to them. Additionally, each was asked to "Draw yourself as you would like to be in one month, one year, and five years" (Brende, 1994, p. 431). Drawings were discussed, and then members were invited to make a group drawing or collage. Members talked about how the group could improve its connections to and better the community.

- **Theme 12** involved **improving relationships with significant others**. Facilitators discussed codependency, relationship addictions, and feelings of isolation. Group members were asked to identify and define different types of love and to generate a list of characteristics of a healthy family. In this last group meeting, participants identified with whom they wanted to have a better relationship and to whom they would like to be more helpful. They also practiced communication skills, such as expressing what they were thinking, feeling, or wanting (Brende, 1994, 432).

Interpersonal Transaction Group

An Interpersonal Transaction Group (IT) was proposed by Landfield (1979) and advanced by Neimeyer (1988). Harter and Neimeyer (1995) compared treatment groups using an Interpersonal Transaction Group (Landfield, 1979; Neimeyer, 1988), a process group (Courtois, 1988; Yalom, 1995), and a control group composed of individuals waiting to get into group treatment. Persons on the waiting list received no group experience. Groups were time-limited and lasted for 10 weeks, with each meeting lasting for 90 minutes. All group members were women who had been molested either by a male who lived with the family (e.g., the father) or by a male outside the family system.

Interpersonal Transition Group members showed less distress (as measured by the SCL-90-R) at post-treatment than members of the process group. Harter and Neimeyer (1995) speculated that the IT group "may have had special advantages to the more severely traumatized women in confronting, sharing, and dealing with their fears" (p. 248) because of the group's structure and predictability. Each group session was separated into three phases:

> (1) a brief introductory phase in which members were given the opportunity to relate important weekly events or to revisit issues remaining from the previous week; (2) a structured 4-minute period of rotating dyadic interactions among all possible pairs of group members focusing upon a topic selected by group therapists or suggested by group members as relevant to recovery from incest (e.g., feelings of being different, issues of trust, family secrets, and ambivalence toward mother and father), and (3) a plenary group discussion in which members had the opportunity to explore issues arising from the dyadic interactions in greater depth. (Neimeyer, Harter, & Alexander, 1991, p. 5)

Topics for discussion in the dyadic groups centered on issues relative to survivors. Issues presented in the beginning sessions were more benign than those chosen as the group progressed and trust was at a higher level. Expressing and sharing feelings and experiences were encouraged to help members recognize their similarities to others who had been abused.

> Whenever possible, topics were framed in a bipolar manner, consistent with personal construct theory, to encourage more flexible and dimensional, rather than black/white constructions of experience. The leaders emphasized the use of bridging questions and comments in the plenary sessions to encourage participants to compare their experiences in the dyadic interactions. . . . They were also encouraged to abstract superordinate constructs that might bridge topics of dyadic discussion to their current life and aspects of their abusive experience . . . with members encouraged to abstract commonalties or superordinate dimensions linking their experiences as children to their current relationships. (Harter and Neimeyer, 1995, p. 244)

Following are some sample topics for dyadic experiences in an Interpersonal Transaction Group (Alexander, Neimeyer, Follette, 1991):

- **Purpose and personal objectives for the group:** What are your fears? What are your expectations?
- **Feeling dissimilar to others:** How are you like other group members? How are you different?
- **Aspects of self:** What are three things you like about yourself? What three areas of yourself do you want to work on?
- **Sharing with others about the incest:** What persons would you feel comfortable telling about the sexual abuse? Who would you not want to know about it?
- **Powerlessness:** How have you experienced feeling powerless in the past and currently?
- **Trust:** Who has been trustworthy for you? In what situations?
- **Secrets:** What family members would be okay if they knew about the incest? Who in your family would you *not* want to know about the incest?
- **Issues relating to mother:** Describe the perfect mother. How would you like to be similar to your mother? Identify how you don't want to be like your mother.
- **Issues relating to father:** Describe the perfect father. How do you want to be like your father? How do you want to be different from him?
- **Anger:** What are constructive ways you express anger? What are destructive ways to express anger?
- **Sexuality:** What things about your sexuality do you feel comfortable with? What do you feel uncomfortable with?
- **Feeling unprotected:** What can you do to feel less vulnerable in future relationships? How is this connected to protecting others?
- **Termination issues:** What did you gain from this group interaction? What did you not gain from this experience? (adapted from p. 223)

"Following the dyadic rotations, the group reconvened as a whole for the remaining 45 minutes of the session in order to further process the disclosures made during the previous one-on-one rotations" (Alexander et al., 1991, p. 223).

Harter and Neimeyer (1995) found a number of different characteristics related to improvements in both kinds of groups. Individuals with lower levels of education did not do as well in the group situations as those women with more education. Married women did not do as well as single women in a group, regardless of their degree of satisfaction in the marriage. Finally, "Women who had suffered more severe forms of sexual abuse showed less substantial improvement, cautioning us against considering time-limited group interventions as a panacea in treating more severely traumatized survivors" (p. 249).

Using Clay in Group Work

Anderson (1995) suggested using clay as a medium in working with sexual abuse survivors:

> [It] has properties that are especially tacitly engaging and invite sensory interaction and playfulness. Clay was also selected because its properties could facilitate a client engaging her inner child. . . . The clay could concretize feelings as well as thoughts. It could also become the focus for client rage and, thus, a means for siphoning off the repressed emotional overloads that many carried. Once some of the affect could be vented, clients could begin to move past the abusive experience(s) toward an integration of affect and intellect and toward recovery. (p. 415)

Anderson (1995) used clay with survivors in a group setting. The group met two hours weekly for nine weeks, and between sessions participants were asked to keep a journal. As part of the journaling process, survivors responded to these three questions:

- Did this week's ceramics group trigger any thoughts, feelings or images? Can you describe these?
- What one or two things did you like best about this week's ceramics group as it related to hands-on work in clay, work with other group members, work with staff?
- Please include any other issue or concern that came up during the time between last week's session and this week's session (Anderson, 1995, p. 24).

Each group session began with members briefly sharing about their week and discussing any topics that had arisen during the week. Following this, the theme for the week was presented. At times examples were provided or a technique demonstrated. Group members were then given about 45 minutes to work on their pieces. The group closed with each member sharing her work. Therapists were conscious of and checked in with each participant to make certain she was at a place to end for the day. Every group participant had to be in ongoing individual therapy.

The clay works were fired between each session to reinforce the client's mastery over the technique and to provide continuity to the process. In week one, survivors were asked to make a pot around their elbows. Another task involved starting a pinch pot but not completing it and passing it to another person to continue working on it. Passing the pots continued until the pots were all completed.

Week two began with the fired clay pots sitting on a table for the participants to view. After clients glazed their pots, they made animals of their own choosing. Anderson noted the importance of client successes in working with this medium in the beginning.

Week three centered on checking-in, collecting their fired pots, and painting on 12"-by-12" clay tiles. Anderson (1995) wrote, "I encouraged them to draw, incise, poke and texture lines and patterns on these tiles in response to descriptive words that I provided . . . [for example] a line that looks like your favorite music" (p. 418).

Weeks four and five centered on the survivors' families of origin. "I asked them to think of a metaphor or symbol for each member of their family when they were about eight years old" (Anderson, 1995, p. 15). Symbols were formed from clay. Quite often group members formed symbols of perpetrators. Anderson suggested that least two weeks is needed to deal with these issues (and four weeks is better). Clients were able to destroy their clay figures in a room during the session if they desired. If their figure was bisque, safety goggles were worn during the breaking. A therapist was with the survivor when the figure was smashed. Thoughts and feelings were processed in the group (Anderson, 1995).

Week six focused on making a family of choice. Participants created symbols from clay that denoted representations of the people in their family of choice.

Weeks seven and eight focused on creating clay message tiles for a mural.

Week nine focused on participants talking about their experiences as group members.

A mural was created from all the tiles. Two weeks following this meeting, a closed reception was held for group members to view the installed mural. Anderson (1995) discussed how the therapy group was evaluated and provided the reader with a few cautions: "Any therapist considering the use of clay in the treatment of incest survivors must be acutely aware of the evocative potential of ceramics and must be prepared to deal with emotions that are triggered" (p. 425).

Brooks's Eight-Session Group Therapy

A different medium was employed by Brooks (1995) in her work with abuse survivors. Using art therapy to raise levels of self-esteem, Brook contended that focusing on shame and anger was the foundation to creating self-esteem.

Eight sessions were included in her project. Drawings were done on white, 8"-by-11" paper. Crayons, chalk, or paint were offered as choices of expressions.

- In session one, each woman was asked: "(1) If you were a color, what color would you be? (2) If you were a shape, what shape would you be? (3) Create a grid with four sectors. Draw a line that represents: sadness, anger, happiness, fear" (Brooks, 1995, p. 455).

- In session two, each survivor was asked to make a self-portrait by pasting a mirror on paper and making a collage or drawing pictures around the mirror.

- Session three centered on the survivor drawing her family inside the house doing something.

- Session four was spent drawing dreams.

- Session five focused on having each survivor draw a monster.

- In session six, each survivor was asked to draw a wish.

- Instructions for session seven asked the clients to draw their favorite animals.

- Session eight was a free draw session, in which survivors could draw whatever they wanted.

ART AS A THERAPEUTIC MEDIUM

Art is an appropriate way to communicate when words are too terrifying. Young (1994) noted, "If psychological trauma is the originator of art, is it any wonder that the creative art therapies hold so much promise as a reparative force?" (p. 13). Several studies have discussed the benefits of art therapy for trauma survivors (Howard, 1990; Johnson, 1987; Kelly, 1984; Naitore, 1982; Peacock, 1991; Powell & Faherty, 1990; Serrano, 1989; Spring, 1985; Stember, 1980; Ticen, 1990; Waller, 1992; Yates & Pawley, 1987). Art provides a modicum of space between the survivor and her feelings and is a vehicle for validating those feelings, which can be freeing for the client.

Figure 9.1. Drawing of stick figures.

One survivor in our study revealed what had been helpful in her healing:

> *Expressing myself creatively has been really important. Drawing, painting, singing, drumming, and writing. Taking classes with creative teachers who are concerned with helping to bring out my voice, not with the finished product being important. We did a lot of improvisation, so it was really me coming out. And so much of my life I had this hand over my throat, preventing me from speaking. Not allowing me to express all the emotions inside of me. I constantly, need to reinforce myself just to speak out loud.*

Individuals who did not experience a soothing self-object in infancy or early childhood move into adulthood believing the world is an adversarial place (Kohut & Wolf, 1978). Art therapy can be a means for the survivor to learn to self-soothe. Personalities working conjointly may be able to draw the abuse they are unable to speak about.

There are many advantages to using art mediums in work with abused individuals. Frye and Gannon (1993) noted,

> Probably the most common use of art is to override the injunction given by abusers "not to tell." . . . Art is also a way to structure time. It is visible evidence of how time has been spent for the patient who loses time. . . . Art media offer freedom of choice, which is a much needed experience of appropriate power and mastery. Art provides a safe alternative to self harm or violence. It is an acceptable way to show the strong aggressive and regressive feelings so frequently disallowed in over-controlled children. . . . Patients can be told, "Don't do it—draw it." . . . Art can foreshadow upcoming therapeutic events. Creative expressions assist in the gentle erosion of denial. . . . Art can depict the whole picture long before the conscious mind can begin to grasp the facts. . . . Art products are a pictorial history showing a personal narrative. . . . Art media provide a visible vehicle for promoting integration of separate experience and function. (p. 12)

Just as art can be therapeutic, it is possible for art to be misused. Clients can avoid issues in therapy by producing significant numbers of drawings or paintings while continuing to resist integrating the traumatic materials.

Much of the artwork produced by clients who have been abused is graphic, violent, and sexual. Simonds (1994) discussed the indicators of trauma in clients' artwork. Her findings were based on Jacobson's (1985) review of the literature. These indicators are

Figure 9.2.   Somewhere a Child Is Crying, by survivor.

Omission of limbs and mouths related to helplessness and immobilization, missing lower torsos, immobilized bodies, small figures, large red mouths, overpowering tongues and excess of teeth, facial expressions that do not fit content depicted, sexual content in the form of trees and monsters, inappropriately sexualized figures. (pp. 64-65)

Therapists need to learn to temper their reactions to these pieces of artwork. They must be careful not to ask, "Which alter drew this piece?" It is more appropriate to ask, "Which part of you is responsible for this drawing?" The goal is to treat all alters in the same fashion and to foster the move toward integration of all parts of the personality. The first question does not seek to do this.

Therapists also should be careful in interpreting the drawings or paintings. Exploration should focus on the client's interpretations of what she has created. This is facilitated by asking, "who, what, when where, and how?" "Why?" is used only minimally.

The Values of Different Art Mediums

Paper and crayons provide an instant freedom for destructive urges. Drawing with pen and ink is a more systematic and regulated medium than crayons; pen and ink provide the user with more control. Using metals or wood conveys potency and structure. Painting enhances opportunities to mix and unfold new symbols. Clay provides the survivor with the opportunity to mold, shape, and create something new.

Frye (1993) suggesting asking the client to, "Show in clay, 'something you need' or 'a gift you would like to give yourself'" (p. 14). Themes for sculptures can be "forgiveness, safety, spirituality, organization, hope, or control" (p. 14). If sculptures are worked on in a group setting, the participants can focus on how these characteristics can be achieved. Another project suggested for group work is a collage with a theme of healing, recovery, potency, or empowerment. Working on a joint project facilitates a sense of belonging and cooperation, something many survivors have never experienced.

Frye (1993) also suggested discussing prototypes of integration from nature, which she called "integrative imagery." She listed some examples of this: "an orchestra, an ant or bee colony, a ball team, a weaving, a completed puzzle, or, as mentioned, a collage" (p. 14). All of these activities foster recovery and healing, thus enabling mastery over events and translating learned behaviors into a healthy life. Expressive modalities include drawing, painting, sculpting, collage-making, journaling, poetry, music, movement or dance, and storytelling.

BIBLIOTHERAPY, POETRY THERAPY, AND OCCUPATIONAL THERAPY

Because recalling abusive incidents can be overwhelming for the survivor, Heller (1993) suggested using poetry therapy in treating dissociative disorders. She defined the goal of this therapy as an attempt "to foster empowerment by providing a means of control, a way of making sense of the world, a way of reducing or tolerating ambiguity, a way to clarify information and feelings, and a means of improving self-concept. The most important goal of poetry therapy, however, is to stimulate creativity" (Heller, 1993, p. 11).

In her therapeutic poetry group for persons with DID, Heller read poetry to the group (for example, "The People, Yes" by Carl Sandburg and haiku by Basho). Group members were encouraged to engage in writing exercises. Heller used J. Ruth Gendler's *The Book of Qualities* (1984) to facilitate this process. Group members were asked to identify a feeling and then have the feeling become a person. Heller (1993) then asked participants a series of questions about the person—for example, how is the person dressed?—and participants wrote their responses on paper. She suggested the following references to use in this treatment format: *Writing Down the Bones,* by Natalie Goldberg; *Writing a Woman's Life,* by Carolyn Heilbrun (1988); and *Writing the Natural Way,* by Gabrielle Rico.

Another medium recommended for facilitating the healing process is occupational therapy. Frye (1993) reminded us that an individual's everyday activities are composed of three factors: "volition (belief in one's own ability to direct one's life), habituation (organizing routines), and performance skills" (p. 12). Frye suggested that the most important aspect of occupational therapy with clients who have experienced long-term trauma is to engage clients in activities that foster independent living skills.

JOURNALING

Writing can be done in almost any setting. It is portable and allows the writer to be as free or as controlling as she needs to be. Erasable boards provide a means to destroy "evidence of telling" if this is needed, and storytelling can help the client begin anew.

Kelly (1955) often asked his clients to write autobiographical accounts of themselves. Here is what he told his clients:

> I want you to write a character sketch of Harry Brown, just as if he were the principal character in a play. Write it as it might be written by a friend who knew him very intimately and very sympathetically, perhaps better than anyone ever really could know him. . . . Be sure to write it in the third person. For example, start out by saying, "Harry Brown is . . . " (p. 323)

Uematsu (1996) discussed how powerful writing can be in helping grievers give voice to their losses, noting how writing is different from talking or speaking:

> The act of writing gives one a chance to capture moments of insight, for the page holds those fleeting thoughts and feelings, does not allow them to escape. After the pen has been put down, one can refer to those words and listen to what occupies the mind. (pp. 19-20)

Uematsu (1996) described writing about loss as an act of despair. Thoughts and feelings that have been scattered find a resting place on the page. Because expressing these thoughts in black and white can create anxiety, the survivor needs to learn a new language to give her trauma a voice, even on paper. "Writing in the midst of disorientation can be an exhausting endeavor, but it can also be the very way to voice the confusion, to reorient the self" (p. 27).

BODY THERAPIES

Traumatic events often result in a survivor being unable to differentiate between bodily cues related to being vulnerable and those related to feeling safe. Just getting through the day may deplete the survivor's physical and emotional energies, especially if she is constantly anxious and struggling to ward off intrusive thoughts or the flooding of her emotions. Attempting to stay numb may facilitate the disconnection between the survivor and "the experience of living in his/her body. Dance/movement therapy, one of the expressive art therapies, allows the client to address these disconnections" (Sutherland, 1993, p. 21).

Oh little one I love you so,
there are so many things you
need to know
    Yet how do I reach you
so tattered and torn.
Wishing so many times you'd
never been born . . .
You were so little and so very young
so very helpless while they had
their fun.
You were not to blame,
yet you're burdened with such shame
after they played their sick demented
game.

    I think often of your poor tortured
soul,
Wondering if you'll ever again be
whole.
As you try so hard to hide all
your pain inside
trying so desperately to salvage
a little bit of pride.
I couldn't be there then, but I'm
here today,
And I hope and pray it will
be to stay.
Maybe with help from the
Father above,
We can salvage your soul with
lots of love.

Figure 9.3.   Journal entry from survivor.

How could this be?

An adult now losing control
was that really my own voice
saying all those mean things
threatening my teenagers
screaming and mean?

Where did it all go, they've
grown up so fast.
When they were little no one
warned me, "Enjoy them, it won't
last"

Now it's too late, they no
longer need me,
they need no one, want no
responsibilities, just to be free...

Oh the pain how long will
it last, will it always haunt
me, my horrible past?

Figure 9.3., continued.

Engaging in **movement therapy** enables the individual to reenact or rewrite an image from the past. Bernstein (1995) wrote this about dance therapy:

> Dance therapy emphasizes improving the survivor's relationship to her body. Through movement she is helped to recognize and change the way she uses, abuses or inhibits her body. In dance therapy the body becomes at once the vehicle for change and the focus of change so that the client can begin to reclaim her body as an ally in her struggle toward health. (p. 42)

In a group for incest survivors, Bernstein (1995) asked group members to do a pattern of movements as a way of reducing shaming: "I asked the women to explore 'stepping out in new ways' on different levels, using asymmetrical movement to the front, side, diagonal, and backward" (p. 95). After the group had practiced these new steps, she asked each member to "Describe how she might be stepping out in new ways in her life" (Bernstein, 1995, p. 45).

Following these exercises, Bernstein asked the participants to remember some of the body postures and movements that were representative of feelings they had assumed as children. These positions correlated to feelings of tension, isolation, being secretive, flaunting, holding, and so on. Bernstein then asked each woman to reenact an incident in which she felt shamed. She described how one group member rushed back and forth across the room to represent the chaos in her past and present life. Bernstein noted that "movement is a bridge to content-laden themes" (p. 46).

The second part of this meeting focused on music and dance. Group members were instructed to dance to Creole drums, with the movements representative of moving the shame out of their bodies. They also were asked to add vocalizations to the movements (Bernstein, 1995).

Body awareness is one of the underpinnings of the psychological self. One way body concept develops is from the recognition of both "internal and external kinesthetic sensations, somatic movements, mental representations, and maturation" (McFarland & Baker-Baumann, 1990, p. 83).

One of the ways the child learns to differentiate herself from her caregivers is by establishing her sense of self. A caregiver who has appropriate boundaries and an established sense of his or her own self is able to help the child in this respect. Unfortunately, some of the hallmarks of dysfunctional families are poorly formed boundaries of self; inappropriate, ineffective, or no communication between members; inflexible rules; unrealistic expectations of children; poor or nonexistent parenting skills; and a struggle with any type of transition or change.

Because of these boundary problems, parents often see their children as extensions of themselves; therefore, these children have no right to their own bodies, their own thoughts, or their own feelings. This, in turn, creates children who are not in touch with their own bodies.

McFarland and Baumann-Baker (1990) discussed the impact on these families of children moving into adolescence:

> The ability of mothers and fathers to respond to their sons' and daughters' bodily and emotional changes at adolescence is a chief contributor in the development of self shame and body shame. If mother and dad share joy in their child's emerging self, embrace the natural alterations arising in the parent-child relationship . . . then the child will experience herself as affirmed both physically and emotionally and will integrate a healthy self-image and body image. (p. 92)

Grounding Techniques and Kinesphere

Grounding techniques are related to movement because "focusing on gravity in relation to the body gradually builds tolerance for previously disowned sensations and helps reconnect disowned or fragmented parts of the body to the whole" (Sutherland, 1993, p. 23).

The grounding techniques of standing—pushing one's feet into the floor to make contact—helps the survivor to view parts of her body differently as she becomes more connected to herself. She can begin to reintegrate body parts that have been anesthetized.

Another way movement therapy can be helpful to a survivor is by helping her focusing on the "kinesphere" or personal space around her body. This helps the survivor begin to establish a relationship with herself in space.

Engaging in new movement behaviors is encouraged as a way of building confidence and self-esteem. The survivor learns where her boundaries end and someone else's begin. She becomes aware of the differing degrees of closeness or distance she needs to have with different persons.

Simonds (1994) suggested asking the survivor to create a picture of a stronger sense of self in the mind's eye, and then to draw it. The therapist should have the survivor assume a body position or a movement that depicts her present situation, then ask her to narrate how it feels. Next, the survivor should create, draw, or depict a body position or a movement that characterizes one of her goals in life or in therapy. Again, the therapist should ask her to describe her feelings while assuming this posture.

If the survivor is reluctant to engage in this process, the clinician should ask her to assume these postures while seated or just to use her hands to convey the positions (Simonds, 1994).

A survivor begins to understand safe touch by learning to touch herself in a self-soothing manner: for example, by brushing her hair; by rubbing body cream on her face, her feet, and her hands; or by gently rubbing her temples.

According to Sutherland (1993), survivors reap several benefits from movement therapy:

> [When they] synchronize their movements and breathing to the rhythm provided by the music, they often report a heightened sense of presence in the body, an awareness of mind/body energies being exerted toward a common goal, and when moving as a group, a sense of cohesion or group synchronicity or "being in tune with others." (p. 23)

Teaching a client rhythmic motions that move from slow to fast or vice versa helps her learn about pacing, moving from a time to rest to a time of activity.

Goodstone (1994) explained how memories can be retained in the body. When abuse is occurring, it is natural for victim to tense her muscles and breathe in a shallow manner, disconnecting from her body on both a feeling and a physical level. "This, coupled with constriction and tension, creates a defensive stature, or shell-like body armor. This armor effectively cuts off body sensation from the victim, and blocks appropriate affect, often leaving childhood trauma deeply embedded in the body" (Goodstone, 1994, p. 20).

When the body experiences habitual abuse, it learns to be withdrawn, aloof, and in a solitary state. As the body learns and is given freedom to relax, it becomes easier to connect with others. Body therapy and healing touch offer freedom because they communicate to the client that it is appropriate to put down her defenses and that any feeling experienced is legitimate.

Bernstein (1995) used a variety of other movements in her work with trauma survivors: "a seal dance from Tierra del Fuego (grunts and scratching included), a leaping butterfly dance from Japan, and a yelling, kicking-out dance from Nigeria" (p. 52). Dance therapy enables the survivor to "bridge her thoughts and feelings with action and to reclaim her body as her own. She becomes expressive, more creative and physically stronger in her own eyes as she develops feelings of control and power" (Bernstein, 1995, pp. 57-58).

According to Goodstone (1994), there are five classes of body therapy: traditional massage, contemporary Western massage, Oriental body work, energetic body massage, and structured/functional movement integration.

Traditional massage is also called Swedish massage, and uses five basic strokes:

> effleurage—long, slow, gentle, soothing strokes; pertissage—grasping, pressing and squeezing muscles and tissues; friction—pressing into one spot with deep often circular pressure; tapotement—quick little cupping and tapping movements on the skin; and vibration—oscillating, quick, fast movements. (Goodstone, 1994, p. 23)

Contemporary Western massage is designed to release pain. Neuromuscular technique and myofascial release are the two most popular forms of Western massage.

Neuromuscular technique involves the body therapist working with trigger points located throughout the body. **Myofacial release** involves skin, muscle, and underlying facial tissue. These are gently palpated by the body therapist. There are many variations of this technique, but the following is an example of one: "One hand [is placed] on the upper back and the other near the collar bone, through gentle physical coaching the tissue may release" (Goodstone, 1994, p. 21).

Oriental body therapy includes **acupuncture** and **accupressure**:

> [These are] based on the theory that the body consists of meridians (lines of energy) associated with the various organs (e.g., lungs, heart, liver, gall bladder) and the emotional ramifications of these organ functions. In this system lungs and large intestines are associated with grief, liver and gall bladder with anger, and bladder and kidneys with fear. (Goodstone, 1994, p. 24)

Energetic body therapies are composed of the disciplines of polarity therapy, therapeutic touch, and Reiki. The body therapist might hold his or her hands inches or more from the survivor's body or actually touch the survivor.

From these techniques the survivor's feelings are brought to her awareness and she can reconnect with herself in a positive manner.

Goodstone (1994) noted, "Effective body therapists are capable communicators who can convey to the client that it is safe to feel any feeling. They also convey that it is okay to 'say no' or refuse any kind of touch or intervention" (p. 25).

Structural/functional movement integration includes the Alexander technique and the Feldenkrais technique. With the **Alexander technique**, survivors are educated on identifying and then letting go of muscular tensions. Conversations between problematic body parts are encouraged as part of this method.

The Feldenkrais technique centers on the client using whole body movements as opposed to using only certain muscles to accomplish a task: for example, "using one's whole body to reach a high shelf, instead of just moving an arm" (Goodstone, 1994, p. 24).

According to Goodstone (1994) some of these techniques might be more attractive to certain individuals than others. Each survivor needs to find the body therapy she is most comfortable with. Yet each of these types has something to offer in terms of working with the body and helping to unlock trauma that has been stored on a nonverbal level.

ACCESSING THE FEELINGS

Clients often describe their feelings as bottled up. Dolan (1991) asked survivors to draw these bottles, label the feelings, and describe and draw ways for the bottled up feelings to get out. Words are simply not enough to give voice to the survivor's pain. Using other mediums is valuable in helping the client give expression and articulation to her thoughts and feelings. Collages, face masks, sculptures, photographs, quilting, and almost anything else can be used.

Dolan (1991) suggested using symbols to represent healing of the self. She told of a client who adopted an animal from her local humane shelter that had been abused. The woman lovingly cared for her new pet, and as she cared for the dog, she began to take better care of herself.

Listed below are activities that have evolved from my own work with a number of clients. It is not an exhaustive list.

- Read a favorite poem or quote.
- Listen to a favorite compact disc.
- Take a walk.
- Visualize a safe place in the mind's eye.
- Call a friend.
- Call a crisis hot line.
- Paint or draw the feeling.
- Journal.
- Squeeze clay.
- Wrap up in a favorite blanket.

The client will need help and support to master her new skills. Drawing, painting, music, dance, journaling, sculpting, running, or any healthy activity in which the survivor can achieve a sense of accomplishment is important for her healing.

Anger

Several nonverbal exercises have been developed to facilitate anger work. Simonds (1994) developed the following anger containment exercise. Once learned within the therapy room, this exercise can be used outside the session as well.

> First, the survivor determines where the anger is being experienced in her body. Next, she is asked to imagine every part of the anger relocating to her left foot. Encourage her to stomp her foot or move her ankle in circular motions to characterize that the anger is indeed in her foot. If she needs to experience the anger in a whole body sense, she can visualize the anger leaving her left foot and being transported to the original places in her body where she experienced it. She may need to practice this a number of times in the therapist's office. (adapted from p. 163)

Another technique suggested by Simonds (1994) is asking the survivor to describe anger as a color and then drawing the feeling using that color.

Some survivors have identified hitting pillows as a great release for anger. Simonds (1994) provided extensive guidelines for pillow-punching exercises (pp. 168-171).

Collage making can be used to help the survivor focus on her anger. The process of choosing the pictures for the collage and her feelings while choosing and then completing the collage are all important.

Tearing paper can be useful in anger work (Simonds, 1994). The therapist asks the survivor to draw the individual(s) with whom she is angry (or she can write his or her name on the paper). Then she tears the paper into little pieces. While tearing it, she should be invited to articulate any thoughts or feelings she is experiencing. After the paper is ripped, torn, or shredded, the survivor needs to decide what kind of closure would be helpful. It might be throwing the paper shreds away, burning them, or crumpling them up.

Burns (1980) suggested asking the client to use the two-column technique in dealing with her anger. This technique involves taking a sheet of paper and drawing a dividing line vertically down the middle, which creates two columns. At the top of one column the survivor writes, "Advantages of My Anger," and at the top of the other she writes, "Disadvantages of My Anger." The therapist then asks the client to generate some ideas and place them in the appropriate column.

Silverman (1991) recommended that the therapist draw a circle on paper for the client who is feeling out of control. Images, designs, and so forth can then be drawn by the client as they relate to her present mood or state of mind. Colors can be chosen to represent feelings.

Drawing symbols or choosing pictures and then pasting them on poster board to create a collage can also be helpful. Pictures are chosen that reflect the angry feelings (Bussard & Kleinman, 1991).

Another suggestion is to give clients a stiff or heavy piece of paper and ask them "to use felt markers to color the whole piece of paper, then cover the entire surface with a dark-colored oil pastel or crayon. Each patient [is] then given a toothpick and instructed to use the toothpick to scratch the surface and create a design which expresses [her] feelings about . . ." (Bussard & Kleinman, 1991, p. 311).

Cohen, Barnes, and Rankin (1995) suggested the following exercise (which is also appropriate for anger work) to help survivors contain thoughts, feelings, and behaviors: First, ask the survivor to identify the thought, feeling, or behavior she wants to contain. Next, have her determine what type of container would be most effective in holding the cognition or the affect. The authors provided these examples: a chained trunk under the sea, a locked room at the end of a long hall, a video cassette in a remote room, and a filing cabinet locked in a vault (p. 11). Finally, provide guideline for how to write about the container.

Another exercise for dealing with anger involves asking the survivor to find a picture in a magazine that helps her complete the statement, "My anger is like a _____ " (Cohen et al., 1995, p. 59). Survivors are encouraged to select pictures representative of something in nature or constructed by human hands rather than a person or an animal. After choosing the picture, the survivor is asked to cut out the picture of her choice and then answer the following questions:

- Describe its texture, weight, size, and temperature.
- What would it feel like to hold this in your hands?
- What sound (if any) does it make?
- What sound would you like it to make?
- What should it say if it could speak?
- Describe the environment in which it could be found.
- Does it move, or is it stationary?
- If it moved, how would you describe its rhythm, speed, and style (p. 59)?

After answering these questions, the client is asked to identify more pictures from magazines that could be "helpful" with the anger picture. All of these pictures are arranged and glued to the paper or poster board. Upon completion, the client is asked eight questions about the art-making experience. She then writes out her responses (Cohen et al., 1995, p. 60).

Containment for Feelings

It is not uncommon for survivors to begin therapy feeling nothing. Then, as therapy progresses, they begin to feel overwhelmed by feelings, as if their emotional floodgates are opening. When this happens, the client can be asked to identify a metaphor for putting her feelings into storage until she feels ready to deal with them. Simonds (1994) listed several suggestions for this storage place: a locked box to which only the survivor has the key; an envelope that is sealed and placed into a purse or desk drawer; or a change purse that is snapped shut. The client might even buy a box with a lock and decorate it. If this is the case, she needs to decide where to keep the box, in sight or out of sight.

Abuse survivors with whom I have worked have carried small sketch pads in their purses. When they began to feel anxious, they drew their feelings inside a circle or in bottles or other containers with stoppers or lids. One client purchased a small pocket diary with a lock and drew her feelings when she became overwhelmed. When she finished drawing, she simply closed the book and locked it up.

Figure 9.4.   Identity, by Jill. In this drawing, I used the butterfly to represent the metamorphosis in the individual from victim to survivor. The circles on the body represent that some healing has occurred.

If containment strategies are not effective, the survivor may need a different constructive outlet to vent her energy, such as walking, playing tennis, or anything else that provides a sense of release.

There are many different ways to help survivors give both voice and form to their experiences. Landgarten (1981) said about the meaning of artwork, "[It is] a symbol of the patient's self-recorded treatment process" (p. 176).

One survivor stated,

> Be really, really gentle. Believe us. I've spent my life not being listened to. Take cues from where we are at, what we are dealing with, and what we can deal with at any one time. Don't push or jump ahead. Validate our stories. Validate our feelings. It's so terrifying a process to go through. ABSOLUTELY TERRIFYING!

She continued,

> Expressing myself creatively has been really important. Drawing, painting, singing, drumming, and writing. Taking classes with creative teachers who are concerned with helping to bring out my voice, not with the finished product. The singing classes have been especially important. So much of my life I had this hand over my throat, preventing me from speaking, not allowing me to express all the emotions inside of me. I constantly need to reinforce myself just to speak out loud.

REFERENCES

Alexander, P. C., & Follette, V. M. (1987). Personal constructs in the group treatment of incest. In R. A. Neimeyer & G. J. Neimeyer (Eds.), *Personal construct therapy casebook* (pp. 211-229). New York: Springer.

Alexander, P. C., Neimeyer, R. A., & Follette, V. M. (1991). Group therapy for women sexually abused as children: A controlled study and investigation of individual differences. *Journal of Interpersonal Violence, 6,* 219-231.

Anderson, F. E. (1991). Catharsis and empowerment through group claywork with incest survivors. *Arts in Psychotherapy, 22*(5), 413-427.

Basho, M. (1977). Haiku. In A. Atwood (Ed.), *Haiku-vision.* New York: Scribner.

Bernstein, B. (1995). Dancing beyond trauma: Women survivors of sexual abuse. In F. J. Levy (Ed.), *Dance and other expressive art therapies: When words are not enough.* New York: Routledge.

Brende, J. (1994). A twelve-theme psychoeducational program for victims and survivors. In M. B. Williams & J. F. Sommers, Jr. (Eds.), *Handbook for post-traumatic stress disorders* (pp. 421-433). Greenwood, CT: JAI Press.

Briere, J. (1989). *Therapy for adults molested as children: Beyond survival.* New York: Springer.

Brooks, S. L. (1995). Art therapy: An approach to working with sexual abuse survivors. *The Arts in Psychotherapy, 22*(5), 447-466.

Burns, D. (1980). *Feeling good.* New York: Signet.

Bussard, A., & Kleinman, S. (1991). Art psychotherapy: An approach to borderline adults. In H. Landgarten & D. Lubbers (Eds.), *Adult art psychotherapy* (pp. 83-110). New York: Brunner/Mazel.

Carozza, P., Heirsteiner, C., & Young, J. (1983). Young female incest survivors in treatment: Stages of growth seen with a group art therapy model. *Clinical Social Work Journal, 10*(3), 165-175.

Cohen, B., & Cox, C. T. (1995). *Telling without talking.* New York: Norton.

Courtois, C. (1988). *Healing the incest wound.* New York: Norton.

Dolan, Y. (1991). *Resolving sexual abuse.* New York: Norton.

Ellingson, M. (1991). A philosophy for clinical art therapy. In H. Landgarten & D. Lubbers (Eds.), *Adult art psychotherapy* (pp. 3-20). New York: Brunner/Mazel.

Frankl, V. (1984). *Man's search for meaning.* New York: Bantam.

Frye, B. (1993). Occupational therapy and trauma recovery. *Treating Abuse Today, 3*(3), 12-15.

Frye, B., & Gannon, L. (1993). The use, misuse, and abuse of art with dissociative/multiple personality disorder patients. *Dissociation, 6*(2/3), 188-192.

Galbraith, N. (1978). A foster child's expression of ambivalence. *American Journal of Art Therapy, 17,* 39-49.

Gendler, J. R. (1984). *The book of qualities.* Berkeley, CA: Turquoise Mountain Press.

Goldberg, N. (1986). *Writing down the bones.* Boston: Shambala.

Goodstone, E. (1994). Body therapy: A survey of methods used in the adjunctive treatment of survivors of physical and sexual abuse. *Treating Abuse Today, 4*(3), 20-26.

Harter, S. L., & Neimeyer, R. A. (1995). Long-term effects of child sexual abuse: Toward a constructivist theory of trauma and its treatment. In R. A. Neimeyer & R. J. Neimeyer (Eds.), *Advances in personal construct psychology* (Vol. 3, pp. 229-269). Greenwich, CT: JAI Press.

Heilbrun, C. (1988). *Writing a woman's life.* New York: Ballantine.

Heller, P. O. (1993). Biblio/poetry therapy in the treatment of multiple personality disorder. *Treating Abuse Today, 3*(4), 10-15.

Howard, M., & Jakab, I. (1969). Case studies of molested children and their art productions. *Psychiatry and Art, 2,* 72-79.

Howard, R. (1990). Art therapy as an isomorphic intervention in the treatment of a client with Posttraumatic Stress Disorder. *American Journal of Art Therapy, 28,* 79-86.

Jacobson, M. L. (1985). Manifestations of abuse in the artwork of an inpatient diagnosed with multiple personality disorder. In B. G. Braun (Ed.), Dissociative disorders: Proceedings of the Second International Conference on Multiple Personality and Dissociative Disorders. Chicago: Rush Presbyterian-St. Luke's Medical Center.

Johnson, D. (1987). The role of the creative arts specialist in the diagnoses and treatment of psychological trauma. *The Arts in Psychotherapy, 14,* 7-13.

Kelly, G. A. (1955). *The psychology of personal constructs.* New York: Norton.

Kelly, S. (1984). The uses of art therapy with sexually abused children. *Journal of Psychosocial Nursing, 22,* 12-18.

Kohut, H., & Wolf, E. G. (1978). The disorders of the self and their treatment: An outline. *International Journal of Psychoanalysis, 59,* 413-425.

Landfield, A. W. (1979). Exploring socialization through the interpersonal transaction group. In P. Stringer & D. Banister (Eds.), *Constructs of sociality and individuality* (pp. 133-151). London: Academic.

Landgarten, H. (1981). *Clinical art therapy.* New York: Brunner/Mazel.

Landgarten , H. B., & Lubbers, D. (1991). *Adult art psychotherapy.* New York: Brunner/Mazel

Lemmon, K. (1984). Hyoanalytic art therapy with victims of rape and incest. *Medical Hypoanalysis, 5*(3), 104-108.

Lubbers, D. (1991). Treatment of women with eating disorders. In H. Landgarten & D. Lubbers (Eds.), *Adult art psychotherapy* (pp. 49-82). New York: Brunner/Mazel.

McFarland, B., & Baker-Baumann, T. B. (1990). *Shame and body image.* Deerfield Beach, FL: Health Communications.

Naitore, C. (1982). Art therapy with sexually abused children. In S. Sgroi (Ed.), *Handbook of clinical intervention in child sexual abuse* (pp. 269-309). Lexington, MA: Lexington Books.

Neimeyer, R. A. (1988). Clinical guidelines for conducting Interpersonal Transition Groups. *International Journal of Personal Construct Psychology, 1,* 181-190.

Neimeyer, R. A., Harter, S. L., & Alexander, P. C. (1991). Group perceptions as predictors of outcome in the treatment of incest survivors. *Psychotherapy Research, 1,* 148-158.

Peacock, M. (1991). A personal construct approach to art therapy in the treatment of post-sexual abuse trauma. *American Journal of Art Therapy, 29,* 100-108.

Powell, L., & Faherty, S. (1990). Treating sexually abused latency girls: A 20 session treatment plan utilizing group process and the creative art therapies. *The Arts in Psychotherapy, 17,* 35-47.

Rico, G. (1983). *Writing the natural way.* Los Angeles: J. P. Tarcher.

Sandburg, C. (1970). *Complete poems.* New York: Harcourt Brace Jovanovich.

Serrano, J. (1989). The arts in therapy with survivors of incest. In H. Wadeson, J. Durkin, & D. Perach (Eds.), *Advances in art therapy* (pp. 114-125). New York: Wiley.

Silverman, D. (1991). Art psychotherapy: An approach to borderline adults. In H. Landgarten & D. Lubbers (Eds.), *Adult art psychotherapy* (pp. 83-110). New York: Brunner/Mazel.

Simonds, S. (1994). *Bridging the silence.* New York: Norton.

Spring, D. (1985). Symbolic language of sexually abused, chemically dependent women. *American Journal of Art Therapy, 24,* 13-21.

Stember, C. (1980). Art therapy: A new use in the diagnosis and treatment of sexually abused children. *Sexual abuse of children: Selected readings* (pp. 59-63). Washington, DC: Government Printing Office.

Sutherland, S. (1993). Movement therapy: Healing mind and body. *Treating Abuse Today, 3,* 21-24.

Ticen, S. (1990). Feed me . . . cleanse me . . . sexual trauma projected in the art of bulimics. *Art Therapy 7,* 11, 17-21.

Uematsu, M. A. (1996). Giving voice to the account: The healing power of writing about loss. *Journal of Personal and Interpersonal Loss, 1,* 17-28.

Waller, C. (1992). Art therapy with adult female incest survivors. *Art Therapy, 9*(3), 135-138.

Yalom, I. D. (1995). *The theory and practice of group psychotherapy* (4th ed.). New York: Basic Books.

Yamamoto-Nading, D., & Stringer, G. M. (1991). *A healing celebration.* Renton, WA: King County Sexual Assault Center.

Yates, M., & Pawley, K. (1987). Utilizing imagery and the unconscious to explore and resolve trauma of sexual abuse. *Art Therapy, 4*(1), 36-41.

Young, W. (1994). EMDR in the treatment of the phobic symptoms in multiple personality disorder. *Dissociation, 7*(2), 129-133.

RELEASE OF INFORMATION FORM

Juliann Mitchell, Ph.D.
37 McMurray Road, Suite 106
Pittsburgh, PA 15241

Release of Information

I, _____(use real name, pseudonym, or anonymous), give Dr. Juliann Mitchell permission to use the information I provide in the questionnaire entitled "Adult Female Survivors of Female Perpetrators." I give my permission with the knowledge that my name will not be used in anything that is published, unless I specifically want my name to be used. I am aware that the information that I provide in filling out the questionnaire could be used to produce research articles, books, films, videos, audio cassettes, etc. No identifying information will be provided in anything that is published, unless I give my written consent for my name to be used.

The information in this questionnaire is being collected for a book to be published that addresses the issue of female perpetrators, a group of abusers that has been grossly underreported in the research literature and professional books. It is my desire to bring this information to the public and to professionals, and to help the courageous women who are adult survivors know that some of their suffering will be brought to light , that they are not crazy, and that, yes, females do abuse other females. It is time for the "secret" of female perpetrators to be told to the world.

Understand that after reading the questionnaire or the release of information form, you are under no obligation to complete any of these materials or participate in this study. If, after reading these materials, you do not wish to participate, please throw all materials away.

If you are interested in participating in a more in-depth interview regarding your childhood, please indicate by checking the appropriate box below.

___ Yes, I am interested in participating in a more in-depth interview.

___ No, I do not want to participate in a more in-depth interview.

Telephone number where you can be contacted: (   ) _____

Checking the "Yes, I am interested " section does not ensure that you will be contacted for an interview; nor does it mean that, if you agree at this time to be interviewed and are contacted at a later time, you are under any obligation to participate in a more in-depth interview. You have the right to change your mind.

These data are being collected with the idea that a book will be published that specifically addresses the issues of female perpetrators of child sexual abuses. If you are interested in having a drawing or a poem published in the book, please indicate by checking the appropriate box.

___ Yes, I am interested in having one drawing or one poem published in the yet to be published book on female perpetrators of childhood sexual abuses. I understand that I will not receive any monetary compensation should a drawing or poem of mine be used in the book. I understand that I can use my real name, a pseudonym, or remain anonymous in anything that is published. (You do not have to use your real name to submit a drawing or a poem.) If a poem or drawing of yours is used, you will receive a complimentary copy of the book when it is published.

If, after reading the above, you are interested in sending a poem or a drawing, please sign your name, pseudonym, or anonymous on the line below, with the understanding that sending a poem or a drawing does not guarantee that it will be published in the book.

I, _____, give my permis-
sion for a poem or drawing of mine to be used in a forthcoming book about
female perpetrators of childhood sexual abuses. (Please send drawing or poem
in return envelope with questionnaire.) If you are unable to do this, you can
send the poem or drawing at a later time to the following address: Juliann
Mitchell, Ph.D., 37 McMurray Road, Suite 106, Pittsburgh, PA 15241. If you
wish to have your drawing or poem returned, please enclose a self-addressed
stamped envelope so that the work maybe returned after it is copied.

Thank you.

Juliann   Date: _____Your Signature: _____

Appendix **B**

QUESTIONNAIRE

Juliann Mitchell, Ph.D.
37 McMurray Road, Suite 106
Pittsburgh, PA 15241
(412) 831-0891

Thank-you very much for your willingness to read the questionnaire. If, at any point in time, answering the questions is too painful, or if you are beginning to have flashbacks, stop immediately. You may want to discuss the questionnaire with your therapist before completing it or share your answers with your therapist. If you do not complete the questionnaire, it is okay. Please answer all of the questions if you can. Your responses are completely confidential. Please feel free to write on the backs of the pages.

Demographic Information

1. State(s) where abuse occurred: _____

2. When the abuse occurred, did you live in a community that was:

   ___ rural ___ suburban ___ urban

3. Social class growing up:

   ___ upper class ___ upper-middle class ___ middle class ___ working class
   ___ lower class

4. Current age: _____

5. Occupation: _____

6. Sex: _____

7. Religious preference: _____

8. Nationality:_____

9. Sexual preference: _____

Sexual Abuse History

10. Were you sexually abused as a child by a female?

    ____ yes ____ no

11. If yes, at what age did the abuse begin? _____

12. How did the abuse start? _____

    _____

    _____

13. At what age did the abuse stop? _____

14. At what age did you first remember being abused? _____

15. Did more than one person abuse you?

    ____ yes ____ no

16. If yes, how many persons? _____

17. Who were you abused by? (Check all that apply.)

    ____ mother
    ____ sister
    ____ grandmother
    ____ aunt
    ____ female cousin at least three years older than you

___ stepmother
___ stepsister
___ female minister
___ scout/campfire leader
___ female neighbor
___ baby-sitter
___ female teacher
___ female family friend
___ other (list all who apply) _____

18. Did the abuse occur more than one time?

    ___ yes ___ no

19. If more than once, how many times _____ or how many months _____
    or how many years _____?

20. How frequently did the abuse occur?

    ___ every day
    ___ every week
    ___ two to three times a week
    ___ more than three times a week
    ___ every two weeks
    ___ every three weeks
    ___ every month (not an established pattern)
    ___ other (please specify frequency)

21. In what manner were you abused? _____

    _____

    _____

22. Did you tell someone about the abuse when you were a child?

    ___ yes ___ no

23. List all persons you told about the sexual abuse: _____

    _____

24. Were you believed?

    ___ yes ___ no

25. If you were believed, did anyone intervene?

    ___ yes ___ no

26. If yes, what happened? _____

    _____

    _____

27. Was the abuse ever reported to children and youth services or some type of child protection agency?

    ___ yes ___ no

28. Was the abuse ever reported to the police?

    ___ yes ___ no

29. If yes, please describe what happened. _____

    _____

    _____

30. If you didn't tell, what prevented you from telling? (Check all that apply.)

    ___ threatened by the abuser
    ___ made to believe it was all your fault
    ___ bribed with money, toys, gifts, by the abuser
    ___ other (please specify) _____

31. How did you deal with being sexually abused at the time it was occurring? _____

    _____

    _____

32. As an adult, who have you told about the abuse? _____

    _____

    _____

    _____

33. What was each person's reaction? _____

_____

_____

34. Describe yourself (as a child) after the sexual abuse was terminated. What were you like socially? _____

_____

Emotionally? _____

_____

Physically? _____

_____

How was your self-esteem? _____

_____

What was your relationship like with males (as a child) after the abuse stopped? _____

_____

What was your relationship like with females (as a child) after the abuse stopped? _____

_____

Long-Term Effects of Sexual Abuse

35. What effect has the abuse you experienced as a child had on you as an adult? Socially? _____

_____

Emotionally? _____

_____

Physically? _____

_____

Sexually? _____

_____

Your relationship with your family? _____

_____

How you feel about yourself? _____

_____

How you relate to men? _____

_____

How you relate to women? _____

_____

36. What are your present feelings about what happened to you as a child?

_____

_____

Family History

37. Describe your mother when you were growing up. _____

_____

38. Describe your father when you were growing up. _____

_____

39. Describe your parents' relationship when you were growing up. _____

_____

_____

40. What was your mother's occupation? _____

41. What was your father's occupation? _____

42. Tell me about your maternal grandparents. _____

_____

43. Tell me about your paternal grandparents. _____

_____

44. What was your role in your family when you were growing up (e.g. clown, caretaker, lost child)? _____

_____

45. What is your current relationship like with your mother? _____

_____

46. With your father? _____

_____

47. With other siblings? _____

_____

48. Did anyone in your family know about the sexual abuse? If so, who? (Please list all who apply.) _____

_____

49. What was their response when they found out? (Please list each family member's response individually.) _____

_____

50. Was anyone in your family addicted to any of the following? (Check all that apply, and circle the family member that applies.)

____ alcohol   mother or father
____ prescription drugs   mother or father
____ illegal drugs (e.g., cocaine, heroin)   mother or father

___ gambling   mother or father
___ pornography   mother or father
___ had an eating disorder (anorexia, bulimia, compulsive overeater)
    mother or father

51. Where were you in your family constellation?

    ___ first born ___ second born ___ third born ___ fourth born

    ___ fifth born ___ sixth born

52. How many brothers did you have? _____

53. How many sisters did you have? _____

54. Were any of your siblings sexually abused by the same person or persons who abused you?

    ___ yes ___ no

The Healing Process

55. What would you say has been helpful to you in your healing process? Please be as specific and in-depth as possible. _____

    _____

    _____

    _____

    _____

56. What has been least helpful in your healing process? _____

    _____

    _____

    _____

57. Check any of the following that has been healing for you as an adult survivor.

___ group therapy with other survivors
___ individual therapy
___ 12-step recovery program
___ church/synagogue, place of worship
___ other (please specify) _____

58. What do you think would be helpful for persons in the mental health field to know about working with survivors? _____

_____

_____

_____

59. What could have occurred that might have prevented the sexual abuse from taking place? _____

_____

_____

_____

60. Comments/suggestions. (Please feel free to add anything you think is relevant.) _____

_____

_____

_____

_____

_____

SUMMARY OF DATA

N = 80

(*Note:* In instances where percentages exceed 100, some participants checked more than one answer; in instances where percentages fall below 100, some participants opted not to answer at all.)

Location Where the Abuse Occurred (%)

United States of America.

Arkansas (1)
California (16)
Colorado (1)
Connecticut (3)
Delaware (1)
Florida (6)
Georgia (4)
Illinois (9)
Indiana (3)
Iowa (1)
Kentucky (4)
Maryland (3)
Massachusetts (6)
Michigan (8)
Minnesota (3)
Missouri (4)
Nebraska (1)
Nevada (1)
New Jersey (4)
New Mexico (1)
New York (20)
North Carolina (3)
Ohio (9)
Oklahoma (1)
Oregon (1)
Pennsylvania (9)
South Carolina (1)
Tennessee (4)
Texas (4)
Vermont (3)
Virginia (3)

271

Washington (3)
West Virginia (1)
Wisconsin (5)
Wyoming (1)
Washington, D.C. (1)

————

149%

Other Areas.

Canada (1)
Germany (1)
Guam (1)
Israel (3)
Nova Scotia (1)
Puerto Rico (3)

————

10%

Type of Community.

Suburban (54)
Urban (34)
Rural (30)

————

118%

The Survivors (%)

Family's Social Class During the Abuse.

Upper (1)
Upper-Middle (24)
Middle (36)
Working (38)
Lower (6)
did not answer (3)

————

108%

Age When Completed Questionnaire.

18 - 29 years old (18)
30 - 39 years old (38)
40 - 49 years old (35)
50 - 59 years old (9)
60 - 69 years old (1)

————

101%

Religious Preference.

Protestant (35)
None (18)
Catholic (15)
Jewish (8)
Goddess/Earth Worship (5)
Spiritual (5)
Christian (4)
Atheist (3)
Native American Beliefs (3)
Agnostic (1)
God as a "higher power" (1)
Jehovah's Witness (1)
Mormon (1)
Myself (1)
Nonorganized religion (1)
Religion lost power (1)
Unitarian (1)

————

104%

Nationality.

Caucasian (90)
Native American (5)
Latina (4)
African American (1)
Dutch (1)
Israeli (1)
Jewish (1)
Polish (1)

————

104%

Sexual Preference.

Heterosexual (51)
Heterosexual, but not certain (4)
Heterosexual, with bisexual
  tendencies (4)
Homosexual (18)
Bisexual (11)
Varies with alters (3)
Unknown (2)
Nonsexual (2)
Omnisexual (1)
Did not answer (4)
_____
100%

Parents' Addictions.

Alcohol:
mothers (26); fathers (50)
Prescription Drugs:
mothers (21); fathers (3)
Illegal Drugs:
mothers (5); fathers (5)
Gambling:
mothers (4); fathers (6)
Pornography:
mothers (6); fathers (18)
Eating Disorders:
mothers (13)
Anorexia: mothers (4)
Bulimia: mothers (4)
Compulsive Overeater:
mothers (33); fathers (10)

Sexual Abuse History (%)

Age Abuse Began.

0 - 2 years (56)
3 - 5 years (21)

6 - 8 years (10)
9 - 11 years (1)
12 - 14 years (4)
15 - 17 years (3)
18 - 20 years (1)
unknown (4)
_____
100%

Age Abuse Ended.

0 - 2 years (1)
3 - 5 years (1)
6 - 8 years (8)
9 - 11 years (10)
12 - 14 years (15)
15 - 17 years (14)
18 - 20 years (14)
21 and up (14)
teens (1)
unknown (20)
_____
98%

Age Abuse Was Remembered.

0 - 5 years (18)
6 - 10 years (6)
11 - 15 years (3)
16 - 20 years (1)
21 - 25 years (13)
26 - 30 years (14)
31 - 35 years (15)
36 - 40 years (9)
41 - 45 years (9)
46 - 50 years (5)
51 - 55 years (1)
56 - 60 years (1)
unknown (8)
_____
103%

Perpetrators.

Mother (84)
Grandmother(s) (25)
Family friend (23)
Aunt (20)
Baby-sitter (14)
Neighbor (10)
Cousin (9)
Nurse/therapist (9)
Cult members (6)
Sister (6)
Step-mother (4)
Step-sister (4)
Teacher (4)
Scout leader (3)
Employee of family business(1)
Foster mother (1)
Minister (1)
Nun (1)
Optometrist (1)
Sunday School teacher (1)
Youth director (1)

Multiple Perpetrators.

Yes (84)
No (16)

_____

100%

Number of Years Abuse Occurred.

1 or 2 (4)
3 or 4 (8)
5 or 6 (9)
7 or 8 (11)
9 or 10 (8)
11 or 12 (4)
13 or 14 (4)
15 or 16 (3)

17 or 18 (13)
19 or 20 (3)
21 or 22 (4)
23 or 24 (1)
25 or 26 (0)
27 or 28 (4)
28 or 30 (3)

_____

79%

Frequency of Abuse.

Every day (20)
Weekly (15)
Two or more times per week (30)
Every month (16)
Ongoing (4)
A few times per year (4)
Not very often (5)
Only once (3)

_____

97%

Did Survivor Tell Anyone About the Abuse When It Was Occurring?

Yes (24)
No (70)

_____

94%

Was She Believed?

Yes (21)
No (79)

_____

100%

Who Survivor Told (as a Child).

Mother (10)
Father (6)

Child protection agency (4)
Doctor (4)
Teacher (4)
Aunt (3)
Priest (3)
Therapist (3)
Friend (1)
Friend's mother (1)
Mother's therapist (1)
Nun (1)
Nurse (1)
Sister (1)
Stranger (1)

44%

Manner in Which the Abuse Occurred.

Digital penetration (44)
Touching/fondling (40)
Object inserted in vagina (39)
Oral sex (38)
Object inserted in anus (24)
Forced to touch others (23)
Tied/held down (20)
Cult/witchcraft (18)
Enemas (17)
Beaten (16)
Kissing (10)
Burned (9)
Locked in places (9)
Bestiality (8)
Cut (5)
Inappropriate conversation (5)
Pornography (5)
At-home abortions (3)
Drugged (3)
Hung upside down (3)
Over-involvement in sexual development (3)
Urinated/defecated on (3)

Douching (1)
Masturbation in front of (1)

Of Those Who Believed, Did Anyone Intervene?

Yes (100)
No (0)

100%

Things That Prevented the Survivor from Telling.

Believed it was her fault (64)
Threaten by the abuser (59)
Bribed (23)
Did not realize anything was wrong (18)
Fear (18)
Told it was a dream/made up (4)
Watched people/animals die (4)
Shame (3)
Thought family would be ruined (3)
Too young to talk (3)
Beaten (1)
Became withdrawn/silent (1)
Destruction of personal property (1)
Dissociation (1)
Felt it would not make a difference (1)
Loved and needed mother (1)
Mind control (1)
Never thought to tell (1)
Threatened to abuse sibling if survivor disclosed abuse (1)
Told she was retarded (1)

Was the Abuse Reported to Child and Youth Services?

Yes (9)
No (80)

89%

Was the Abuse Reported to the Police?

Yes (8)
No (80)

―――――

88%

Ways Survivors Dealt with Abuse While It Was Occurring.

Dissociation (66)
DID (35)
Repression (14)
Did what she was told (15)
Denial (6)
Became loose (3)
Became tense (3)
Drugs/alcohol (3)
Fantasized (3)
Ran away (3)
Angry outbursts (1)
Ego states (1)
Listened to music (1)
Never dealt with it (1)
Stopped talking (1)
Took the blame (1)
Waited for it to end (1)
With total dread (1)

Adult Disclosures and Reactions (%)

Who the Survivors Have Told About the Abuse.

Therapist (83)
Friend (58)
Group members (38)
Spouse (36)
Sister (28)
Children (20)
Mother (19)

Brother (15)
Father (11)
Lover/partner (9)
Aunt (8)
Cousin (8)
Coworkers (6)
Everyone (6)
Minister/priest (5)
Public speeches/writing (5)
Family (4)
Strangers (3)
Teacher/professor (3)
Acquaintances (1)
Daughter's therapist (1)
Dentist (1)
Doctor (1)
Editor of *S.O.F.I.E.* (1)
Foster family (1)
In-laws (1)
Lawyer (1)
Mother-in-law (1)
Newspaper columnist (1)
Police (1)
Roommate (1)
Soulmate (1)
Step-father (1)
Uncle (1)

Reactions.

Support (63)
Denial (50)
Belief (43)
Do not want to know/talk about it (24)
Shock (23)
Anger at abuser (15)
Sympathy (15)
Did not respond (11)
Anger at survivor (9)
Did not support (6)
Told survivor to forget it/get on with her life (6)

Acceptance (5)
Encouraged survivor to talk (5)
Felt it was not as bad as described (5)
Comfort (4)
Concern (4)
Curiosity (4)
Empathy (4)
Understanding (3)
Called the survivor crazy (1)
Confusion (1)
Disgust (1)
Embarrassed (1)
Felt threatened (1)
Filed for divorce (1)
Made excuses for abuser (1)

Boundary problems (1)
Caretaker (1)
Clung to people (1)
Clown (1)
Did not like attention (1)
Everyone hated survivor (1)
Felt different (1)
Fought (1)
Jealous (1)
Overly friendly with strangers (1)
Needed to belong (1)
Never connected (1)
Very religious (1)

Effect of the Abuse on the Survivor as a Child (%)

Socially.

Withdrawn/shy/introverted (60)
Unpopular/few friends (25)
Drank/used drugs (8)
Fearful (6)
Tried to be perfect (6)
Did not function well (5)
Insecure (5)
Promiscuous (5)
Became extroverted (4)
Did not trust anyone (4)
Many friends (4)
Angry (3)
Became active (3)
Busy/joined groups (3)
Fearful of adults (3)
Inadequate (3)
Initiated sex play with boys (3)
Overachiever (3)
People pleaser (3)
Rebellious (3)

Emotionally.

Withdrawn/numb/shut down (45)
Afraid (25)
Depressed (20)
Suicidal (11)
Needy (10)
Fragile (9)
Angry (8)
Cried often (6)
Did not trust (6)
Ashamed (5)
Immature (5)
Insecure (5)
Confused (5)
Unstable (5)
Tried too hard (4)
Imitated others (3)
Anxious (1)
Happy (1)
Jealous (1)
Never envisioned a future (1)
Proud (1)
Schizophrenic (1)
Trusting (1)
Did not know how to cry (1)

Physically.

Overweight (24)
Underweight (14)
Healthy (11)
Eating disorders (10)
Headaches (10)
Stomach problems (6)
Active (5)
Afraid of team sports (5)
Did not sleep well (5)
Always sick (4)
Accident prone (4)
Cramps (4)
Did not want to be touched (4)
Excellent shape (4)
Good at individual sports (4)
Hypertension (4)
Self-injury (4)
Tall (4)
Constipation (3)
Could not eat (3)
Diarrhea (3)
Hospitalized (3)
Not very active (3)
Scars (3)
Tired (3)
Allergies (1)
Asthma (1)
Awkward (1)
Bad back (1)
Bladder infections (1)
Bruises (1)
Diabetes (1)
Did not feel pain (1)
Felt overweight (1)
Handicapped (1)
Hated to expose body (1)
Heart problems (1)
Heavy menstrual periods (1)
Learned karate (1)
Many problems (1)

Obsessed with urination (1)
Paralyzed (1)
Seizures (1)
Severe nosebleeds (1)
Small (1)
Vomited often (1)
Weight fluctuated (1)
Wished to be neither sex (1)
Wished to not have a body (1)
Wore baggy clothes (1)
Wore glasses (1)
Yeast infections (1)

Self-Esteem.

Low (39)
Zero/nonexistent (36)
Hated herself (6)
Knew peers thought she was weird (5)
Was good (5)
Based on people liking her (3)
Considered herself bad (3)
Considered herself different (3)
False (3)
Fluctuated (3)
Insecure (3)
Knew she was intelligent (3)
Tried to please others (3)
Avoided thinking about herself (1)
Based on material items (1)
Thought she was desirable (1)
Thought she was retarded (1)

Relationships with Males.

Scared (23)
Promiscuous (21)
Males abused also (16)
Avoided (9)
Did not trust (9)
Nonexistent (8)
Playmates (8)

Pleased males (8)
Poor friendships (8)
Relate better with males (6)
Afraid of sex (5)
Leery of male strangers (5)
Friend/not someone to date (5)
Compliant (4)
Easily used (4)
Quiet/shy around (4)
Wanted a boyfriend (4)
Felt she needed to be perfect to be loved (3)
Felt safer with (3)
Good/trusting (3)
Isolated (3)
Wanted big brother/rescuer (3)
Competitive (1)
Hated (1)
Indifferent (1)
Overly friendly (1)
Polite (1)
Poor communication (1)
Resentful (1)

Relationships with Females.

Not close (14)
No trust (13)

Fearful (10)
Few friendships (10)
Many friendships (10)
Close (9)
Looked for mother figure (9)
Avoided (6)
Needy of love (6)
Hateful (5)
Leery of all (5)
Acted how others wanted her to (4)
Felt not as good (4)
Liked one-on-one (4)
Looked for approval (4)
Sexual (4)
Angry (3)
Bad with groups (3)
Caregiver (3)
Competitive (3)
Did not like them to touch (3)
Fell in love with many (3)
Nonexistent (3)
Preferred their company (3)
Quiet (3)
Thought they were boring (3)
Fear of being consumed (1)
Feel betrayed by them (1)
Indifferent (1)
Jealous of them (1)
Need to be in control (1)

RESOURCES

ORGANIZATIONS

Abuse & Trauma Recovery Program
Dominion Hospital
2960 Sleepy Hollow Rd.
Falls Church, VA 22044

Association of Child Advocates
P.O. Box 5873
Cleveland, OH 44101-0873
(216) 881-2225

Center for Trauma & Dissociation
4400 E. Cliff Ave.
Denver, CO 80222
Attn: Dr. Nancy Cole

Child Abuse Institute of Research
P.O. Box 1217
Cincinnati, OH 45201

Child Sexual Abuse Institute
P.O. Box 453
Wooster, OH 44691

Child Welfare League Of America
440 1st St., NW, Ste. 310
Washington, DC 20001
(202) 638-2952

Clearinghouse for Child Abuse
 Prevention
2314 Auburn Ave.
Cincinnati, OH 45219

Clearinghouse on Child Abuse
 & Neglect
P.O. Box 1183
Washington, DC 20013

DD Institute of SW, Inc.
P.O. Box 820983
Dallas, TX 75382-0983
Attn: Phila Hall, Executive Director

DD Unit—Sheppard Pratt
6501 N. Charles St.
Box 6815
Baltimore, MD 21285-6815
Attn: Dr. Susan Walt

Defense for Children International,
United States of America
201 Forsyth St.
New York, NY 10002
(212) 343-0951

Incest Resources, Inc.
46 Pleasant St.
Cambridge, MA. 02139

International Society for Prevention
of Child Abuse & Neglect
1205 Oneida St.
Denver, CO 80220
(303) 321-3963

International Society for the Study
of Multiple Personalities
& Dissociation
5700 Old Orchard Rd., First Floor
Skokie, IL 60077
(708) 966-4320

Loved Ones of Multiples
P.O. Box 4367
Boulder, CO 80306-4367

MPD/DD Resource & Education
Center
P.O. Box 2356
Brentwood, TN 37024-2346
Attn: Elizabeth Power

National Center for Treatment of
Dissociative Disorder
1290 S. Potomac
Aurora, CO 80012
Attn: Nancy Cole, Psy.D.

National Council on Child Abuse
and Family Violence
1155 Connecticut Ave., NW, Ste. 300
Washington, DC 20036
(202) 429-6695

National Organization for Victim
Assistance
1757 Park Road N.
Washington, DC 20010

National Resource Center
on Child Sexual Abuse
106 Lincoln St.
Huntsville, AL 35801

One of Many Voices
1275 4th Street, #231
Santa Rosa, CA 95404
(For survivors who have PTSD)

Progress in DD
c/o Ridgeview Institute
3995 S. Cobb Dr.
Smyrna, GA 30080
Attn: Richard Kluft, M.D.

Sidran Foundation
2328 W. Joppa Rd., Ste. 15
Lutherville, MD 21903

VOICES in Action, Inc. (Victims
of Incest Can Emerge Survivors)
P.O. Box 148309
Chicago, IL 60614
(312) 327-1500

Women Incested Needing
Group Support
8007 W. Colfax Ave.
C.S. #27, Box 129
Lakewood, CO 80215

Women's Growth in Connecticut
Stone Center for Development
   Services & Studies
Wellesley College
Wellesley, MA 02181

Women's Trauma Recovery Services
806 West 60th Terr.
Kansas City, MO 64113
Attn: I. Lisa McCann, Ph.D.

12-Step Programs

Adult Children Of Alcoholics
P.O. Box 3216
Torrance, CA 90505

Al-Anon Family Groups, Inc.
P.O. Box 862
Midtown Station
New York, NY 10018-0862

Alcoholics Anonymous World Service
475 Riverside Dr.
New York, NY 10115

Co-Dependents Anonymous
P.O. Box 5508
Glendale, AZ 90017

Debtors Anonymous
P.O. Box 20322
New York, NY 10025-9992

Emotions Anonymous
P.O. Box 4245
St. Paul, MN 55104

Narcotics Anonymous
World Service Office
16155 Wyandotte St.
Van Nuys, CA 91496

Overeaters Anonymous
World Service Office
2190 190th St.
Torrance, CA 90504

Sexaholics Anonymous
P.O. Box 300
Simi Valley, CA 93062

Sexual Abuse Survivors Anonymous
World Service Headquarters
P.O. Box 241046
Detroit, MI 48224
(313) 882-9646

Survivors Of Incest Anonymous
World Service Office
P.O. Box 21817
Baltimore, MD 21222-2365
(415) 433-2365

**Organizations for Nonverbal
Treatment**

American Dance Therapy
   Association
2000 Century Plaza, Ste. 108
Columbia, MD 21044
(410) 997-4040

American Massage Therapy
   Association
820 Davis St.
Evanston, IL 60201-4444
(708) 864-0123

American Oriental Bodywork
   Therapy Association
6801 Jericho Turnpike
Syosset, NY 11791
(516) 364-0808

American Polarity Therapy
  Association
2888 Bluff St., Ste. 149
Boulder, CO 80301
(303) 545-2080

Associated Bodywork and Massage
  Professionals
P.O. Box 1869
Evergreen, CO 80439-1869
(303) 674-8478

PUBLISHERS
AND DIRECTORIES

Above & Beyond
P.O. Box 2672
Ann Arbor, MI 48106-2672
(800) 821-5341
(Books, tapes, and information on
healing resources and sexual abuse
survivor issues.)

American Psychiatric Press
1400 K St., NW
Washington, DC 20005

Button & Dietz, Inc.
Human Resources Consultants
P.O. Box 19243
Austin, Texas 78760-9243
(Free reading list and resource list
for survivors of sexual abuse.)

Child Abuse & Neglect & Family
Violence Audiovisual Catalog
Clearinghouse on Family Violence
  Information
P.O. Box 1182
Washington, DC 20013
(703) 821-2086

Child Abuse & Neglect: An
Information & Reference Guide
Galand Publishing, Inc.
136 Madison Ave.
New York, NY 10001
(212) 686-7942

Guilford Publications
72 Spring St.
New York, NY 10012

Incest Resources
46 Pleasant St.
Cambridge, MA 02139

Incest Survivors Resource
  Network International
P.O. Box 7375
Las Cruces, NM 88006-7375
(Quaker educational resources
for survivors of any denomination.)

Learning Publications
P.O. Box 1338
Holmes Beach, FL 34218-1338

Psychology Book Club
230 Livingston St.
P.O. Box 941
Northvale, NJ 07647

Safer Society Press
P.O. Box 340
Brandon, VT 05733
(802) 247-3132

Sexual Abuse Prevention: An
Annotated Bibliography
Network Publications
P.O. Box 1830
Santa Cruz, CA 95601

Sexual Assault & Child Abuse:
A National Directory of Victim
Services & Prevention Programs
Oryx Press
4041 N. Central, #700
Phoenix, AZ 85012

Sidran Press
211 Southway
Baltimore, MD 21218

Stearn's Book Service
2004 W. Roscoe St.
Chicago, IL 60618
Attn: Book Buyer

NEWSLETTERS AND JOURNALS

Above a Whisper
P.O. Box 2588
Ann Arbor, MI 48106-2588

Beyond Survival Magazine
1278 Glenneyre St., #3
Laguna Beach, CA 90504

International New Journal of Abuse
Survivorship & Therapy
2272 Eastlake Ave., #300
Seattle, WA 98102
Attn: David L. Calof, Editor

Journal of Dissociation
Riverside Institute
3995 S. Cobb Dr.
Smyrna, GA 30080

Many Voices
P.O. Box 2639
Cincinnati, OH 45201

MP Dignity
P.O. Box 4367
Boulder, CO 80306-4367

MPD Reaching Out
Royal Ottawa Hospital
1145 Carling Avenue
Ottawa, Ontario,
Canada K12 7K4

Soundings
Echoes Network Counseling Center
1622 N.E. 8th
Portland, OR 97232

Stand Fast
P.O. Box 9107
Warwick, RI 02889

Survivor
P.O. Box 11315
Knoxville, TN 37939-1315

THE BANNER PROJECT

The banner project was begun in 1989, by members of an incest support group in Madison, Wisconsin. Currently there are more than 900 handprint sections from survivors. The handprints represent the many uses of hands: nurturance, love, and connecting to others. Each individual's handprint is unique.

Sections are sewn together to create hands because, "Hands joined together signify unity and strength." Write to the address below for information on making a section or to request the banner for display:

Wisconsin Committee for Prevention of Child Abuse
214 N. Hamilton Street
Madison, WI 53703
Phone: (608) 256-3374
Fax: (608) 256-3378

BIBLIOGRAPHY

Bernstein, E. M., & Putnam, F. W. (1986). Development, reliability, and validity of a dissociation scale. *Journal of Nervous and Mental Disease, 174,* 727-735.

Calof, D. L. (1993). A conversation with Pamela Freyd, cofounder and executive director, False Memory Syndrome Foundation. Part I. *Treating Abuse Today, 3*(3), 25-39.

Capacchione, L. (1979). *The creative journal: The art of finding yourself.* Athens, OH: Swallow Press.

Fowler, C. A., Hilsenroth, M. J., & Handler, L. (1995). Early memories: An exploration of theoretically derived queries and their clinical utility. *Bulletin of the Menniger Clinic, 59*(1), 79-98.

Harvey, M. R. (1996). An ecological view of psychological trauma and trauma recovery. *Journal of Traumatic Stress, 9*(1), 3-23.

Kohut, H., & Wolf, E. G. (1978). The disorders of the self and their treatment. An outline. *International Journal of Psychoanalysis, 59,* 413-425.

Lifton, R. (1979). *The broken connection.* New York: Simon & Schuster.

Ross, C. A., Heber, S., & Norton, G. R. (1990). Dissociation and abuse in multiple personality patients, prostitutes, and exotic dancers. *Hospital and Community Psychiatry, 41,* 328-330.

287

Ross, C. A., Heber, S., Norton, G. R., Anderson, G., & Barchet, P. (1989). The Dissociative Disorders Interview Schedule: A structured interview. *Dissociation, 2*(3), 165-189.

Sgroi, S. (Ed.). (1982). *Handbook of clinical intervention in child sexual abuse.* Lexington, MA: Lexington Books.

Simonds, S. (1992). Sexual abuse and body image: Approaches and implications for treatment. *The Arts in Psychotherapy, 19,* 289-293.

Steele, K., & Colrain, J. (1990). Abreactive work with sexual abuse survivors: Concepts and techniques. In M. A. Hunter (Ed.), *The sexually abused male. Volume 2. Applications of treatment strategies* (pp. 1-55). Lexington, MA: Lexington Books.

Turner, M. T., & Turner, T. N. (1994). *Female adolescent sexual abusers: An exploratory study of mother-daughter dynamics with implications for treatment.* Brandon, VT: Safer Society Press.

Wallis, L. (1983). *Stories for the third ear.* New York: Norton.

INDEX

ABOUT THE AUTHORS

Dr. Juliann Mitchell is a licensed psychologist in private practice in Pennsylvania. She is also available as a speaker, consultant, and workshop presenter. Dr. Mitchell collects zebras for her office.

Jill Morse graduated from Point Park College, Pittsburgh, Pennsylvania, with a B.A. in English and a minor in psychology. She currently works in child care.